GEOMORPHIC
HAZARDS

INTERNATIONAL ASSOCIATION OF GEOMORPHOLOGISTS

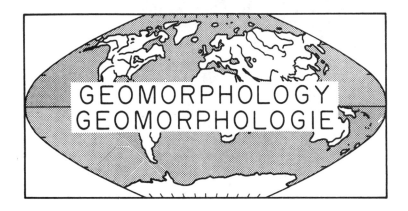

Publication No. 1

THE EVOLUTION OF GEOMORPHOLOGY
A Nation-by-Nation Summary of Development

Edited by H. J. Walker *and* W. E. Grabau

Publication No. 2

RIVER GEOMORPHOLOGY

Edited by Edward J. Hickin

Publication No. 3

STEEPLAND GEOMORPHOLOGY

Edited by Olav Slaymaker

Publication No. 4

GEOMORPHIC HAZARDS

Edited by Olav Slaymaker

GEOMORPHIC HAZARDS

Edited by

OLAV SLAYMAKER
University of British Columbia, Canada

JOHN WILEY & SONS
Chichester · New York · Brisbane · Toronto · Singapore

Copyright © 1996 by John Wiley & Sons Ltd,
    Baffins Lane, Chichester,
    West Sussex PO19 1UD, England

    National   01243 779777
    International (+44) 1243 779777

Other Wiley Editorial Offices

John Wiley & Sons, Inc., 605 Third Avenue,
New York, NY 10158-0012, USA

Jacaranda Wiley Ltd, 33 Park Road, Milton,
Queensland 4064, Australia

John Wiley & Sons (Canada) Ltd, 22 Worcester Road,
Rexdale, Ontario M9W 1L1, Canada

John Wiley & Sons (SEA) Pte Ltd, 2 Clementi Loop #02-01,
Jin Xing Distripark, Singapore 0512

Library of Congress Cataloging-in-Publication Data

Geomorphic hazards / edited by Olav Slaymaker.
        p.   cm. — (Publication / International Association of
    Geomorphologists ; no. 4)
        Papers from the Third International Geomorphological Conference
    held at McMaster University, Hamilton, Ont., Aug. 1993.
        Includes bibliographical references and index.
        ISBN 0-471-96213-9
        1. Natural disasters—Congresses. 2. Geomorphology—Congresses.
    I. Slaymaker, Olav, 1939—   . II. International Geomorphological
    Conference (3rd : 1993 : McMaster University) III. Series:
    Publication (International Association of Geomorphologists) ; no. 4.
    GB5001.G47   1996
    363.3′4—dc20   95-42363
                                                              CIP

British Library Cataloguing in Publication Data

A catalogue record for this book is available from the British Library

ISBN 0-471-96213-9

Typeset in 10/12pt Times by MHL Typesetting Ltd, Coventry
Printed and bound in Great Britain by Bookcraft (Bath) Ltd
This book is printed on acid-free paper responsibly manufactured from sustainable forestation,
for which at least two trees are planted for each one used for paper production.

Contents

vi   *Contents*

Contributors

P. Ballerini Department of Earth Science, University of Florence, 50121 Florence, Italy

C. Bechini Department of Earth Science, University of Florence, 50121 Florence, Italy

Mohamed Tahar Benazzouz Geomorphology Laboratory, Earth Science Institute, University of Constantine, Algeria

F. Brunori Department of Earth Science, University of Florence, 50121 Florence, Italy

N. Casagli Department of Earth Science, University of Florence, 50121 Florence, Italy

N. H. D. T. Cremers Department of Physical Geography, Utrecht University, PO Box 80115, 3508 TC Utrecht, The Netherlands

D. de Brum Ferreira INIC, Centro de Estudios Geográficos, Faculdade de Letras, Cicade Universitaria, 1699 Lisbon Codex, Portugal

Morgan De Dapper Department of Geography, University of Ghent, ITC, Krijgslaan 281 (S8), B 9000 Ghent, Belgium

A. P. J. De Roo Department of Physical Geography, Utrecht University, PO Box 80115, 3508 TC Utrecht, The Netherlands

Mohamed El Badawi National Authority for Remote Sensing and Space Sciences, Kasr El Eini Street 101, Cairo, Egypt

Carlo Elmi Department of Geological Science, University of Bologna, Via Zamboni 67, 40127 Bologna, Italy

S. Fiaschi Department of Earth Science, University of Florence, 50121 Florence, Italy

Abd-Alla Gad National Authority for Remote Sensing and Space Sciences, Kasr El Eini Street 101, Cairo, Egypt

C. A. Garzonio Town and Land Planning Department, University of Florence, 50121 Florence, Italy

Rudi Goossens Department of Geography, University of Ghent, ITC, Krijgslaan 281 (S8), B 9000 Ghent, Belgium

Anna Groot Department of Geography, University of Lethbridge, Lethbridge, Alberta, Canada T1K 3M4

Masaru Iwamoto Department of Civil Engineering, Nishi-Nippon Institute of Technology, 1633 Kanda, Fukuoka 800-03, Japan

Ricarte S. Javelosa Department of Environment and Natural Resources, Bureau of Mines and Geosciences, Manila, Philippines

S. Moretti Department of Earth Science, University of Florence, 50121 Florence, Italy

Olivia Nesci Institute of Geology, University of Urbino, Via S. Chiara 27, 61029 Urbino, Italy

Jan. J. Nossin ITC, Department of Earth Resources Survey, Division of Applied Geomorphology, Enschede, The Netherlands

K. Oostindie Department of Soil Physical Transport Phenomena, The Winand Staring Centre, PO Box 125, 6700 AC Wageningen, The Netherlands

Gerald Osborn Department of Geology and Geophysics, University of Calgary, 2500 University Drive NW, Calgary, Alberta, Canada T2N 1N4

M. Teresa Ramírez-Herrera Institute of Geography, UNAM, Ciudad Universitaria, 01000 Mexico DF. Present address: Department of Geography, University of Edinburgh, Edinburgh EH4 9XP, UK

C. J. Ritsema Department of Soil Physical Transport Phenomena, The Winand Staring Centre, PO Box 125, 6700 AC Wageningen, The Netherlands

A. Sidorchuk Department of Geography, State University of Moscow, Moscow 119899, Russia

Olav Slaymaker Department of Geography, University of British Columbia, Vancouver, Canada V6T 1Z2

Ian Spooner Department of Geology, Acadia University, Wolfville, Nova Scotia, Canada B0P 1X0

M. A. Verzandvoort Department of Physical Geography, Utrecht University, PO Box 80115, 3508 TC Utrecht, The Netherlands

C. G. Wesseling Department of Physical Geography, Utrecht University, PO Box 80115, 3508 TC Utrecht, The Netherlands

Series Preface

The Third International Geomorphological Conference was held at McMaster University, Hamilton, Ontario, in August of 1993. No consistent format has yet been established for publishing papers presented at these conferences. Short contributions from the first conference (Manchester) were published in two large volumes, and selected papers from the second conference (Frankfurt) have appeared in a number of special issues of *Zeitschrift für Geomorphologie*. Although some papers from the third conference will be published in special issues, independently of the International Association of Geomorphologists, others will appear in a series of volumes dealing with specific geomorphological themes. The first of these conference volumes, *River Geomorphology*, was edited by Ted Hickin of Simon Fraser University, British Columbia, and the second, *Steepland Geomorphology*, by Olav Slaymaker of the University of British Columbia. *Geomorphic Hazards*, edited by Olav Slaymaker, is the third of the conference volumes to be published in the "International Association of Geomorphologists Series" by John Wiley & Sons Ltd. All the papers submitted to this volume were independently reviewed before being accepted for publication. It is anticipated that two other volumes, dealing with the geomorphological effects of minor climatic change and the plenary sessions will be published in this series.

A. S. Trenhaile, Series Editor
University of Windsor, Ontario

1

Introduction

OLAV SLAYMAKER

Department of Geography, University of British Columbia

1.1 DEFINITION AND CATEGORIES OF A GEOMORPHIC HAZARD

A geomorphic hazard results from any landform change that adversely affects the geomorphic stability of a site (Schumm, 1988) and that intersects the human use system with adverse socioeconomic impacts (White, 1974). The hazard is commonly defined by geomorphologists as the probability of a change of a given magnitude occurring within a specified time period in a given area; the associated risk is the consequent damage or loss of life, property and services (Varnes et al., 1984). Whyte and Burton (1980), on the other hand, define risk as the product of the probability of occurrence of a hazard and its societal consequences. In both definitions, hazards and risks are connected: in the former, the hazard assessment is central and is perceived as an objective scientific discipline; in the latter, the focus is on risks as societally evaluated phenomena, and the concept of risk supersedes that of hazard. Geomorphologists have made little contribution to risk studies, though engineers have recognized the importance of the field (e.g. Morgan, 1992). Recent discussions (Bobrowsky, 1992; Gardner, 1993) have confirmed the central interest of geomorphologists in hazard assessment.

Geomorphic hazards are characterized by magnitude, frequency and areal extent. Table 1.1 attempts to discriminate between the various categories of hazard whether endogenous (caused by "normal" tectonic or volcanic processes), exogenous (caused by "normal" subaerial processes) or induced by climate and land-use change. The use of the term "normal" is open to criticism but it accepts, as a convenient working hypothesis, that there exists a long-term geophysical average condition on which trends are superimposed by global warming or land-use changes. The table fails to capture the distinction between site, local, regional and national impacts but it does bring out the potential importance of low-magnitude hazards *vis-à-vis* high magnitude hazards quite well. In geomorphology, one of the early discussions of this issue was provided by Hewitt (1972) building on a more general discussion (Hewitt and Burton, 1971); Mann and Hunter (1988) have reinforced a probabilistic approach to geomorphic hazards. Slaymaker (1991) discussed a typology of geomorphic hazards relevant to consideration of sustainable development.

Geomorphic Hazards. Edited by O. Slaymaker.
© 1996 by John Wiley & Sons Ltd

TABLE 1.1   Categories of geomorphic hazard (numbers in brackets refer to the relevant chapter in this volume)

Geomorphic hazard	High magnitude Low frequency	Low magnitude Continuous	Low magnitude High frequency
Endogenous	Volcanism (2,6,7) Neotectonics (3,7)		Neotectonics (3,7)
Exogenous	Floods (2,6) Karst collapse Snow avalanche Channel erosion (6,11) Sedimentation (6) Mass movement (2,4,5,6,7) Jokulhlaups (2) Tsunamis Coastal erosion	Solution Mass movement (5)	Floods (2,6) Solution Snow avalanche Channel erosion (6,11) Sedimentation (6) Mass movement (5) Tsunamis Coastal erosion
Climate or land-use change	Desertification (8,12,13) Permafrost Degradation (11) Soil erosion (8,9,10,11) Salinization (12) Floods (2)	Desertification (8,12,13)	Desertification (8,12,13) Permafrost Degradation (11) Soil erosion (8,9,10,11) Salinization (12)

1.2 COMPONENTS OF RISK STUDIES IN RELATION TO GEOMORPHIC RISK ZONATION

There are four well-recognized areas of the risk studies field: risk assessment, risk perception and decision science, risk communication and public policy, and risk management and/or mitigation (Slovic, 1986).

1. Risk assessment seeks to give precise descriptions of the nature of the hazard and the extent and type of exposure to the hazard in various populations. Risk is commonly described as the product of probability of occurrence of a natural hazard and its societal consequences (Whyte and Burton, 1980). Almost always, risk assessment is carried out in the context of incomplete data and uncertainty.

2. Risk perception is the "common sense" understanding of hazards, exposure and risk, arrived at by a community through intuitive reasoning. It is usually expressed in qualitative terms such as "safe" or "unsafe". Public policy decisions are almost always driven by perceived risk among the population affected and among decision-makers. These perceptions are commonly at variance with "technical" risk assessments.

3. Risk communication is the social dialogue about risk by a variety of parties. This dialogue is commonly only characterized by strong disagreements between different stakeholders. It has the practical objective of searching for consensus on how to assess and manage hazards. It also includes overcoming misperceptions, such as safety of development in river floodplains.

4. Risk management is the process of determining an adequate response to hazards which incorporates risk assessment, risk perception and risk communication. Strategies include controlling, mitigating or sharing the adverse impact of hazards and indeed can include enhancing beneficial outcomes of hazards. Educational, economic and regulatory approaches to hazards can also generate benefits that outweigh the adverse impact of hazards.

1.2.1 Risk Assessment

There are three steps in the determination of composite risk zonation: (a) mapping of geomorphic hazard domains, (b) assessment of vulnerability, and (c) prioritizing of georesources (Nossin, 1989; Nossin and Javelosa, Chapter 6, this volume).

(a) Geomorphic hazard domains are established by geomorphic mapping and remotely sensed images utilizing either a historical approach or a dynamic geomorphology approach. Ranking is based on the degree and extent of instability.
(b) Vulnerability means the degree of loss (severity and cost of damage) resulting from the hazard (UNDRO, 1979).
(c) The georesource domain includes discrimination of priorities of land use as between urban, agricultural and woodland. The value of human life guarantees that urban land will have highest priority. [For a contrary perspective, examples from Austria (Aulitzky, 1994), Switzerland (Kienholz and Mani, 1994), Norway (Hestnes and Lied, 1980) and Japan (Kadomura, 1980) should be consulted.]

1.2.2 Risk Perception and Communication

Information processing with respect to people''s attitudes and behaviour towards impending disasters and changes in risk-taking behaviour over human life spans, as researched in developmental psychology, have given rise to a distinct subfield of risk communication. In part, this field deals with disparities between the meaning of risks as assessed by experts and understood by the general public. Given that these disparities exist, how can we improve the quality of dialogue about risk across the gap that separates experts from the general public? Secondly, how can we apply this improved dialogue about risk towards achieving a higher degree of social consensus on the inherently controversial aspect of managing environmental risk (Leiss, 1990)?

To this end, a classification of firmly held perspectives on risks, following the discussion of Krimsky and Golding (1992) can be helpful. As far as I am aware, geomorphologists have not ventured into this discussion and I am raising it here to indicate my sense of its importance and immediate relevance (Table 1.2). This table illustrates the dominant contribution of geomorphologists to risk assessment and management as exemplified by contributions to this volume.

1.2.3 Risk Management

A recent discussion by Cave (1992) demonstrates this empirical approach to hazard acceptability adopted by geomorphologists in the absence of hard information on risk

TABLE 1.2 Classification of risk perspectives (modified from Krimsky and Golding, 1992)

	Geomorphology	Probability	Economics	Psychology	Social	Cultural
Input term	Mapped/modelled value	Expected value (synthesized)	Expected utility	(Subjective) Expected utility	(Perceived) Fairness	Shared values
Methodology	Historical record Experiments	Event analysis	Risk/benefit analysis	Psychometrics	Surveys/structured analysis	Grid group analysis
Scope	Environment	Safety	Universal	Individual perception	Social interest	Cultural cluster
Application	Science and protection of the environment Management	Safety Engineering Mitigation	Decision-making		Policy making and regulations Conflict resolution and mediation Risk communication	
Function (instrumental)	Standard setting for early warning	Improving early warning system	Resource allocation	Individual assessment	Fairness Equity Political acceptance	Cultural identity
Function (social)	Assessment	Risk reduction and policy selection	Coping with uncertainty		Political legitimation	

TYPE OF DEVELOPMENT APPLICATION	TYPE OF HAZARD			
	PROBABILITY OF OCCURRENCE HIGH ←————→ LOW			
	ANNUAL RETURN FREQUENCIES			
PROJECT	>1:50	1:50 to 1:200	1:200 to 1:500	<1:500
Minor repair < 25%				
Major repair > 25%				
Reconstruction				
Extension				
New building				
Subdivision				
Major rezoning				

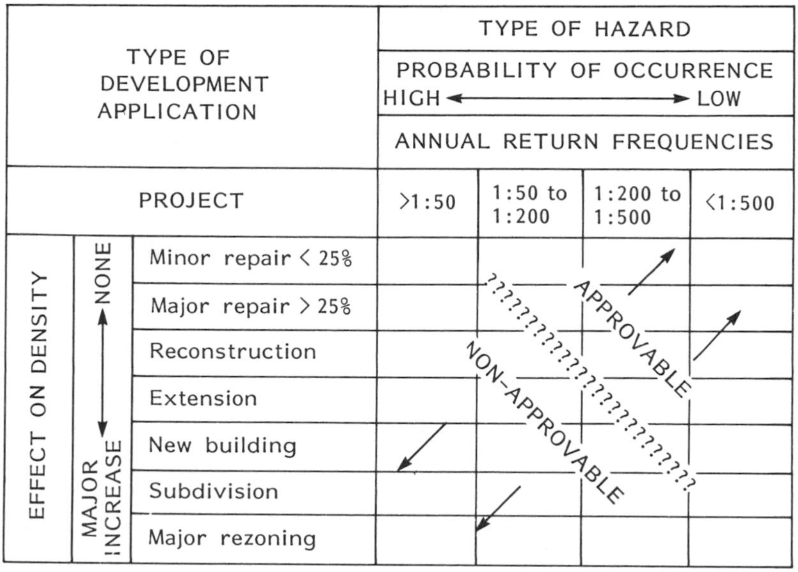

(EFFECT ON DENSITY: NONE / MAJOR INCREASE) — diagram with APPROVABLE / NON-APPROVABLE zones and ???? boundary

(a)

INUNDATION BY FLOOD WATERS FROM FRASER RIVER & TRIBUTARIES				
	1:40	1:40 to 1:200	1:200 to 1:500	1:500 to 1:10000
Minor repair (<25%)	2	1	1	1
Major repair (>25%)	4	3	3	1
Reconstruction	4	3	3	1
Extension	4	3	3	1
New building	4	3	3	1
Subdivision (infill/extend)	5	4	4	1
Rezoning (for new community)	5	5	5	1

(b)

FIGURE 1.1 Hazard acceptability for development: (a) approvable projects (Cave, 1992); (b) scale of acceptability for inundation by flood waters (Cave, 1992) (Modified from Fig. 6.11, Nossin — this volume)

perception and communication. Whether a development application is approved by local government in British Columbia depends on the nature of the project and the annual return frequencies of individual hazards. In the case illustrated — that of inundation by flood waters (Figure 1.1) — the scale of acceptability of a hazard (1−5) shows that rezoning for a new community is unacceptable on land that may be inundated once in 500 years, whereas a project described as "minor repair" is approvable on that same land area. From a professional geoscientist's perspective, this approach provides a practical rule of thumb for decision-making in hazard management. It seems clear that research into risk perception and communication is urgently needed to provide a more transparent and robust approach to hazard mitigation and management.

1.3   THE ROLE OF GEOMORPHOLOGISTS IN HAZARD AND RISK STUDIES

Geomorphic hazards occupy a central role in hazard assessment and new methods of hazard assessment draw heavily on satellite remote sensing and geomorphological survey. As can be seen from the contents of this volume, there is comparatively little discussion by geomorphologists of the limitations of geomorphic hazard assessment in isolation from consideration of societal goals and cultural value systems.

The risk approach to geomorphic hazards enables a fuller incorporation of both expert analysis and societal synthesis in the solution of the natural hazards problem. In this volume, the best example of such an approach is provided by Nossin and Javelosa (Chapter 6). However, Chapter 2 (Spooner et al.) provides an innovative approach to hazard assessment by exploration of resident oral histories in a remote part of British Columbia: they incorporate hazard perception and hazard communication in their research methodology.

But the main message of the volume is the enormous emphasis by geomorphologists on careful hazard assessment and a not inconsiderable application to hazard mitigation and management. Chapters 6 (Nossin and Javelosa), 7 (Iwamoto), 8 (Brum Ferreira), 10 (De Roo et al), 11 (Sidorchuk), 12 (De Dapper et al) and 13 (Benazzouz) all discuss the management implications of their hazard assessments.

1.4   ACKNOWLEDGEMENTS

Each of these papers was originally presented at the 3rd International Conference of Geomorphologists held at McMaster University, Hamilton, Ontario in August 1993. The assistance of the following manuscript reviewers is gratefully acknowledged: Matt Brunengo, Rorke Bryan, Mary Lou Byrne, Tom Dunne, Pierre Gangloff, Ken Hewitt, Shiu Luk, Jean Poesen, Andre Roy and Hanspeter Schreier. Expert assistance in the preparation of the final manuscript was received from Sandy Lapsky, Jeanne Yang and Linda Suss.

The patience and assistance of Wiley's editorial staff is also acknowledged.

REFERENCES

Aulitzky, H. 1994. Hazard mapping and zoning in Austria: methods and legal implications. *Mountain Research and Development*, **14**, 307−313.

Bobrowsky, P. (ed.) 1992. *Geologic Hazards in British Columbia*. BC Geological Survey Branch, Open File, 1992−15.

Cave, P.W. 1992. Hazard acceptability thresholds for development approvals by local government. In Bobrowsky, P. (ed.), *Geologic Hazards in British Columbia*. BC Geological Survey Branch, Open File, 1992−15, 15−26.

Gardner, J. 1993. Mountain hazards. In French, H.M. and Slaymaker, O. (eds.), *Canada's Cold Environments*. McGill-Queen's Press, Montreal and Kingston, 247–270.

Hestnes, E. and Lied, K. 1980. Natural hazard maps for land use planning in Norway. *Journal of Glaciology*, **26**, 331–343.

Hewitt, K. 1972. The mountain environment and geomorphic processes. In Slaymaker, O. and McPherson, H.J. (eds), *Mountain Geomorphology*. Tantalus Research, Vancouver, 17–34.

Hewitt, K. and Burton, I. 1971. *The Hazardousness of a Place*. University of Toronto, 154 pp.

Kadomura, H. 1980. Erosion by human activities in Japan. *GeoJournal*, **4**, 133–144.

Kienholz, H. and Mani, P. 1994. Assessment of geomorphic hazards and priorities for forest management on the Rigi North Face, Switzerland. *Mountain Research and Development*, **14**, 321–328.

Krimsky, S. and Golding, D. (eds) 1992. *Social Theories of Risk*. Praeger, Westport, Connecticut.

Leiss, W. 1990. Managing the risks and consequences of innovation. In Salter, L. and Wolfe, D. (eds), *Managing Technology*. Garamond Press, Toronto. 185–206.

Mann, J.C. and Hunter, R.L. 1988. Probabilities of geologic events and processes in natural hazards. *Zeitschrift für Geomorphologie*, Supp. Vol. **67**, 39–52.

Morgan, G.C. 1992. Quantification of risks from slope hazards. In Bobrowsky, P. (ed.), *Geologic Hazards in British Columbia*. BC Geological Survey Branch, Open File, 1992–15, 57–70.

Nossin, J.J. 1989. Aerospace survey of natural hazards: the new possibilities. *International Institute for Aerospace Survey and Earth Sciences (ITC) Journal*, 3/4, 183–188.

Schumm, S.A. 1988. Geomorphic hazards–problems of prediction. *Zeitschrift für Geomorphologie*, Supp. Vol. **67**, 17–24.

Slaymaker, O. 1991. Implications of the process of erosion and sedimentation for sustainable development. In Dorcey, A.H.J. (ed.), *Perspectives on Sustainable Development in Water Management*. Westwater Research Centre, Vancouver, 93–114.

Slovic, P. 1986. Informing and educating the public about risk. *Risk Analysis*, **6**, p. 403–415.

United National Disaster Relief Co-ordinator (UNDRO) 1979. *Natural Disasters and Vulnerability Analysis*. Report of Expert Group Meeting, Geneva, 49 pp.

Varnes, D.J. et al 1984. *Landslide Hazard Zonation: a Review of Principles and Practice*. International Association of Engineering Geology, Commission on Landslides and Other Mass Movements on Slopes, UNESCO, Paris.

White, G.F. 1974. *Natural Hazards*. Oxford University Press, Oxford.

Whyte, A.V. and Burton, I. 1980. *Environmental Risk Assessment*. Scientific Committee on Problems of the Environment (SCOPE), No. 15, 176 pp.

2

Resident Oral Histories: A Tool for the Study of Recent Environmental Change on the Stikine Plateau of Northwestern British Columbia

Ian Spooner

Department of Geology, Acadia University

Gerald Osborn

Department of Geology and Geophysics, University of Calgary

AND

Anna Groot

Department of Geography, University of Lethbridge

ABSTRACT

Resident oral histories are potentially powerful tools for both the spatial and temporal resolution of past changes in the physical environment, particularly in remote, isolated areas. Although subsequent physical verification is desirable, oral histories may provide the initial evidence of past events. This methodology is most likely to be effective when researchers have some knowledge of the social structure and ethical code of the community. We have obtained information on Late Holocene landslide and flood activity, volcanism and jokulhlaup drainage in northwestern British Columbia, in stories related by both the Tahltan natives and non-native settlers, some of whose ancestors have resided in the area for over 100 years. Landslide activity has occurred sporadically and most often has been associated with spring runoff during high snowpack years. A landslide along the Tuya River blocked the migratory route of salmon to Tuya Lake, altering settlement patterns. A landslide along the Tahltan River (*c.* 20 years ago) altered river hydraulics and overran a traditional gathering place. The potential exists for future landslide activity and possible blockage of the river at this site, the most important migratory route for sockeye salmon in the Stikine River drainage. A flood caused by the failure of a rock-avalanche-created dam once reversed the flow direction of the Stikine River. Both legends and resident histories indicate that volcanic activity on Mount Edziza may have occurred within the last millennium, indicating that the eruptive history of Mount Edziza should be re-evaluated, especially in light of proposed economic development of the region. Recollections of jokulhlaup drainage on the lower Stikine River further document a major event that is not well understood or documented.

Geomorphic Hazards. Edited by O. Slaymaker.
© 1996 by John Wiley & Sons Ltd

2.1 INTRODUCTION

In 1992 a study aimed at the detailed resolution of aspects of Holocene environmental change in the Stikine Plateau region of northwestern British Columbia was initiated. Among the active processes affecting the region are mass movement and volcanism: numerous landslide scars are found in major stream valleys of the Stikine Plateau (Figures 2.1 and 2.2) and Mount Edziza has been the centre of over 30 Holocene eruptive events (Figure 2.1) some of which have dammed major rivers and produced extensive lava and pumice fields. Our initial research focused on determination of the cause and regional distribution of these phenomena and the assessment of their impact on the inhabitants of the region.

Resolving the timing of late Holocene environmental change is generally difficult. Radiocarbon dating is not a suitable method for determining the age of very young samples. Furthermore, it is difficult to determine the season during which an event occurred, although this information may be required when examining phenomena that might be related to short-term climate change. Methods such as dendrochronology and lichenometry can be used in select cases, but were not universally applicable in the study area. Analytical methods do not allow us to judge the impact of such change on the resident population. These problems prompted us to consider resident oral history as a possible aid in locating, dating and resolving the cause and impact of recent changes to the environment. We were encouraged by the work of de Laguna (1958, 1972), Souther (1970), Albright (1984), Fladmark (1985), Gottesfeld et al. (1991) and Moodie et al. (1992) in the same region, which suggested that records of specific geomorphic events were preserved in oral histories.

In the following text we will outline the methodology that we employed, present our results and discuss the validity and benefits of this approach. This paper is an attempt to relate some of our experiences in the hope that they may serve as a guide to other non-specialists considering resident history as a resolution tool. We would like to stress that the research protocol and experiences of past anthropological, archaeological and geological researchers in the area (Fladmark, 1985; Albright, 1984; Souther, 1992) served as a valuable guide to us.

2.2 GEOLOGICAL SETTING, QUATERNARY HISTORY AND REGIONAL CLIMATE

The Stikine Plateau (Figure 2.1) lies within the Lower Triassic to Middle Jurassic Whitehorse Trough of the Intermontane Belt, which consists mainly of volcanic rocks (Souther, 1992). The Whitehorse Trough lies between the plutonic and metamorphic rocks of the Coast Plutonic Complex to the west and those of the Omineca Crystalline Belt to the east. The northeasterly trending Stikine Arch crosses the area and forms the northern margin of the Bowser Sedimentary Basin. The Mount Edziza Volcanic Complex dominates the study area and consists of the Mount Edziza volcano, dissected lava domes of the Spectrum Range (outside the study area) and a host of satellitic cones that surround the main vent. On the north edge of the study area the Stikine River has cut through a series of basalt flows believed to have originated from Mount Edziza. The eroded river course forms the Stikine River Canyon (Figure 2.1) which is, in places, over 500 m deep.

11

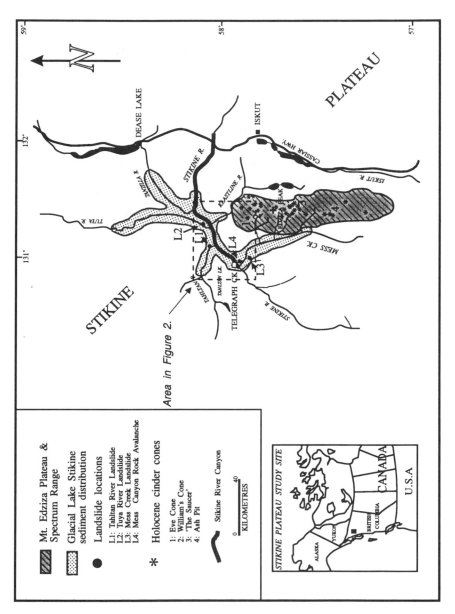

FIGURE 2.1 General location map showing Holocene volcanic and landslide sites. Glacial Lake Stikine sediment distribution modified from Ryder and Maynard (1991). Volcanic sites from Souther (1992)

Geomorphic Hazards

To the north of the Stikine River the Cassiar Mountains produce a rolling mountain relief while to the south, west and east, the Edziza Plateau and the Stikine River are enclosed by the jagged, glacier-capped peaks of the Coast and Skeena Mountains.

Differential advance and retreat of regional ice sheets in the Coast Mountains and the Skeena Mountains during the Fraser (Wisconsin) glaciation resulted in the damming of the Stikine River drainage and the formation of a pre-glacial lake, Glacial Lake Stikine (Ryder and Maynard, 1991). Glacial Lake Stikine sediments are overlain by Fraser Till (Figure 2.3) and this 300 m thick sediment package underlies an extensive plateau in the central portion of the study area (Figure 2.1). A similar lacustrine and glacial sediment succession, but of middle Pleistocene age, has been preserved between basalt flows in the Stikine River Canyon, providing evidence of middle Pleistocene glaciation and an indication that early advance of Coast Mountain ice also occurred during this time (Spooner, 1993). The Holocene epoch was characterized by rapid incision of late Wisconsin sediments, and by climate fluctuation that culminated in the Little Ice Age event about 200 years ago. Though not well documented in the study region, this cold period has been recognized by Ryder (1987), Miller and Anderson (1974a) and Fladmark (1985), and was thought by the latter author to have had a significant effect on the indigenous population.

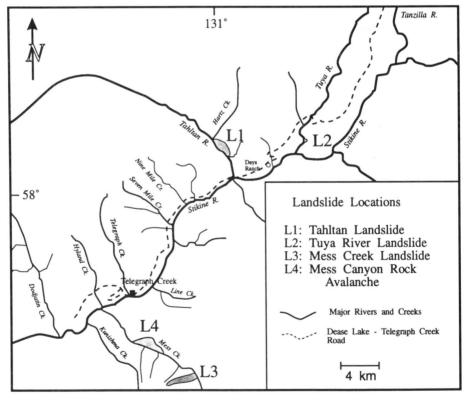

FIGURE 2.2 Location of landslide sites

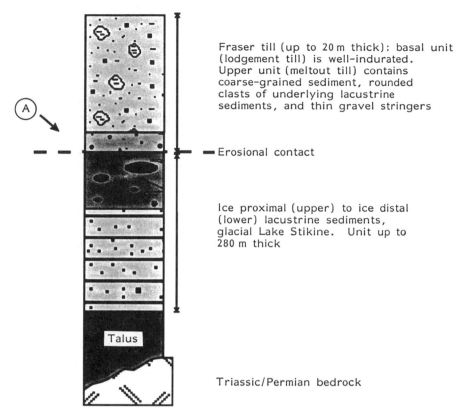

Fraser till (up to 20 m thick): basal unit (lodgement till) is well-indurated. Upper unit (meltout till) contains coarse-grained sediment, rounded clasts of underlying lacustrine sediments, and thin gravel stringers

Erosional contact

Ice proximal (upper) to ice distal (lower) lacustrine sediments, glacial Lake Stikine. Unit up to 280 m thick

Talus

Triassic/Permian bedrock

FIGURE 2.3   Stratigraphy of the Tahltan landslide sediments (L1, Figure 2.2). The contact between the relatively permeable meltout till and the impermeable lodgement till and the underlying sediments creates a plane that channels meltwater. It is along this plane that initial failure may have occurred

The study area is situated within the rain shadow of the Coast Mountains and typically has precipitation levels of 300–850 mm annually (Albright, 1984). These amounts increase eastward as elevation increases. Alpine Tundra, Spruce–Willow–Birch and Boreal White and Black Spruce Zones can be found within the study area. A drier microclimate exists in the middle section of the Stikine River valley, where total annual precipitation is rarely greater than 370 mm (Albright, 1984).

2.3   PREVIOUS RESEARCH

2.3.1   Archaeology

Fladmark (1985) noted that the Stikine Plateau is a region of dynamic environmental change, and that the original inhabitants of the region may have been aware of many of these changes. Though sparsely populated (*c.* 1500 persons in 1900; Albright, 1984), the region was heavily travelled, as game was plentiful and obsidian was available for trade and local use (Fladmark, 1985). Fladmark (1985) has studied the Stikine Plateau and Mount Edziza as an obsidian source and suggests that prehistoric native utilization of obsidian may date to 10 000 years BP.

2.3.2 Anthropology

Teit (1906), Emmons (1911) and Helm (1956) were involved in documenting the histories and legends of the Tahltan Indians. Ethnoarchaeological (Albright, 1984) and anthropological (Sheppard, 1983) studies have focused on the indigenous population (Tahltan of the Athapaskan linguistic group) and have established the research protocol guidelines and habitation histories referred to in this paper. These studies also served as important sources for literary references to environmental change.

2.3.3 Geology

Souther (1992) has produced an extensive body of work on the Mount Edziza Volcanic Complex and has conducted detailed investigations on the Holocene eruptive history of the area. Souther (1992) has shown that the youngest eruption on the northern portion of the Edziza Plateau (Desolation Lava Field) emanated from Williams Cone (Figure 2.1) about 1340 ± 130 BP. Twelve eruptive centres exist on the southern side of the Edziza Plateau (Figure 2.1) and constitute the Snowshoe Lava Field (Souther, 1992). Though Souther equates the age of these eruptive centres with the Desolation Lava Field, no dates have been obtained. Souther (1992) notes that the eruptive centres in the Snowshoe Lava Field and those near Walkout Creek and Mess Lake (most notably the Ash Pit, Figure 2-1) could potentially be younger than the Williams Cone eruptive event.

   Hamilton (1981) completed a geological investigation of the Level Mount Volcanic Complex, 60 km north of Mount Edziza. Cockfield (1926), Kerr (1926) and Johnson (1926) completed the first regional geological surveys of the area. Watson and Mathews (1944) extended this work to the north.

2.3.4 Geomorphology/palynology

Alley and Young (1978) noted that landslide activity has been pervasive throughout the Holocene and could potentially have an effect on settlements and transportation routes. Miller and Anderson (1974a, b) completed research on Holocene climatic trends in an area north of the Stikine drainage. They indicate that the timing of Holocene climate fluctuations in northwestern British Columbia may be out of phase with climate change recorded elsewhere in western North America.

2.4 ORAL HISTORIES AND GEOLOGICAL RESEARCH

Geologists have long used oral tradition as a tool to resolve environmental change during the late Holocene. A pioneer in this regard was de Laguna (1958, 1964, 1972) who equated Tlingit oral tradition of changes in the ice cover of Yakutat and Icy Bay in southwestern Alaska with glacial advance during the Little Ice Age. Stories of floods and earthquakes were also collected and related to events in the 19th century. More recently,

Souther (1970), Blong (1982), and Moodie et al. (1992) have collected stories that relate directly to volcanic activity and have found that these stories both confirm dated occurrences and validate hypotheses based on observation.

An important theme in these studies is that the oral traditions were specific to events that occurred during the past century and were collected from native peoples or were related to previous collectors (often missionaries) by natives. In addition, most of the studies document notable environmental events that affected either a significant regional population base, as is the case with the Tlingit population studied by de Laguna, or affected a large area, as is the case with the White River Ash study by Moodie et al. (1992).

For events thought to have occurred in the past century, we access oral histories in a manner similar to that employed by de Laguna (1972) and others. We have relied heavily on the writings of Teit (1906, 1909, 1919, 1921), Emmons (1911), Helm (1956) and the interpretations (as well as collected stories) of Fladmark (1985) and Albright (1984). However, there are several aspects of our study that differ from the studies previously discussed. The use of conventional data-gathering techniques (aerial photographs, meteorological and engineering reports) has been inhibited by the remote location and low population density. The dating of samples has been inhibited by the recency of some of the events. We consider oral histories as a possible means of locating, dating and assessing the impact of relatively recent and local environmental change events such as landslides, floods and related phenomena. Our experiences have shown that until very recently (within the last 20 years) there have been no written records of these events save those events that directly affected transportation routes or were recorded by happenstance observation. We have collected oral histories from both natives (Tahltan) and non-natives, as the latter have inhabited the Stikine Plateau since about the turn of the century and represent a small but potentially important source of information. We do not distinguish between these sources but refer to the collective as residents and the stories and remembrances as resident oral histories.

2.5 METHODOLOGY: RESIDENT ORAL HISTORY

We first obtained permission to gather non-written information from the Tahltan Band office in Telegraph Creek. The majority of the native population now resides in the villages of Telegraph Creek, Dease Lake and Iskut (Figure 2.1). Our method of gathering information was simple and direct. Our questions were directed towards older members of the community, and were neither leading nor complicated. The objective of our research was explained before the interview began and all interview subjects were asked if they felt comfortable contributing to such a project. Notepads and recording apparatus were not used. The initial questions included the following:

1. Are earth slides common? When did they occur?
2. Did anyone ever tell stories about smoke coming from Ice Mountain (a common local name for Mount Edziza)?
3. Did anyone ever talk about the earth shaking and why it shook?
4. Have the salmon always come up the river? If not, how many seasons did they not come? Do you know why?

5. Are there any stories about really poor hunting and poor berry-picking seasons?
6. Has there always been enough food?

We found it essential to employ a local resident as a guide and intermediary. A local guide is aware of ethics and points of protocol that are specific to the community and can solve logistical problems promptly. Our intermediary was a non-native who had been born and raised in the community. The guide's advanced education and familiarity with all residents was instrumental in helping us translate our scientific interests to other residents of the community, many of whom were not formally educated, and in directing us towards individuals most receptive to our research interests.

Ethical guidelines established by Sheppard (1983) were also instructive; we refrained from asking for the names of individuals interviewed and in some instances we were invited to help in a chore, as many individuals felt that their "giving" of information placed a debt upon the interviewer. This was done gladly as both a courtesy and repayment for the information that individual had given to us.

We also obtained information from literary sources, many obscure and out of print, that would normally not have been found in an earth-science-focused literature review. References were found in anthropological studies (Albright, 1984; Sheppard, 1983) and archaeological and geological studies (Fladmark, 1985), and were made available to us by local historians and long-term residents. Among these were the notes of missionaries (Teit, 1906, 1909, 1919, 1921; Emmons, 1911) and passages on regional geography and native legend in accounts of travels and explorations in the region (Patterson, 1966).

After identification of a site or region of interest, field examination was initiated. Flight surveys and, when available, aerial photographs were used to evaluate remote and inaccessible sites (L3 and L4, Figure 2.2). Sites that were accessible were examined in detail; in some cases interview subjects were "re-interviewed" as an understanding of the site progressed.

2.6 OBSERVATIONS

2.6.1 Oral remembrances as related during interviews

A total of eight people were spoken with formally. Seventeen additional people were interviewed informally during the course of our tenure in the community.

An elderly native woman related stories to her caregiver during the last winter of her life (1989). Of particular interest was a story told to her by her great-grandmother whose mother recalled smoke rising from Ice Mountain. Another elderly resident remembered being told, as a child, of there being smoke and fire on Ice Mountain. These were the only oral recountings of a volcanic event.

Along the Tahltan River (L1, Figure 2.2; Figure 2.4) is an important fishing and fish processing location that local residents call "The Cannery". A landslide was thought, by five interview subjects, to have occurred there during the middle 1960s, most likely 1965. Others in the community also agreed with this date and all thought that this event occurred in the spring. This landslide was also noted by fisheries personnel; a weir has been operated by the Department of Fisheries and Oceans on Tahltan Lake (Figure 2.1) since 1958 (P. Etherington, personal communication, 1993). During 1965 local residents were employed to help transport spawning salmon around the obstruction created by the landslide. Two of the residents who regularly frequented this area remembered that for some years prior to the failure, snow had failed to stay on the site of the future landslide.

Several subjects recounted that they were told that the salmon had once migrated up the Tuya River to spawn in Tuya Lake (Figure 2.1), an event that no longer occurs. None could recall when the salmon ceased to spawn. Others recounted that fish cache pits were known to exist in the immediate vicinity of Tuya Lake.

A landslide in the Mess Creek Valley (Figure 2.2) was noted in late April 1992 by the local bush pilot. The slide lies along a regular flight path and was first observed after a period of sustained rain and snow. This landslide was not noted on flyovers in previous months.

Telegraph Creek residents related stories of the Stikine River flowing the "wrong" way (i.e. upstream). Particularly pervasive was the remembrance of the Stikine River flowing east (Figure 2.2) near the village of Telegraph Creek for part of one day in the late summer of 1949. The river was a deep brown colour and was choked with fresh foliage. Although this story was originally remembered by two individuals, several others within the community corroborated this story later. Two older residents who had fished and trapped on the lower Stikine River (near the United States border) had heard numerous stories that the river, on occasion, had reversed its flow in the vicinity of the Flood Glacier, a glacier in the Coast Mountains that has its terminus near sea level and 5 km inland from the banks of the Stikine River.

FIGURE 2.4   The Tahltan River and incised Tahltan landslide debris. The rapids created by the boulder lag of the landslide are a major obstacle for Chinook, Coho and Sockeye salmon migrating to upstream spawning grounds. Arrows point to blocks of basement rock transported by the landslide

Stories of severe climate were not pervasive within the community, although most older interview subjects thought that precipitation in both the winters and the summers had been greater during, and previous to, their childhood (before *c*. 1920).

2.6.2 Recollections of Late Holocene environmental change obtained from literary sources

Both Helm (1956) and Fladmark (1985) indicate that eruptions have been recounted in oral remembrances and resulted in inhabitants being forced to move their camps quickly. Fladmark (1985) refers to a story collected by Albright (1984) about a toad, translated by Teit (1919) as E'dista, whose breath would come out through holes in the mountains and whose breathing hole was at the top of a mountain. Fladmark (1985) suggests that these cryptic references to volcanic activity may relate to events that are ". . . sufficiently far removed in time to cloud them in supernatural symbolism" (Fladmark, 1985, p. 40). Emmons (1911) documented the disappearance of moose from the region from 1800 to about 1877. The loss of this important food source affected the Tahltan peoples greatly; this period was also remembered as a time of long, harsh winters (Emmons, 1911). Dawson (1898) recounted the travels of McLeod and Simpson, who in 1838 encountered a severe rapid on the lower Tuya River, the significance of which will be discussed later.

2.6.3 Field observations and interpretations

Three landslides and one rock avalanche of significant volume were identified as late Holocene in age on the basis of resident oral histories. The three landslides (L1−L3, Figure 2.2) occurred in unconsolidated lacustrine (Glacial Lake Stikine; Ryder and Maynard, 1991) and glacial (Fraser Glaciation) strata believed to be middle to late Wisconsin in age. The rock avalanche (L4, Figure 2.2) occurred in Permian and/or Triassic bedrock (GSC Map 9-1957).

2.6.3.1 Tahltan River landslide (L1)

The failure of a 250 m thick package of horizontally bedded Glacial Lake Stikine sediments and overlying Fraser Till (Figure 2.3) along the Tahltan River (L1, Figure 2.2) resulted in a landslide 2·8 km wide and 0·9 km long and the movement of *c*. 6×10^6 m^3 of sediment. The landslide overran a traditional fish-processing site and the coarse fraction that was not transported downstream during subsequent river incision altered the hydraulics of the river, creating a series of cascading rapids at this point (Figure 2.4). The slope on which the landslide occurred averaged 14°, was faced southwest and was grassy with isolated stands of trembling aspen (*Populus tremuloides*) and alder (*Alnus* sp.). Movement of material was complex, with rotational movement dominating the upper portion of the landslide mass (Figure 2.5). Debris flow was the dominant sediment transport mechanism in the lower portion of the landslide. Near the base of the landslide trees have been inverted and buried to the root ball in slide debris. Blocks of sedimentary basement rock were incorporated and transported in the debris flow (see arrows, Figure 2.4). The contact between the relatively permeable meltout till and the underlying impermeable lodgement till and lacustrine sediment is a plane of groundwater transport

FIGURE 2.5 Headscarp of the Tahltan landslide. Note person at left-hand side of photo for scale. The site is still active with continued rotational slumps occurring almost yearly. The arrow points to the scarp headwall formed on the Glacial Lake Stikine terrace that is elevated about 300 m above the Tahltan River

and a favourable location for the initiation of slip. The contact between these two layers is visible on undisturbed slopes as a conspicuous band of tree and shrub growth.

Aerial photographs taken in 1949 offer poor resolution of the site but do indicate that some soil creep had taken place by this time. Aerial photographs taken in 1974 indicate that slope creep and rotational movement at the scarp head have occurred since the initial slide; many minor landslides have occurred within the landslide scar. The site remains active at present.

2.6.3.2 Tuya River landslide (L2)

A debris avalanche along the Tuya River Canyon (L2, Figures 2.2 and 2.6) of a similar sediment package to that observed at site L1 resulted in the movement of about 64 000 m^3 of horizontally bedded sediment into the Tuya River channel. Both bedrock and unconsolidated sediments make up the canyon walls; slopes are typically from 60° to 80°. The landslide created a 130 m high scarp. Coarse material that was not transported downcurrent produced a short but violent set of cascading rapids (Figure 2.7). Aerial photographs indicate that this slide had occurred prior to 1949.

2.6.3.3 Mess Creek Landslide (L3)

Failure of Glacial Lake Stikine sediments and overlying Fraser Till along Mess Creek (L3, Figure 2.2) resulted in a debris flow that incorporated about 1 × 10^6 m^3 of sediment. The slope at the landslide site before failure was about 8°. This landslide was observed only from the air owing to its inaccessible location. The head of the landslide lies on the terrace created by the incision of Mess Creek into Fraser Till and the underlying fine-grained silts and clays of Glacial Lake Stikine. This stratigraphic sequence is similar to that observed at sites L1 and L2.

2.6.3.4 Mess Canyon Rock Avalanche (L4)

The Mess Canyon rock avalanche (Figure 2.8) occurs in highly fractured Triassic and Permian bedrock in the 500 m deep Mess Creek Canyon. Adjacent slopes are steep, about 60° to 70°, and are unforested. A 1·5 km wide scarp defines the near-vertical fault plane on which displacement is about 100 m. Mess Creek Valley and Mess Creek Canyon fall along a series of faults, collectively called the Mess Creek Fault. The rock avalanche created a 30 m high dam, portions of which are evident on aerial photographs. Slide debris that was too large to be transported downstream has created cascading waterfalls and rapids. Aerial photographs taken between 22 and 30 August 1949 indicate that a slide scarp had developed by that time. The slide surface is hummocky, disturbed and unvegetated and the sediment that was deposited in the short-lived lake is now exposed upvalley from the slide; these observations indicate that the slide probably took place shortly before the aerial photographs were taken.

FIGURE 2.6 Tuya River landslide scarp. The scarp reveals the horizontally bedded lacustrine Glacial Lake Stikine sediments and overlying Fraser Till (see Figure 2.3). The elevation drop from the top of the scarp to the Tuya River is about 300 m

FIGURE 2.7 Tuya River rapids. These rapids developed from the coarse fraction of the landslide debris that could not be transported by the Tuya River. The river obstruction occurred prior to 1790 and is believed to have halted the upstream migration of salmon

2.7 RESULTS

The determination of the absolute timing (including the season) of landslide occurrence in the region can help determine the cause of the events. Oral recollections revealed that the Tahltan (spring, 1965) and Mess Creek (April 1992) landslides occurred in the spring; in the case of Mess Creek this followed substantial meltwater runoff. The landslides formed in similar sedimentary settings (Figure 2.3). The probable cause of the landslides was loss of cohesion and slip along the plane that separates impermeable and permeable strata. The initial slope of the slide area does not have to be great, as the variability of this component for each slide demonstrates. From a geotechnical perspective, the occurrence of landslides does not appear to be predictable; however, areas of potential instability can be determined. The Mess Canyon rock avalanche (L4, Figure 2.2) is located along the trend of the Mess Creek Fault and occurred primarily in bedrock. The reversal of Stikine River flow near Telegraph Creek probably resulted from the catastrophic breaching of the rock-avalanche-created dam. Subsequent to the collection of the oral remembrance of this event, the rock avalanche that created this dam was located on aerial photographs (Figure 2.8, L4 on Figure 2.2). Owing to its location in bedrock (as opposed to the origins in sediment for the Tahltan, Tuya and Mess Creek landslides) and along the trend of the Mess Creek Fault, which has been active during the Quaternary (Souther, 1992), there exists the possibility that this slide occurred as a result of tectonic activity. An interpretation of the aerial photographs and the oral record of this event both indicate that the landslide probably took place in August 1949. It is possible that a series of earthquakes, one of which was a magnitude 8·1 event off the coast of the Queen Charlotte Islands (22 August 1949), activated this rock avalanche; however, the precise timing of this event could not be fixed from the oral history record.

Mass movement events have the potential to impact lifestyles and alter settlement patterns. The Tahltan landslide (L1, Figures 2.2 and 2.5) overran a traditional gathering spot and transformed the hydraulics of the Tahltan River. If the newly formed rapids had proved to be a barrier to salmon migration, a significant component of the west coast salmon fishery would have been affected. It is estimated that as much as 60% of the sockeye salmon that returned up the Stikine watershed each year to spawn hatched in Tahltan Lake (see Figure 2.1; P. Etherington, personal communication, 1993). Meanwhile, the Tuya landslide created rapids which almost certainly blocked a salmon spawning route and affected native settlement patterns. Literary sources (Dawson, 1898) indicate that this event occurred before 1838, the date of the arrival of non-natives to the region. A programme to core the sediments of Tuya Lake is underway and should resolve the absolute timing of the Tuya slide and the subsequent shift in habitation patterns, through the dating of the termination of deposition of salmon macrofossils.

The oral recollections of volcanic activity combined with the recounting of possible volcanic events in legends (Fladmark, 1985; Albright, 1984) suggests that volcanic activity took place on the Edziza Plateau/Spectrum Range subsequent to the radiocarbon-dated Williams Cone eruption (*c.* 1340 BP). How recently the last eruption may have taken place is unclear. If a generation span in considered to be 20 years, one oral

FIGURE 2.8   Mess Canyon rock avalanche (A). This rock avalanche occurred in the 1940s and was believed to have dammed Mess Creek. Subsequent catastrophic breaking of the dam resulted in an upflow floodwave at the town of Telegraph Creek. The landslide may have been triggered by earthquake activity off the Queen Charlotte Islands

FIGURE 2.9   Late Holocene cinder cones of the Snowshoe Lava field, southern Edziza Plateau. The collected remembrances indicate that eruptive activity on the Edziza Plateau/Spectrum Range may have occurred as little as 160 years ago

recollection indicates that an eruption may have taken place on Mount Edziza within the last 160 years. De Laguna (1958) has shown that oral tradition can possibly record events that occurred as much as 450 BP. If this is considered to be a temporal limit to oral tradition (a conservative assumption at best) we can further constrain the age of volcanic activity on Mount Edziza to between 450 and 160 BP (Figure 2.9).

The story of a short-lived dramatic increase in river volume in the lower Stikine River, as related by older native fishermen, is also interesting. Such occurrences were believed to be fairly common. It may be that water trapped under the glaciers along the lower Stikine River is released periodically, causing quick but short-lived rises in river volume. Drainage of subglacial lakes is common, and has been noted on the Taku River drainage by Souther (1971), but has yet to be physically observed in modern times along the Stikine River drainage.

References to climate change (Emmons, 1911) were not pervasive. Fauna habitation pattern shifts and recollections of harsher winter conditions that may predate this century may be related to regional cooling that was associated with the culmination of the Little Ice Age event (Ryder, 1987).

2.8   DISCUSSION

Our study was not designed to, and hence not capable of, determining the presence or lack of an oral history tradition. However, we suspect that native oral history of long-term environmental change is not present within the study region. We do not feel that this can be related to a general lack of interest in the environment, as most residents were keenly aware of recent changes (Figure 2.10). It appears more likely to us that long-term oral traditions were greatly affected by non-native contact. Over half the population died either from smallpox or from starvation in two separate epidemics in the 1800s (Albright, 1984). It is possible that many of the clan leaders and oral historians died between 1832 – 1838 and 1847 – 1849, "... resulting in a weakening of such traditional institutions as the clan story tellers guild" (Albright, 1984, p.17). The study was also constrained by the limited number of elders that were both available and receptive to the interview process. Sheppard (1983) recognized that acceptance within the community requires that one spend a prolonged period of time in the region, participating in daily life and assuming a position of responsibility and utility within the community. This was not an option that was available to us.

As the summary of results (Table 2.1) illustrates, the different investigative techniques appear to be most effective when used in concert with each other. Anthropological technique is particularly useful in locating study sites and obtaining "rough", often minimum, ages for relatively recent (this century) events. The resolution of older events, which often requires an estimation of generation span, becomes increasingly inexact. Palynological and archaeological techniques can be used to identify trends in environmental (climate) change, the latter technique being especially useful in assessing the impact of that change (change in habitation patterns). Geomorphological, geological and anthropological data can be combined to further resolve the absolute timing of an

FIGURE 2.10 Tahltan Andy Carlick with salmon at the Department of Fisheries and Oceans weir on the Little Tahltan River. The importance of resources such as salmon to residents of the Stikine Plateau led us to suggest that changes in the environment that affected these resources are most likely to be preserved in the oral record

TABLE 2.1 Summary of investigative technique and age

Site	Physical process	Investigative technique[a]	Estimated age/ date of occurrence[b]
L1	Landslide	Anthropology/geomorphology/geology	Spring 1965
L2	Landslide	Anthropology/geology/archaeology	>156 BP (<450 BP ??)
L3	Landslide	Anthropology/geology	April 1992
L4	Rock avalanche	Anthropology/geomorphology/geology	August 1949
Mount Edziza	Volcanic eruption	Anthropology/geology/archaeology	>160 BP (<450 BP ??)
Regional	Regional cold period	Anthropology/archaeology/palynology/geology	Pre-1900?
Upper Stikine River	Flooding	Anthropology	August 1949
Lower Stikine River	Flooding	Anthropology	Not known

[a] Anthropology refers mainly to oral histories and collected remembrances
[b] Question marks (?, ??) refer to decreasing levels of confidence in the age or date

event. Dating of the Tuya River landslide (L2 on Figure 2.2, Figure 2.5 and Figure 2.6) is a good example of the rather elaborate but effective way in which a variety of techniques can be used to date an event. This landslide was noted by the authors before the oral history study was initiated. As its scarp is nearly vertical and all slide debris, save the incompetent coarse lag, has been removed, there remains no conventional means of dating the event. The oral history study uncovered four separate but connected recollections relating to it: (i) salmon had once migrated up the Tuya River; (ii) the remains of fish cache pits could be found on the shore of Tuya Lake; (iii) cascading rapids on the lower Tuya River are the present barrier to salmon migration (P. Etherington, personal communication, 1993); and (iv) the rapids predate the arrival of non-natives to the region. Connecting these events led to the summation that these rapids formed the original barrier to salmon migration at least 156 years ago and revealed a means (lake coring) by which the absolute age of the landslide could be determined.

An oral historian is ''. . . governed in what he can do by the amount and quality of the evidence he believes he can uncover . . .'' (Henige, 1982, p.24). This is not necessarily so for a geologist using oral history as a tool. Some remembrances have been verified geologically; for others, geological evidence must still be found to physically verify the event(s). The importance to geologists of oral histories appears greatest when they are considered as an investigative tool and are used primarily to locate sites of interest and verify specific events. Oral history is also the only technique available with which to gauge the impact of an event on both the environment and the resident population. In the study area, the accuracy of oral history as a dating method was limited by the small population size, imprecise determination of generation spans and the questionable status of a continuing oral tradition.

In many cases, determination of the cause of an event is more desirable than its absolute age. When investigating landslide phenomena the season and the precipitation levels (spring runoff/ heavy rains, etc.) are desirable information as they can lead to an understanding as to why initial slope failure occurred and under what conditions future slope failure should be expected. Resident histories are one of the very few investigative techniques that offer the possibility of determining the season and local moisture conditions at the time of failure.

2.9 SUMMARY

The small sample group in this study negates the use of statistical methodology to ascertain authenticity. We were able to locate recent landslides that postdate aerial photograph coverage and in specific cases the stories provided year and season of the slope failure. Both resident histories and site investigation support the conclusion that failure of Glacial Lake Stikine sediments commonly occurs in the spring, is associated with periods of peak runoff resulting in sediment saturation, loss of cohesion and subsequent failure, and is not related to tectonic activity. The coarse lags of the landslide debris have altered river hydraulics. These landslides have the potential to disrupt transportation routes and alter the migratory routes of salmon.

Stories suggesting that volcanic activity on Mount Edziza may have occurred in the last millennium give added impetus to studies of the eruptive history of the Stikine volcanic belt. Continued volcanic studies involve the coring of lakes to the east of the volcanic plateau in an attempt to locate and date ash and cinders that may have been transported by the dominantly westerly winds.

It is our belief that in isolated locales, where the lifestyle of the resident population is tied closely to the environment, changes to that environment will be noticed. To those carrying out research on late Holocene environmental change in remote, rugged regions, where traditional means of location and observation are not readily available, the oral histories of those who populate the region are another tool that can be used to resolve the timing, magnitude and social impact of environmental change.

ACKNOWLEDGEMENTS

We would like to thank the people of Telegraph Creek and the Tahltan Band Council for their interest and cooperation in this project. We owe a great debt to Ron Janzen, the owner of Tel-Air 1987 Flight Services. Not only did he introduce us to many within the community, without whom much of this work could not have been completed, but his knowledge of the geography of the region led to many interesting discoveries. Rick, Barb and Rosemary McCutcheon and Jim Bourquin and family provided helpful advice and guidance. We would like to thank Peter Etherington and Andy Carlick (Canadian Department of Fisheries and Oceans) for their interest in this project. Funding for this project was provided by the Geological Society of America, the Canadian Circumpolar Institute, the University of Calgary, NSERC and the Northern Science Training Program Grants through the Arctic Institute of North America. We thank Olav Slaymaker, Rick McCutcheon and two anonymous reviewers for their helpful comments and suggestions.

REFERENCES

Albright, S.L. 1984. *Tahltan Ethnoarchaeology*. Department of Archaeology, Simon Fraser University, British Columbia, Canada, Publication No. 15, 127 pp.

Alley, N.F. and Young, G.K. 1978. *North Central British Columbia: Environmental Significance of Geomorphic Processes*. Bulletin—Ministry of the Environment, Resource Analysis Branch, No. 10, 83 pp.

Blong, R.L. 1982. *The Time of Darkness: Local Legends and Volcanic Reality in Papua New Guinea*. University of Washington Press, Seattle.

Cockfield, W.E. 1926. *Explorations Between Atlin and Telegraph Creek*, British Columbia. Canada Department of Mines Geological Survey Summary Report, 1925, Part A, No. 2113, 25–32.

Dawson, G.M. 1898. *Report on an Exploration in the Yukon District, N.W.T. and Adjacent Northern Portion of British Columbia*. Geological Survey of Canada Paper, Queen"s Printer, Ottawa, Canada.

de Laguna, F. 1958. Geological confirmation of native traditions, Yakutat, Alaska. *American Antiquity*, 23, 434.

de Laguna, F. 1964. *Archaeology of the Yakutat Bay Area*. Bureau of American Ethnology Bulletin No. 192, Smithsonian Institution, Washington, DC.

de Laguna, F. 1972. *Under Mt. St. Elias. The History and Culture of the Yakutat Tlingit*. Smithsonian Contributions to Anthropology, No. 7, Smithsonian Institution Press, Washington, DC.

Emmons, G.T. 1911. *The Tahltan Indians*. The Museum of Anthropological Publications, Philadelphia University Museum, Wisconsin Historical Society, Vol. 6.

Fladmark, K.R. 1985. *Glass and Ice: The Archaeology of Mt. Edziza*. Department of Archaeology, Simon Fraser University, Publication No. 15, 217 pp.

Gottesfeld, A.S., Mathewes, R. and Gottesfeld, L. 1991. Holocene debris flows and environmental history, Hazelton area, British Columbia. *Canadian Journal of Earth Sciences*, **28**, 1583−1593.

Hamilton, T.S. 1981. *Late Cenozoic Alkaline Volcanics of the Level Mountain Range, Northwestern British Columbia: Geology, Petrology and Paleomagnetism*. PhD Thesis, Department of Geology, University of Alberta, Canada, 474 pp.

Helm, J. 1956. Field notes on the Tahltan and Kaska Indians: 1912−15. *Anthropologica*, **3**, 39−171.

Henige, D. 1982. *Oral Historiography*, Longman, New York.

Johnson, W.A. 1926. *Gold Placers of the Dease Lake Area*. Canada Department of Mines Geological Survey Summary Report, 1925, Part A, No. 2113, 33−75.

Kerr, F.A. 1926. *Dease Lake Area, Cassiar District British Columbia*. Canada Department of Mines Geological Survey Summary Report, 1925, Part A, No. 2113, 75−100.

Miller, M.M. and Anderson, J.H. 1974a. Out-of-phase Holocene climatic trends in the maritime and continental sectors of the Alaska−Canada Boundary Range. In Mahaney, W.C. (ed.), *Quaternary Environments: Proceedings of a Symposium*, York University, Geographical Monographs, No. 5, 33−58.

Miller, M.M. and Anderson, J.H. 1974b. Alaskan Glacier Commemorative Project, Phase IV: Pleistocene−Holocene sequences in the Alaska−Canada Boundary Range. In Oehser, P.H. (ed.), *National Geographic Society Reports, Abstracts and Reviews of Research and Exploration Authorized under Grants from the National Geographic Society during the year 1967*, National Geographic Society, Washington DC, 197−223.

Moodie, D.W., Catchpole, A.J.W. and Abel, K. 1992. Northern Athapaskan oral traditions and the White River Volcano. *Ethnohistory*, **39**(2), 148−171.

Patterson, R.M. 1966. *Trail to the Interior*. William Morrow, New York, 225 pp.

Ryder, J.M. 1987. Neoglacial history of the Stikine — Iskut area, northern Coast Mountains, British Columbia. *Canadian Journal of Earth Sciences*, **24**, 1294−1301.

Ryder, J.M. and Maynard, D. 1991. The Cordilleran Ice Sheet in Northern British Columbia. *Geographie Physique et Quaternaire*, **45**(3), 355−363.

Sheppard, J. 1983. *The Histories and Values of a Northern Athapaskan Indian Village*. PhD Dissertation, The University of Wisconsin-Madison, Ann Arbor, MI, USA.

Souther, J.G. 1970. Recent volcanism and its influence on early native cultures of northwestern British Columbia. In Smith, R.A. and Smith, J.W. (eds), *Early Man and Environments in Northwest North America*. Students Press, Calgary, 53−64.

Souther, J.G. 1971. *Geology and Mineral Deposits of the Tulsequah Map-area, British Columbia*. Geological Survey of Canada, Memoir 362.

Souther, J.G. 1992. *The Late Cenozoic Mount Edziza Volcanic Complex, British Columbia*. Geological Survey of Canada, Memoir 420.

Spooner, I.S. 1993. Comparison of Early Pleistocene and Wisconsin glacial successions in northwestern British Columbia: Implications for the repeatability of large-scale ice sheet dynamics. In *Program with Abstracts and Field Guide*. Canadian Quaternary Association Biennial Meeting, 18−21 April 1993, A44.

Teit, J.A. 1906. Notes on the Tahltan Indians of British Columbia. In Laufer, B. (ed.), *Boas Anniversary Volume*, G.E. Stechert, New York, 337−349.

Teit, J.A. 1909. Two Tahltan traditions. *Journal of American Folklore*, **22**, 314−318.

Teit, J.A. 1919. Tahltan tales. *Journal of American Folklore*, **32**, 198−250.

Teit, J.A. 1921. Tahltan tales. *Journal of American Folklore*, **34**, 223−258 and 335−356.

Watson, K. DeP. and Mathews, W.H. 1944. *The Tuya−Teslin Area, Northern British Columbia*. British Columbia Department of Mines Bulletin No. 19.

3

Morphological Evidence for Neotectonic Activity and Seismic Hazard in the Acambay Graben, Mexican Volcanic Belt

M. Teresa Ramírez-Herrera

Instituto de Geografía, Universidad Nacional Autónoma de México

ABSTRACT

Relevant geomorphic evidence indicative of neotectonic activity in the Acambay graben, a major structure in the central part of the Mexican Volcanic Belt, was derived from remote sensing analysis, employing large-scale aerial photos and digitally enhanced Landsat imagery, as well as topographic maps, in conjunction with detailed field mapping.

The Acambay—Tixmadeje, Pastores, Venta de Bravo, and Temascalcingo fault systems, which are generally oriented east—west, expose linear ridges, sag ponds, offset drainage, shutter and compression ridges which indicate a left-lateral component. Prominent fault scarps and triangular facets show vertical displacement along the faults flanking the graben. The existence of such morphological features implies that these faults have been active since the Quaternary. Tectonic landforms in the Acambay graben reflect faulting characterized by normal south-facing and normal north-facing faults combined with left-lateral displacement.

Morphological evidence and the historical occurrence of seismic activity along the Venta de Bravo fault system suggest that it is the most tectonic and potentially seismic active fault system in the Acambay graben.

3.1 INTRODUCTION

Despite a number of case studies of the large-scale tectonics of central and southern Mexico (López, 1984; Johnson, 1987; Pasquaré et al., 1987; Ortiz and Bocco-Verdinelli, 1989; Johnson and Harrison, 1989, 1990; Martínez-Reyes and Nieto-Samaniego, 1990; Ramírez-Herrera, 1990), there has been little application of geomorphological techniques to understanding the nature of recent seismic activity, and the relationship between the genesis of micro- to mesoscale tectonic landforms and the regional geodynamic setting. An integrated meso- and microscale morphotectonic approach has yet to be applied to improve understanding of the neotectonic regime in southern Mexico.

As a step towards such an understanding a field study is presented here of active and Quaternary tectonics. The specific aim of the research is the identification of

---

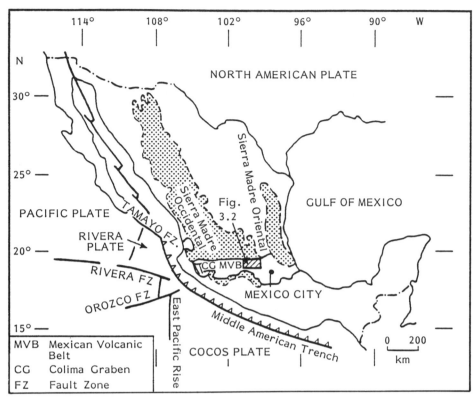

FIGURE 3.1 Tectonic setting of the Mexican Volcanic Belt (MVB). Shaded square shows the location of the Acambay graben

geomorphological evidence indicating neotectonic activity in the Acambay graben, a major structure in the central part of the Mexican Volcanic Belt, and an assessment of its relationship to regional-scale geodynamics and local seismicity. This study involved a combination of detailed field mapping and remote sensing analysis employing large-scale aerial photography (scales 1:50 000 and 1:25 000) and digitally enhanced Landsat (TM) imagery.

3.2 MAJOR TECTONIC FEATURES OF THE CENTRAL MVB AND HISTORIC SEISMICITY

The Acambay graben is located in the central part of the Mexican Volcanic Belt between latitude 19°45′−20°00′ north and longitude 99°45′−100°25′ west (Figure 3.1). The Mexican Volcanic Belt is a structure 20−150 km broad extending for around 1000 km in an approximately east−west direction from the Pacific Ocean to the Gulf of Mexico. It is an active, mostly calc-alkaline volcanic chain (Verma, 1987), genetically associated with subduction of the Cocos plate beneath the North American plate along the Middle

American trench. The central part of the Belt is characterized by generally east—west striking faults which form a series of *en echelon* grabens along its length. This structural style, which is indicative of an extensional regime, is clearly related to the volcanism and regional-scale tectonics of the area. Northwest—southeast-trending lineaments in the Belt's central section are thought to be older, reactivated structures related to the subduction of the Farallon Plate (Mooser and Ramírez-Herrera, 1989). It has been proposed by Mooser and Ramírez-Herrera (1989) that the Acambay graben, along with the other series of *en echelon* graben and horsts of the Mexican Volcanic Belt, is the product of episodically active left-lateral shear in the upper brittle section of the crust generated in the Middle American trench and the newly developing Colima graben to the west (Luhr et al., 1985).

Analysis of aerial photographs in conjunction with digitally enhanced Landsat imagery has revealed east—west trending faults of Quaternary age which give rise to pronounced scarps over a distance of around 70 km. Continuing tectonic activity in the Acambay graben is confirmed by recent well-documented seismic episodes such as the Acambay event of 1912 (Urbina and Camacho, 1913) and the Venta de Bravo event of 1979 (Astiz, 1980), both of which caused significant vertical displacements along faults flanking the graben. Earthquakes have been recorded on several of the faults in the region during historic time (based on newspaper reports in *Diario Oficial* of 25 January 1854, and *Siglo XIX* of 10 March 1854, cited in Suter et al., 1992). The Acambay event ($M_s = 6 \cdot 9$) of 19 November 1912 generated vertical displacements of up to $0 \cdot 5$ m (Urbina and Camacho, 1913), (M_s — surface-wave magnitude). The most recent significant seismic activity occurred in 1979 and involved approximately 90 individual events extending over several months (from February to June), with the main shock, the Venta de Bravo event ($M_b = 5 \cdot 3$), occurring near the beginning of the sequence on 22 February (Astiz, 1980, (M_b — body-wave magnitude)). The focus of the main shock was located $27 \cdot 8 \pm 4 \cdot 2$ km east of Maravatío at a depth of $8 \cdot 2 \pm 2 \cdot 9$ km, with the epicentre being close to the outcrop of the Venta de Bravo fault (Astiz, 1980).

3.3 MORPHOLOGICAL EVIDENCE OF NEOTECTONIC ACTIVITY IN THE ACAMBAY GRABEN

Morphological observations were gathered from the field, airphoto-interpretation and the interpretation of digitally enhanced satellite imagery in order to identify neotectonic structures in the Acambay graben. Detailed geomorphological mapping was carried out at a scale of 1:50 000 and focused on the eastern part of the graben as far west as Maravatío (longitude 100°25′ W) (Figure 3.2) since this is the area in which the geomorphological expression of faults is most evident. Five major fault systems related to specific neotectonic structures were identified:

1. the Pastores fault;
2. the Venta de Bravo fault system on the southern margin of the graben;
3. the Acambay—Tixmadeje fault system;
4. Tepuxtepec faults on the northern flank of the graben; and
5. the Temascalcingo faults in the centre of the graben (Figure 3.2).

32

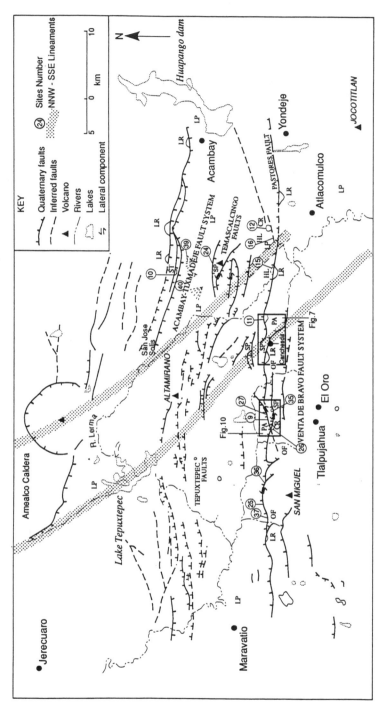

FIGURE 3.2 Morphotectonic map of the Acambay graben. Ticks on fault lines indicate downthrown side. Symbols: LP — lacustrine plain, LR — linear ridge, HL — high level of lake deposits, CR — compression ridges, PA — pull-apart basins, SP — sag ponds, ST — shutter ridges, OF — offset drainage

Detailed aspects of the morphology will be discussed along with the description of specific faults in the following sections.

3.3.1 Pastores fault

The east—west-trending normal Pastores fault forms the southern boundary of the eastern part of the Acambay graben (Figure 3.2). The scarp of the Pastores fault is formed in basaltic andesites, the Pastores volcanic rocks (Late Miocene?). These rocks appear to be partly mantled by andesitic conglomerates and pumice-rich tuffs (Sánchez-Rubio, 1984). The Pastores fault also truncates volcanic rocks of the Atlacomulco Formation (Early Miocene) (Sánchez-Rubio, 1984). The Pastores fault as well as the lacustrine tuff beds in the area of Atlacomulco appear partially covered by the Pleistocene Atlacomulco andesites that form a lava field. However, there is morphological evidence of the displacement of the fault in this area.

The fault is 30 km in length and is associated with a scarp 200—250 m high with a gradient of approximately 21°—46°. The fault has a clear continuous topographic expression over a distance of 14 km, while at its eastern end its presence is evident through the displacement of cinder and scoria cones. At San Pedro Potla at the foot of the Pastores fault scarp, the proximity of elevated lake deposits to the fault suggests that they may have been displaced by faulting, although they do not show evidence of tilting in this area (Site 15, Figure 3.2).

Terraces with small scarps can be seen on the Toxi Plain north of the Pastores fault (Site 16, Figure 3.2), and may have a tectonic origin, similar to those reported after the 1912 earthquake (Urbina and Camacho, 1913). They may be interpreted as "short-term" evidence (Armijo et al., 1986) of Late Quaternary tectonic movements, but it is difficult to distinguish them from agricultural terraces. North of the Pastores fault (Site 12, Figure 3.2), however, there are deformed lake deposits (86° inclination and east—west trend and some deformed into recumbent folds). There is also an apparently 30° WSW-trending fault at this location while a reverse fault exposed at this site indicates the presence of compressional stresses (Figure 3.3). The deformed lake deposits are apparently part of a small compression ridge which is bounded by two arroyos associated with two ENE—WSW-trending faults which displace lake deposits. It is probable that this area between the two faults has experienced both extension and compression, but further investigations are required to confirm this interpretation.

A swampy depression between the two fault segments at Canchesdá is indicative of a pull-apart basin representing an extensional off-set (Suter et al., 1991) (Site 11, Figure 3.2). This structure provides further evidence that movement along the two fault segments includes a minor left-lateral strike-slip component (Figure 3.4).

3.3.2 Venta de Bravo fault system

The oldest outcropping rocks truncated by the Venta de Bravo fault system are folded and slightly metamorphosed Mesozoic sediments (Flores, 1920) which in the El Oro region (Fries et al., 1977) and at Cerro San Miguel (Silva-Mora, 1979) are overlain by andesitic-dacitic volcanic rocks (Silva-Mora, 1979). Higher in the sequence lake deposits occur south of Canchesdá, and ignimbrite deposits (Las Americas Formation) cover the mainly

Geomorphic Hazards

FIGURE 3.3 Reverse fault displacing lake deposits near the eastern end of the Pastores fault.
Symbols: a — displaced layer

flat surfaces forming mesas. North of Tlalpujahua, on the northern border of an ignimbrite mesa, dissection has occurred, possibly due to the posterior faulting in this region (Fries et al., 1977). The hanging wall of the Venta de Bravo master fault is composed of the lake deposits of the Ixtapantongo Formation (Sánchez-Rubio, 1984), scoria cones with associated basalt flows (Silva-Mora, 1979), and alluvial fan deposits. According to Suter et al. (1992), the east−west-trending normal faults of the study area have been active in the Late Quaternary. Further age constraints on seismic activity are provided by the lake deposits of the Ixtapantongo Formation, which have a minimum thickness of 5 m and ^{14}C ages of <23 ka (Sánchez-Rubio, 1984). They are displaced by the Pastores fault and are truncated by the Venta de Bravo fault south of Canchesdá (Figure 3.2).

The Venta de Bravo fault consists of a master fault with several shorter east−west-striking normal fault segments to the north and south. It is expressed topographically by a continuous, 45 km long, north-facing fault scarp which attains a maximum height of 300 m near the strato-volcano of San Miguel (Figure 3.2). At this location in the central section of the fault, the scarp exhibits "long-term" morphological evidence (Armijo et al., 1986) of probable Quaternary activity: triangular facets associated with deeply incised V-shaped valleys (Figure 3.5). This area of maximum relief along the fault system is located approximately 10 km west of the epicentre of the main shock of the 1979 series of seismic events (Suter et al., 1992).

South of Venta de Bravo town an almost parallel associated minor fault, with a downthrown block facing to the north, joins the master fault on its western side and creates a rhomboid depression between the two faults (Figure 3.6), (for location see

Figure 3.2). The presence of a sediment-filled sag pond at the base of the scarp of the associated minor fault to the south, and the left-lateral displacement observed on the Encinal River where it crosses segments of the fault, both provide evidence of recent left-lateral movement (Figure 3.6). This structural configuration is interpreted as an incipient pull-apart feature which indicates extension within the area (Suter et al., 1991, 1992). However, a ridge (Site 26, Figure 3.2) indicative of local compression is present in the zone of intersection between the two faults.

Along the Venta de Bravo master fault near the Encinal River (Site 27, Figure 3.2) the presence of triangular facets along the scarp formed by V-shaped valleys cut into andesitic volcanic rocks is indicative of recent fault activity. Other indicators of recent seismicity in this part of the fault scarp include offset drainage and rock slides (Figure 3.6). The Venta de Bravo fault scarps reveal fault planes at several locations (Sites 35, 36 and 37, Figure 3.2) and at some of these, such as at Site 25 (Figure 3.2) at the western end of the fault, subvertical striations and a "tool track" (Hancock and Barka, 1987) are

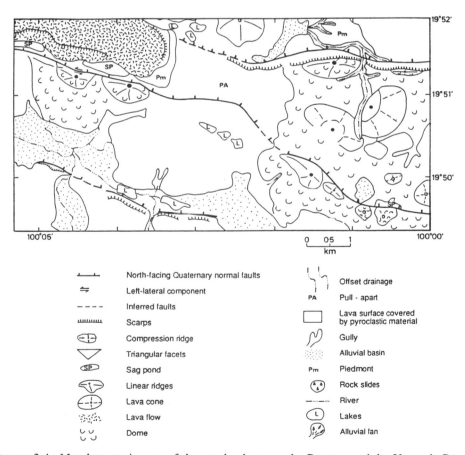

FIGURE 3.4   Morphotectonic map of the overlap between the Pastores and the Venta de Bravo faults (Site 11, Figure 3.2)

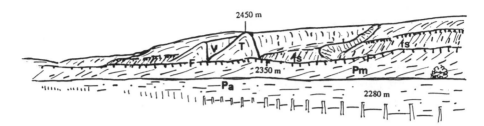

T - Triangular facets   Pm - Piedmont
F - Fault   fs - Fault scarp
Pa - Alluvial plain   V - V-shaped valley

FIGURE 3.5 Morphological sketch of tectonic landforms along the Venta de Bravo fault

visible. Fault planes exposed along the Encinal River are associated with friction breccia, mylonite and black soapstone, which provide evidence of slip along the fault.

3.3.3 Acambay – Tixmadeje fault system

The Acambay – Tixmadeje fault system, which extends from Acambay to San José Solís and forms the northern boundary of the Acambay graben, is characterized by east – west-trending normal faults (Figure 3.2). Some of the individual faults are up to 30 km long and are associated with fault scarps averaging 400 to 450 m in height. The boundary between the Acambay and Tepuxtepec faults is marked by the valley of the Lerma River and a 180° change in dip azimuth of the normal fault that cuts the southern fringe of the Amealco caldera (Suter et al., 1991). Fault planes can be observed in the hanging wall of the Acambay – Tixmadeje master fault. They have slickensides and show steps and

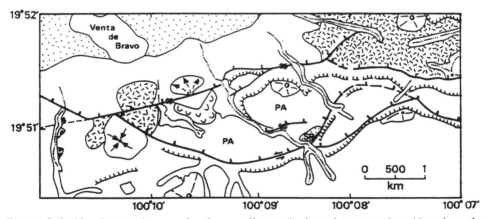

FIGURE 3.6 Morphotectonic map showing a pull-apart basin and compression ridge along the Venta de Bravo fault (for location see Figure 3.2). Key as for Figure 3.4

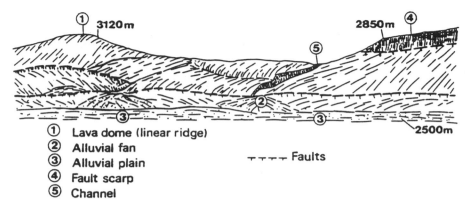

FIGURE 3.7   Morphological sketch of a mountain front of the northern flank of the
Acambay graben

subvertical striations as also observed by Suter et al. (1991). This micromorphological
evidence may represent recent tectonic movement. Along the scarps of the
Acambay—Tixmadeje fault system (Site 40, Figure 3.2) there are well-defined triangular
facets. The scarp, which has a relatively low gradient of approximately 25°, has been
deeply eroded and incised and at its foot it is partially covered by colluvium and in some
places by alluvial fans (Figure 3.7). Drainage channels have been blocked by a second
fault on the scarp apparently displaying some strike-slip component. Basaltic cones and
linear ridges appear along this part of the fault (Figure 3.8). The linear ridges are
probably shutter ridges (Sylvester, 1988) and therefore indicate a strike-slip component
along the fault (Site 10, Figure 3.2).

3.3.4   The Tepuxtepec fault system

The Tepuxtepec fault system which extends from Mount Altamirano to a point north of
Maravatío, is characterized by east—west normal faults (Figure 3.2). Although the
northern flank of the Acambay graben is predominantly characterized by south-facing
normal faults, there are some north-facing faults which, where present, give rise to small
graben and horst structures. Overall the fault system is approximately 40 km long, but
individual faults are limited to 8 km in length. The Tepuxtepec system is composed of
several truncated faults which have a clear topographic expression and a mean height of
around 30 m. Changes in the direction of the drainage and long straight segments of the
Lerma river clearly show the location of several faults in the Tepuxtepec system. In its
central part the fault system is partially buried beneath the sediments of Lake Tepuxtepec.

3.3.5   Temascalcingo faults

The deeply eroded peak of Temascalcingo, which reaches an elevation of 3220 m, is
located in the central part of the Acambay graben (Figure 3.2). This volcano is a complex
structure formed by massive andesitic lavas as well as by a thick agglomerate of andesitic

composition. A dome-like body of dacitic composition, with a K—Ar age 8·5 Ma (Sánchez-Rubio, 1984), occurs inside the graben by the eastern foot of the volcano, where it is partly mantled by tuffs and alluvium. The Temascalcingo volcanic structure is truncated in its central part by a series of east—west-trending faults, the Temascalcingo faults, which form a small graben structure within the volcano (Figure 3.2). The overall fault system extends for 18 km, with individual fault segments reaching 11 km in length and associated fault scarps up to 150 m high. Small sediment-filled depressions (sag ponds) occur along a fault flanking the north of Temascalcingo (Site 24, Figure 3.2). The scarp at this location is approximately 50 m high.

A series of faults is exposed along the arroyo of Tinajal, located on an alluvial fan on the northwest flank of Temascalcingo (Site 39, Figure 3.2). The northern fault encountered has a direction of 80°E, and, on the basis of the dislocation of the underlying conglomeratic horizon, it has a vertical throw of 0·87 m and a horizontal displacement of approximately 1 m (Figure 3.9). It appears to be a strike-slip fault with a left-lateral component. Upstream there are several other faults that displace a tuff deposit and the lower conglomeratic horizon. On the western flank of Temascalcingo, lava flows are cut by a series of ESE—WNW-trending, northward, dipping faults arranged *en echelon*, giving rise to scarps 20 m in height. Some of these faults are associated with small sag ponds, but there is no clear evidence of a lateral component to the faulting in this area.

Further west of the Temascalcingo volcano there are several ESE—WNW-trending faults that cross and cut a rhyolitic lava field of Quaternary age and form lava domes with a K—Ar age of 1·57 ± 0·15 Ma (Demant and Robin, 1975). Some of these faults are shown by the alignment of lava cones and the presence of scarps. There are also small swampy depressions along some of the faults that might indicate tectonic activity.

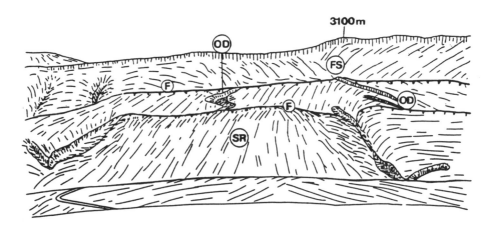

OD   Offset drainage
SR   Shutter ridge
F   Fault
FS   Fault scarp

FIGURE 3.8 Morphological sketch of the northern flank of the Acambay graben. Linear ridges are exposed on the frontal part of the slope and offset drainage shows the location of displacement by a fault of the Acambay—Tixmadeje system

FIGURE 3.9 Exposure showing a fault with a 0·87 m vertical displacement of a conglomerate on a component of the Temascalcingo fault system

3.4. DISCUSSION AND CONCLUSION

A range of geomorphological evidence indicates recent tectonic activity along the faults bounding the Acambay graben. Such morphological indicators are most evident along the southern flank of the graben, particularly along the Venta de Bravo fault system, in the northern flank along Acambay – Tixmadeje fault system and in the central part along Temascalcingo faults. Here, prominent fault scarps, triangular-faceted spurs, offset drainage, sag ponds and compression ridges are clearly developed, and high slope gradients demonstrate the freshness of the scarps. In contrast, faults in the Tepuxtepec system exhibit shallow gradient slopes and low fault scarps which may indicate either more prolonged erosion or a lower rate of tectonic activity in this part of the graben. Except for limited historical evidence, there is as yet no absolute dating available for the most recent fault displacements, and consequently estimates have to be based on the degree of fault scarp degradation.

The geomorphological evidence indicative of neotectonic activity described here shows that the faults in the southern flank of the graben have experienced slip combining normal north-facing faulting and left-lateral displacement, with significant lateral displacements being most clearly expressed morphologically along the Venta de Bravo fault system. The Acambay—Tixmadeje fault system consists of normal south-facing faults with a component of left-lateral displacement. By contrast, the Tepuxtepec faults are mainly north-facing and where combined with south-facing normal faults give rise to small graben structures. The Temascalcingo faults, in the centre of the graben, are also characterized by a combination of normal south- and north-facing faults with a component of left-lateral displacement, giving rise to a graben structure within the volcano of Temascalcingo. Although the Acambay graben is a complex zone of extension, it also shows some evidence of compression. This is indicated by two compression ridges, one located on the western end of the pull-apart structure along the the central part of the Venta de Bravo fault, and the other situated at the eastern end of the Toxi plain. Since other morphological features indicative of compression have not been detected in the region, these compression ridges are probably secondary structures related to left-lateral motion at fault junctions.

In summary, this study demonstrates that: (1) the tectonic landforms of the Acambay graben reflect fault activity characterized by normal north- and south-facing faults combined with left-lateral displacement; (2) geomorphological data for the Acambay graben are consistent with systems of faults which have experienced transtensive, large-scale, left-lateral shear along the Mexican Volcanic Belt; and (3) the clarity of the geomorphological evidence and the historical occurrence of seismicity along the Venta de Bravo system of faults suggest that this is the most tectonically active structure in the Acambay graben. Further analysis of neotectonic activity in the region is recommended in order to document more precisely both spatial and temporal variations in seismicity.

ACKNOWLEDGEMENTS

This research was financially supported by the Universidad Nacional Autónoma de México (UNAM). Travel funds were granted by the Instituto de Geografía, UNAM. It is a pleasure to acknowledge the help of Dr M. Summerfield for his thorough review and advice.

REFERENCES

Armijo, R., Tapponier, P., Hang, J.L. and Tong-Lin. 1986. Quaternary extension in southern Tibet: Field observations and tectonic implications. *Journal of Geophysical Research*, **91** (B14), 13803–13872.

Astiz, L.M. 1980. *Sismicidad en Acambay, Estado de México. El Temblor del 22 de Febrero de 1979*. BS Thesis, Universidad Nacional Autónoma de México, México, 130 pp.

Demant, A. and Robin, C. 1975. Las fases de vulcanismo en México: una síntesis en relación con la evolución geodinámica desde el Cretácico. *Revista del Instituto de Geología, Universidad Nacional Autónoma de México*, **75** (1), 70–82.

Flores, T. 1920. Estudio geológico-minero de los distritos de El Oro y Tlalpujahua. *Boletín, Instituto de Geología, UNAM*, **43**, 85 pp.

Fries, J., Ross, C.S.A. and Obregón 1977. Mezcla de vidrios en los derrames cineríticos Las Américas de la región de El Oro-Tlalpujahua, Estados de México y Michoacán, parte centromeridional de México. *Boletín del Instituto de Geología, Universidad Nacional Autónoma de México*, **70**, 1−84.

Hancock, P.L. and Barka, A.A. 1987. Kinematic indicators on active normal faults in Western Turkey. *Journal of Structural Geology*, **9**, 573−584.

Johnson, C.A. 1987. *A Study of Neotectonics in Central Mexico from Landsat Thematic Mapper Imagery*. MS Thesis, University of Miami, Coral Gables, Florida, 112 pp.

Johnson, C.A. and Harrison, C.G.A. 1989. Tectonics and volcanism in central Mexico: a Landsat Thematic Mapper perspective. *Remote Sens. Environ.*, **28**, 273−286.

Johnson, C.A. and Harrison, C.G.A. 1990. Neotectonics in Central Mexico. *Physics of the Earth and Planetary Interiors*, **64** (2−4), 187−210.

López, G.G. 1984. *Tectonic Structure and Development of the Trans-Mexican Volcanic Belt*. PhD Thesis, Moscow State University, Moscow (in Russian).

Luhr, J.F., Nelson, S.A., Allan, J.F. and Carmichael, I.S.E. 1985. Active rifting in southwestern Mexico: manifestations of an incipient eastward spreading-ridge jump. *Geology*, **10**, 37−48.

Martínez-Reyes, J. and Nieto-Samaniego, A.F. 1990. Efectos geológicos de la tectónica reciente en la parte central de México. *Revista de Instituto de Geología, Universidad Nacional Autónoma de México*, **9** (1), 33−50.

Mooser, F. and Ramírez-Herrera, M.T. 1989. Faja Volcánica Transmexicana: Morfoestructura, tectónica y vulcanotectónica. *Boletín de la Sociedad Geológica Mexicana*, **T. XLVIII** (2), 75−85.

Ortiz-P, M.A. and Bocco-Verdinelli, G. 1989. Análisis morfotectónico de las depresiones de Ixtlahuaca y Toluca, México. *Geofísica Internacional*, **28** (3), 507−530.

Pasquaré, G., Ferrari, L., Perazzoli, V., Tiberi, M. and Turchetti, F. 1987. Morphological and structural analysis of the central sector of the Transmexican Volcanic Belt. *Geofísica Internacional*, (special volume on Mexican volcanic belt) **26** (3B), 177−193.

Ramírez-Herrera, M.T. 1990. *Análisis Morfoestructural de la Faja Volcánica Transmexicana (centro-oriente)*. MSc Thesis. Universidad Nacional Autónoma de México, México DF, 86 pp.

Sánchez-Rubio, G. 1984. *Cenozoic Volcanism in the Toluca − Amealco Region, Central Mexico*. MPhil Thesis. University of London, Imperial College of Science and Technology, 275 pp.

Silva-Mora, L. 1979. *Contribution à la Connaissance de l'Axe Volcanique Transmexicain: Etude Géologique et Pétrologique des Laves du Michoacán Oriental*. Thèse de Docteur Ingénieur, part I, *Université de Droit, d'Economie et des Sciences d'Aix − Marseille France*, France, 145 pp.

Suter, G., Aguirre, J., Siebe, C., Quintero, O. and Komorowski, J.C. 1991. Volcanism and active faulting in the central part of the Trans-Mexican volcanic belt. In Walawender, M.J. and Hanan, B.B. (eds), *Geological Excursions in Southern California and Mexico*. Guidebook of Annual Meeting of the Geological Society of America, San Diego, California, 21−24 October 1991, 224−243.

Suter, G., Quintero, O. and Johnson, C.A. 1992. Active faults and State of Stress in the Central Part of the Trans-Mexican Volcanic Belt, Mexico. Part 1: The Venta de Bravo fault. *Journal of Geophysical Research*, **97** (B8), 11983−11993.

Sylvester, A.G. 1988. Strike-slip faults. *Geological Society of America Bulletin*, **100**, 1666−1703.

Urbina, F. and Camacho, H. 1913. La zona megasísmica Acambay-Tixmadeje, Estado de México, conmovida el 19 de noviembre de 1912. *Boletín del Instituto Geológico de México*, **32**, 125 pp.

Verma, S.P. 1987. Mexican volcanic belt: Present state of knowledge and unsolved problems. *Geofísica Internacional* (special volume on Mexican volcanic belt), **26** (3B), 309−340.

4

Landslides in Flysch Formations in the Northern Apennines, Italy

CARLO ELMI

Dipartimento di Scienze Geologiche, Università di Bologna

AND

OLIVIA NESCI

Istituto di Geologia, Università di Urbino

ABSTRACT

In the Northern Apennines three main flysch formations are present, covering more than 60% of the entire area: the Monghidoro Formation (Upper Cretaceous), the Macigno Formation (Upper Oligocene – Middle Miocene), and the Marnoso-arenacea Formation (Middle – Upper Miocene). Different types of rock movements occur in the three formations, owing to their different tectonic styles and jointing patterns: mainly rock block slides are observed in the Marnoso-Arenacea Formation; rock slumps are more frequent in the Monghidoro and Macigno Formations. Thirty large landslides, still active or dating from the last 400 years, have been examined from the geomorphic and geotechnical viewpoint: they range from 1 to 3 km in length and from 1×10^5 to 1×10^7 m³ in volume. The back-analysis showed that, notwithstanding the high values of peak friction angles (28 – 30°), the slides occurred on slopes from 15° to less than 10°, generally linked to intense rainfall. Some statistical analyses on the main parameters have been performed, aimed at obtaining detailed knowledge of the most common and most unstable formations of the Northern Apennines.

4.1 INTRODUCTION

The aim of this paper, which extends previous work (Elmi et al., 1993), is to study and compare landslides that occur in the most common flysch formations covering more than 60% of the Northern Apennines, Italy (Figure 4.1). The examined area is part of the Adriatic side of the chain, between the Reno and Bidente Rivers, and between the main divide and the Po River Plain. Elevations range from 200 to 1200 m. The climate is temperate (subcontinental); the rainfall varies from 700 to 1500 mm a^{-1} and is

Geomorphic Hazards. Edited by O. Slaymaker.
© 1996 by John Wiley & Sons Ltd

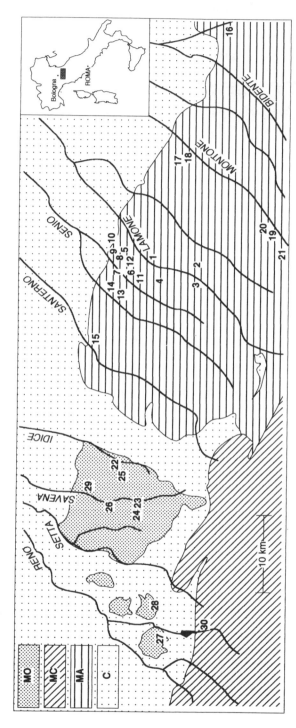

FIGURE 4.1 Geological sketch and location of landslides (1–30): MA = Marnoso-Arenacea Formation (Fm) (middle to upper Miocene); MO = Monghidoro Fm (upper Oligocene–lower Miocene); MC = Macigno Fm (upper Cretaceous); C = Liguride Nappe (mainly clays) and Neogenic Clays

concentrated in early spring and late autumn, with peak intensity values around 50 mm h^{-1}.

The main flysch formations are: the Monghidoro Formation (MO, upper Cretaceous), the Macigno Formation (MC, upper Oligocene−lower Miocene), the Marnoso-arenacea (marly-sandy) Formation (MA, middle−upper Miocene) (Figure 4.1). They are formed by regular and rhythmical alternation of thinly bedded clayey marls, sandy shales and sandstones (graywacke).

Thirty large landslides were examined from the geomorphic and geometric point of view. The landslides are recent, dating from the last four centuries; most of them are still active. Historical records of their age, rate of movement and other data are quite scarce. In many cases, the landslides affected uninhabited areas and there is a trace of them only in toponymy (for example, Lame = sheets or "laminar" landsliding, Cigno or Ciglio = sharp edge or scarp, Rovine = ruins). Borehole data or laboratory tests, geotechnical and hydrological data, maps or airphotos preceding the movement were available only in a few cases.

Whereas a strong connection with rainfall is documented at least in some recent cases, the effect of seismic activity is not clearly demonstrated, even if some events have a rough relationship with seismic shocks (see below).

Where no other direct data were available, the quantitative data, i.e. the position and the shape of failure surfaces, the preslide slope profiles and the debris volumes, have been obtained from the slope morphology, from the position, shape and dip of main scarps and from other morphological indicators.

All available data are summarized in Table 4.1.

4.2 THE LANDSLIDES

The Marnoso-arenacea Formation is characterized by a sequence of asymmetrical folds and large monoclines, with a rectangular drainage pattern that is structurally controlled. The main valleys are perpendicular to the structures; the secondary subsequent valleys are asymmetrical with gentle dip slopes and steeper opposite scarp slopes. The formation has a regular structure and presents a low degree of jointing ("slabby" to "buttressed rock" type). Translational movements (*rock block slides*) along the bedding planes are frequent. Rotational failures (*rock slumps*) are less common and can develop only in jointed rocks, as for example in the anticline cores. Therefore the landslides develop mainly on dip slopes. Nearly all of them were shaped by rock slides.

In the Monghidoro and Macigno Formations, the general geomorphologic and structural conditions are similar to those of the Marnoso-arenacea Formation, but they have a higher degree of jointing because they underwent stronger tectonization: the rock mass may be classified as "blocky rock". Therefore rock slumps on scarp slopes are more frequent than in the Marnoso-arenacea Formation, even if translational failures on dip slopes can also be seen.

4.2.1 Rock slides

The movements develop in two different ways: (a) rock block slide, extended to the entire slope (Figures 4.2.1, 4.2.3, 4.2.4, 4.2.6, 4.2.12, 4.2.25, 4.2.27) on a single bedding

TABLE 4.1 Landslide characteristics. For geographic locations, see Figure 4.1 and relevant numbered sites

No.	Locality (age)	Formation[a]	Type[b]	Menu Elevation (m)	Relief (in)	ϕ^c	β^d	Volume (10^3 m³)
1	S. Eufemia (1939)	MA	j	400	445	27	13	12500
2	Casoni d. Tura	MA	j-g	350	400	23	15	10300
3	M. Romano (1690? <1813)	MA	j	450	400	21	15	33000
4	Purocielo (1690)	MA	j	425	340	23	13	29000
5	Torretta (1978)	MA	j	275	125	20	10	850
6	Cavinella	MA	j	300	200	20	12	2800
7	Zattaglia (1978)	MA	j	290	180	18	10	620
8	S. Stefano in Z. (1500?)	MA	z	250	175	19	10	1850
9	Lame (active)	MA	j-g	200	210	17	8	24500
10-	Boesimo (1690)	MA	g	275	350	22	11	20000
11	Rio Pozza	MA	j	375	195	21	11	4300
12	S. Croce	MA	j	350	175	23	15	5500
13	M. Castellaro Renzuno	MA	j	410	170	18	10	480
14	Ca'd. Antonio	MA	j	285	230	19	10	6800
15	Fontanelice	MA	j	250	110	19	10	8250
16	Teodorano (active)	MA	j	225	80	21	11	1500
17	M. Casole (active)	MA	j	300	200	21	11	7600
18	M. Paolo (active)	MA	j	300	175	19	10	7300
19	Cesita (active)	MA	j	350	90	25	13	3500
20	Cuzzano	MA	j	420	150	25	13	10500
21	Pianaccia	MA	j	650	230	26	14	7500
22	Campeggio (1890)	MO	g	650	430	22	13–19	4250
23	Castel dell'Alpi a (1951)	MO	g	760	225	24	15	8400
24	Castel dell'Alpi b (1951)	MO	g	925	100	22	15	2600
25	F.so delle Macchie	MO	j	750	160	19	10	6600
26	Balzo del Cigno (<1935)	MO	g	600	281	25	20–32	5300
27	Castel di Casio (1874)	MO	j	610	480	19	10	28700
28	Camugnano (<1930)	MO	g-m	560	225	18	14	22900
29	Rio Lognola	MO	j	550	160	32	18	6700
30	S. Giorgio (1500?–1873)	MC	g	815	690	32	20–24	18900

[a] Ma = Marnoso-arenacea Formation; MO = Monghidoro Formation; MC= Macigno Formation

[b] Landslide type according to Varnes (1978): j = rock slide, g = rock slump, m = lateral spread, z = earthflow

[c] ϕ = back calculated friction angle

[d] β = slide surface dip (rock slides) or former slope dip (rock slumps)

surface; (b) sliding occurs at different times along gradually lower bedding planes, forming a typical terraced profile (Figures 4.2.5, 4.2.11).

At the crest, an isolated slab or "castle" often remains where the uplift water force was not high enough to trigger the movement (Figures 4.2.1, 4.2.6, 4.2.11, 4.2.12, 4.2.13, 4.2.21, 4.2.25). At the toe the rivers are progressively displaced, and on the opposite side active faceted spurs develop (Figures 4.2.2, 4.2.3, 4.2.4, 4.2.12).

The main scarp is frequently rectilinear, and coincides with joint sets. The shear surfaces are often exposed on large extensions. Other cases have been reconstructed by subsurface data (see Zattaglia in Table 4.1) or are conjectural. The shear planes follow the argillaceous layers within the turbidite sequence, or coincide with the bedding planes.

The failures generally happen at one time. The velocities vary from low ($1 \cdot 5$ m a^{-1}) to moderate ($1 \cdot 5$ m day^{-1}). Movement of the detached blocks is often stopped owing to the rapid fall of the uplift water forces. Measurements or reported information on water level, velocities and geomechanical parameters are available only in some active cases (e.g. Torretta, Zattaglia and Pianaccia).

The slide debris is quickly disrupted and eroded, particularly in the youngest sections of the Marnoso-arenacea Formation, where the rock is weakly cemented. Therefore in many of the examples (Figures 4.2.1, 4.2.11, 4.2.12, 4.2.13, 4.2.17) there is a discrepancy between the volume of the debris still in place and the volume that can be inferred from the former slope profile. Some slides are recent and still active (e.g. Torretta, Pianaccia) and they give direct indications of the failure evolution.

The shear strength parameters (ϕ, c) have been obtained mainly from back-analysis, where we assumed the worst conditions, i.e. the phreatic line at slope surface. In some recent occurrences (e.g. Zattaglia, Teodorano) the water table has been reported at ground level or even slightly higher, flowing over the well rims. That simplified assumption, in the absence of measured (or observed) data, was made in order to compare large movements that occurred over a wide area in similar geological and geomorphic conditions. In a further step, we assumed that only frictional resistance (cohesion = 0) had been mobilized, otherwise unusually low friction angles and higher uplift water forces are required.

The study area shows high seismic activity, but only indirect influence on the slides can be inferred: for instance in the S. Eufemia landslide (April 1939) a local seismic shock of VI–VII on the Mercalli scale had occurred two months before. An earthquake occurred in 1688, two years before the M. Romano, Purocielo and Boesimo landslides.

4.2.2 Rock slumps

These landslides are more common on the scarp slope sides in the Monghidoro and Macigno Formations, where the rock masses are densely jointed. Landsliding is often retrogressive (Figure 4.2.10, Marnoso-arenacea Formation; Figures 4.2.22, 4.2.23/24, Monghidoro Formation; Figure 4.2.30, Macigno Formation). The slope angles are higher (mean value 18°) than in the rock slides (about 13°).

The slide mass once again causes deviation of the rivers and erosion of the opposite slopes: a condition of alternate and repeated landsliding (slides and slumps) may therefore develop on both slopes ("see-saw" slides, as in Castel dell'Alpi landslide where a cycle of four alternate landslides — *c.* 1850, 1870, 1909 and 1951 — has been reconstructed) (Elmi, 1990).

48

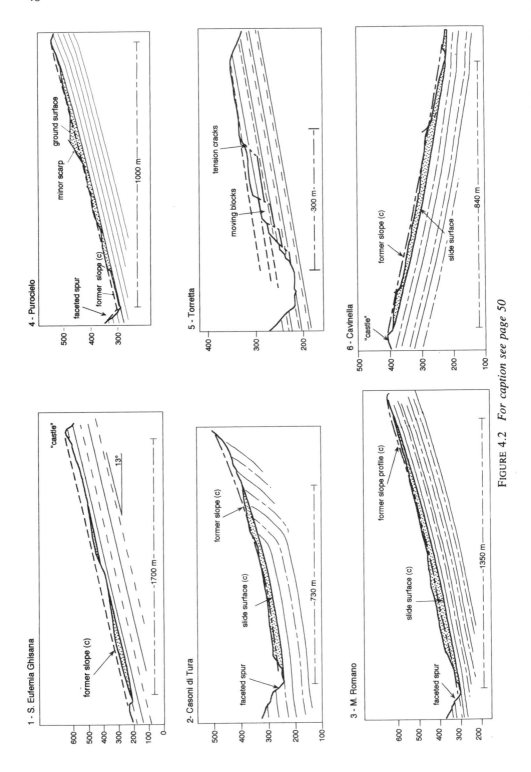

1 - S. Eufemia Ghisana

"castle"

former slope (c)

13°

—1700 m—

600
500
400
300
200
100
0

2 - Casoni di Tura

former slope (c)

slide surface (c)

faceted spur

—730 m—

500
400
300
200
100

3 - M. Romano

former slope profile (c)

slide surface (c)

faceted spur

—1350 m—

600
500
400
300
200

4 - Purocielo

ground surface

minor scarp

faceted spur

former slope (c)

—1000 m—

500
400
300

5 - Torretta

tension cracks

moving blocks

—300 m—

400
300
200

6 - Cavinella

"castle"

former slope (c)

slide surface

—840 m—

500
400
300
200
100

FIGURE 4.2 *For caption see page 50*

49

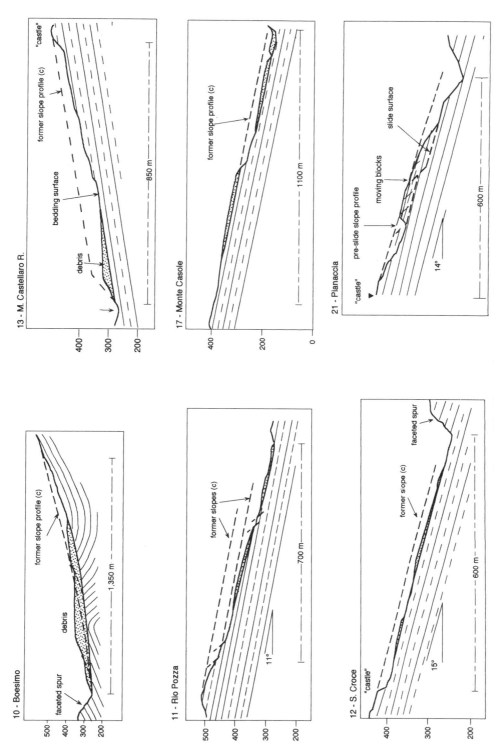

13 - M. Castellaro R.

"castle"

former slope profile (c)

bedding surface

debris

850 m

400
300
200

17 - Monte Casole

former slope profile (c)

1100 m

400
200
0

21 - Planaccia

"castle"

pre-slide slope profile

moving blocks

slide surface

14°

600 m

10 - Boesimo

former slope profile (c)

debris

faceted spur

1,350 m

500
400
300
200

11 - Rio Pozza

former slopes (c)

11°

700 m

500
400
300
200

12 - S. Croce

"castle"

former slope (c)

faceted spur

15°

600 m

400
300
200

FIGURE 4.2   For caption see page 50

50

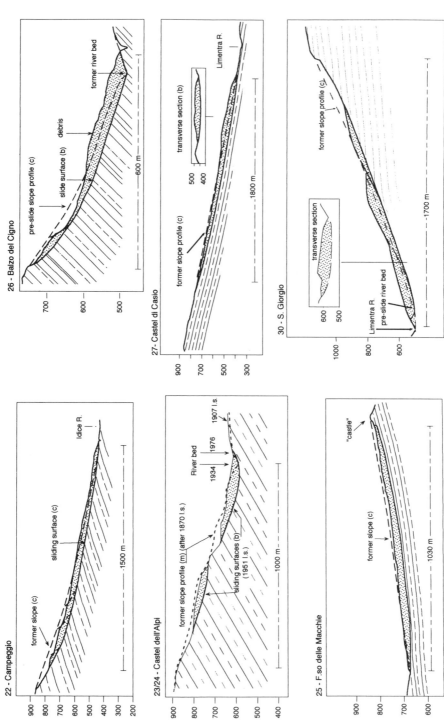

FIGURE 4.2 Sections of some landslides (numbers refer to Table 4.1). Numbers 1–21 are MA Fm, 22–27 are MO Fm and 30 is MC Fm; b = datum from boreholes or geophysical investigation; c = conjectural datum; m = datum from older maps. Sections 4, 13, 23/24 and 30 are reproduced by permission of A.A. Balkema from Chowdhury, R.N. and Sivakumar, S.M. (eds). *Environmental Management, Geo-water and Engineering Aspects, Proceedings of the International Conference, Wollongong, Australia, 8–11 February 1993.* Balkema, Rotterdam

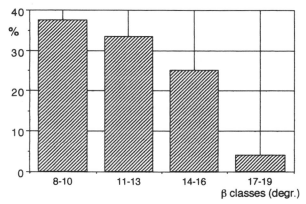

FIGURE 4.3 Frequency classes of slide surface dip (21 cases)

Back-analyses were performed with the Janbu method under conditions of limiting equilibrium ($F = 1$) and varying c', ϕ' and pore pressure u inputs. Once again we assumed $c' = 0$ conditions and groundwater table at the slope surface.

4.3 DISCUSSION AND CONCLUSIONS

From statistical analysis of data we observe that in rock slides the maximum frequency of the slip surface dip angle (β) for the Marnoso-arenacea Formation is found in the $8-10°$ class; more than 65% of the cases considered show values of β between $8°$ and $13°$ (Figure 4.3). No significant difference between Marnoso-arenacea Formation and Monghidoro Formation β values was found.

In more than 60% of all Marnoso-arenacea cases (Figure 4.4) the friction angle ϕ, obtained with water table at the ground surface, is between $18°$ and $23°$ (minimum value

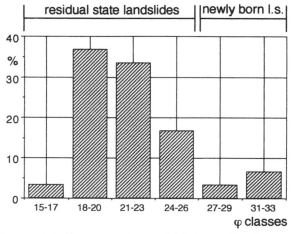

FIGURE 4.4 Frequency classes of friction angle (all cases)

Geomorphic Hazards

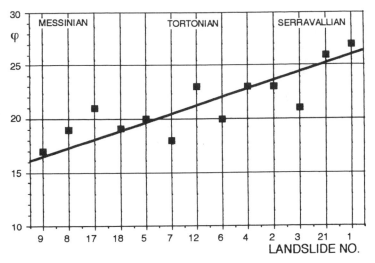

FIGURE 4.5   Relation between friction angle and relative age of rocks (MA Fm only)

17°, maximum 27°, and mean 21°). The peak friction angles of clays obtained from laboratory tests are far higher than those values ($\phi = 28-32$).

In the Marnoso-arenacea Formation landslides, the friction angles seem to be related to their stratigraphic position: the more ancient the rocks, the higher the friction angle (Figure 4.5). This probably means a difference in lithological assemblage or in diagenetic evolution.

In the *rock slumps* the back-calculated friction angles (mean value 23°) are perhaps slightly higher than in the *rock slides* (mean value 21°) because circular slip surfaces intersect all the rock mass, i.e. materials with higher shear resistance such as jointed sandstones (Figure 4.6).

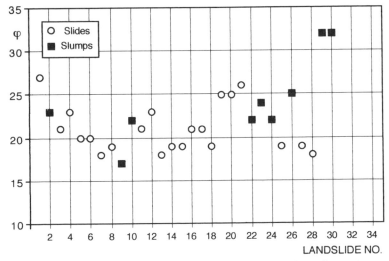

FIGURE 4.6   Values of back-calculated friction angles (all cases)

In all landslides (rock slides and slumps in Marnoso-Arenacea, Monghidoro and Macigno Formations) the back-calculated friction angle values are smaller than the peak ones obtained by laboratory tests (only a few data available). This might mean that (a) the pore pressure has been underestimated and in some cases conditions of confined aquifers were present (pore pressure ratio r_u tending to unity); (b) only residual shear resistance is mobilized on the failure surfaces. Field evidence or historic records indicate that only a few landslides are newly born (for example Figures 4.2.26 and 4.2.30); in most cases, either rock slides or slumps are "residual state landslides", linked to progressive failure phenomena or to an interstratal slip of neotectonic origin.

The reported results could be extended as a first approach to all areas showing similar geomorphic and tectonic features or climatic conditions. Thereby the margin of uncertainty in the assessment of the slope stability or of geologic hazards in small-scale planning can be reduced.

ACKNOWLEDGEMENTS

The study was funded by Consiglio Nazionale delle Ricerche, project SCAI, Studio Centri Abitati Instabili, Contract no. 9102585 M2, to C. Elmi, and by MURST (Ministry of University, Scientific Research and Technology) to O. Nesci.

REFERENCES

Elmi, C. 1990. I movimenti franosi di Castel dell'Alpi. *Previsione e Prevenzione di Eventi Franosi a Grande Rischio*. Convegno su Cartografia e monitoraggio dei movimenti franosi, Bologna, 10–11 Nov. 1988, CNR, GNDCI.

Elmi, C., Fini, A., Francia, R., Lizzani, A. and Genevois, R. 1993. Large landslides in flysch formations in the Northern Apennines (Italy): analysis and comparison of the geomorphologic features and geomechanical behaviour. In Chowdhury, R. and Sivakumar, M. (eds), *Environmental Management, Geo-water and Engineering Aspects, Proceedings of the International Conference, Wollongong, Australia, 8–11 February 1993*.Balkema, Rotterdam, 299–304.

Varnes, D.J. 1978. Slope movements types and processes. In *Landslides: Analysis and Control*. Transportation Research Board, National Academy of Science, Special report 176.

5

Landslide Hazard Mapping in Tuscany, Italy: An Example of Automatic Evaluation

F. Brunori, N. Casagli, S. Fiaschi

Earth Science Department, University of Florence

C.A. Garzonio

Town and Land Planning Department, University of Florence

AND

S. Moretti

Earth Science Department, University of Florence

ABSTRACT

Research dealing with landslide hazard assessment often focuses on the relationships between parameters affecting the slope instability process. This leads researchers to evaluate the relative influence of each factor such as land-use, slope gradient and lithology. This way of operating is sometimes subjective. In this chapter, a statistically based methodology is presented for establishing an objective ranking within the classes of the parameters and among the parameters themselves. A new method of variable definition is presented, using dimensionless ratios based on actual landslides occurring in the different classes of the parameters.

5.1 INTRODUCTION

This paper deals with the study of the main geomorphic factors influencing slope stability in order to evaluate the hazard with respect to mass movements. The problem is dealt with by means of a statistical approach which enables us to quantify and establish the rank of each parameter on the basis of its influence on the slope stability conditions.

Geomorphic Hazards. Edited by O. Slaymaker.
© 1996 by John Wiley & Sons Ltd

This procedure is based on the assumption that the factors which caused a mass movement in the past are the same factors that will cause the same process in the future. Furthermore, a forecast of the evolutionary tendencies of an area is a projection of probability, which is more reliable the larger the number of samples taken into consideration for the analysis. One of the main problems in studying and managing the geomorphic parameters statistically is their representativeness; in other words, the number of data records considered is often very low with respect to the number of variables taken into consideration.

Traditionally, methods for assessing the relative hazard are based on the overlying of thematic information and on some simple analytical combinations of different parameters (Varnes et al., 1984; Carrara et al., 1978, 1985; GNGFG, 1987; Hartlén and Viberg, 1988; Einstein, 1988). This procedure is often performed automatically by means of computer-aided systems such as a Geographical Information System (GIS). The factors which are most commonly considered in hazard analysis are climatic conditions, groundwater, structure, lithology, land use, geotechnical properties, slope morphology and geomorphology. The choice of the relative importance to be given to each parameter is very difficult. The traditional methods of hazard assessment are mainly based on an interpretation of relative importance and on the attribution of "ratings" to the different parameters. The hazard assessment cannot then be considered as an objective and reproducible document. In this paper, a new methodology is presented for the definition of geomorphic variables, using the data of a landslide inventory in order to perform a zonation of landslides on the basis of different thematic conditions. This procedure allows a series of variables to be obtained with a statistically meaningful number of records; the procedure is based on actual slope failure phenomena and is therefore representative of instability conditions. Moreover, we propose a method for "weighting" the relative influence of the parameters, based on multivariate statistical data processing. The methodology is applied on a test site in Tuscany, near the historic town of Certaldo, characterized by hilly slopes cut in Pliocene marine sediments. The analysis is performed automatically using a GIS, and computer software developed at the Earth Science Department of Florence. A flow chart of the methodology is presented in Figure 5.1.

5.2 GEOLOGICAL AND GEOMORPHIC FEATURES OF THE TEST SITE

The site chosen for testing the methodology is located on the Tyrrhenian side of the Northern Apennines in Tuscany (central Italy), about 30 km south of Florence, near the town of Certaldo (Figure 5.2).

The landscape is characteristic of the gently sloping hilly areas of the Pliocene deposits present in the central part of Tuscany. This landscape is a consequence of the vertical and horizontal variability of the lithology, with deposits having different physical and mechanical characteristics (alternations of gravels, sands and clay). The flat-top areas and the typical profiles along valley sides present an alternation of slopes with different gradients, which coincide with the lithological variations.

This area is also representative of climatic, vegetation and land-use conditions common to wider agricultural areas in Tuscany. It is largely an agricultural area where nowadays the principal activity is represented by vineyards and olive groves. These activities, especially the wine production, have also been the principal cause of hillside reprofiling

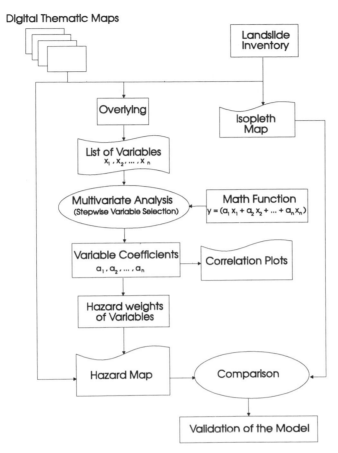

FIGURE 5.1 Flow chart of the methodology

as the vineyards had to be made accessible to mechanized farm equipment. This transformation has produced some advantages for productivity but, in many cases, it reduces slope stability and induces soil erosion and mass movements.

The zone under consideration extends over an area of about 10 km². The scale of the survey is 1:5000 for the thematic maps; the landslide inventory is performed at the more detailed scale of 1:2500. The final hazard map is produced at a 1:10 000 scale.

5.3 PARAMETER SELECTION AND THEMATIC MAPPING

The first step in any method of landslide hazard assessment is the selection of parameters which are meaningful for the specific conditions of the test site under consideration (GNGFG, 1987).

In fact, some of the parameters which influence slope stability do not vary in this sample area and cannot be considered as independent variables for a relative hazard

assessment. In this case the climatic conditions can be considered uniform and the strata
are characterized by horizontal bedding.

Other parameters are closely linked to each other, for example the lithology and the
hydrogeological characteristics, and so only one of them can be considered in the
analysis. The lithological variations in the zone under examination are due mainly to
granulometry changes of the marine Pliocene deposits (Sestini, 1970). Therefore
lithological classes are identified by the name of grain-size classes.

Bearing in mind these considerations, the analysis is based on three parameters only:
lithology, land-use and slope morphology. Thematic digital maps are compiled for each
of these parameters and are fed into the GIS. In particular, lithological and land-use maps
are drawn, taking different classes into consideration (Table 5.1); a slope gradient map is
obtained from the digital terrain model, taking into consideration five slope classes
representative of the conditions of the sample area (Table 5.1).

5.4 LANDSLIDE INVENTORY

An accurate landslide inventory is the best tool for the calibration of methodologies of
hazard zonation, since it provides direct information on the location and on the
geomorphic characteristics of actual slope movements.

Eighty-nine landslides of different types are surveyed on the test site; morphometric
and geomorphic data are systematically collected, geographically referenced, and fed into
the GIS. The distribution of the landslides is represented by means of an isopleth map
(Figure 5.3) (Campbell, 1973; de Graff and Canuti, 1988).

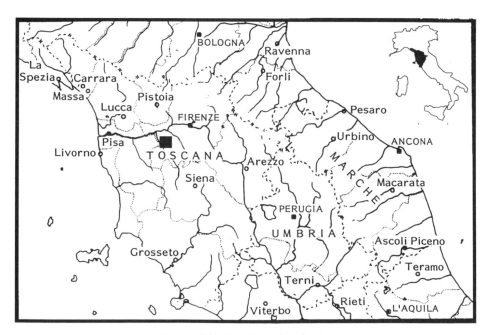

FIGURE 5.2 Location of study area

TABLE 5.1   Parameters considered in the analysis

Lithology	Slope	Land-use
Q = alluvial clays and sands	P1 = 0−5%	B = wood and poplar trees
dt = slope debris	P2 = 6−13%	C = brush
Pegs = pebbles, gravels and sands	P3 = 14−19%	I = abandoned areas
Ps = sands	P4 = 20−25%	SA = mixed arable olive groves
Psag = clays and sands	P5 >25%	U = urban areas
Pag = clays		PAS = rangelands
		V = vineyards
		S = arable

5.5   DEFINITION OF VARIABLES

The definition of the variables to be used for the statistical data processing is based on a comparative analysis of the different thematic parameters and the landslide inventory. In practice, by overlying the lithological, land-use and slope gradient maps on the landslide map, a zonation can be made of each of the 89 landslides into plots with homogeneous characteristics; 233 plots were identified in this way. Each one represents a portion of landslide area with a given lithology, land-use and slope gradient (Figure 5.4). With reference to the parameter class codes listed in Table 5.1, a plot can be identified by a three-element code (e.g. Ps-P2-B: landslide element in sands, with slope between 6 and 13%, covered by wood). These 233 plots provide a statistically meaningful set of records to be used for definition of the variables.

The dependent variable y is defined, in a dimensionless way, as the ratio (expressed as a percentage) between the area of each plot and the total area involved in landslides, by a method analogous to that method proposed by de Graff (1978).

One independent variable x is defined for each of the different classes of the three thematic parameters. With reference to Table 5.1, six variables are defined for lithology, five for slope gradient and eight for land use. Each variable is defined as the ratio (expressed as a percentage) between the area of the plot characterized by the corresponding thematic class and the total area in which this class is represented. For example, the variable Ps (associated with the thematic class Ps−sand) is defined, for any plot with a sand lithology, as the ratio between the plot area and the total area of sand outcrop. For the plots characterized by lithologies different from sand, the variable Ps is set as zero.

5.6   MULTIVARIATE ANALYSIS

The next step in the procedure consists of a synthesis in which the relative influence of each variable on slope instability is weighted by performing a multivariate statistical analysis. This type of analysis has been tested in Italy by Carrara (1983) and Carrara et al. (1985).

A multiple regression analysis is applied using a linear function:

$$y = a_0 + a_1 x_1 + a_2 x_2 + \ldots + a_i x_i + \ldots + a_n x_n$$

where a_i represents the vector of coefficients and x_i the vector of independent variables.

Geomorphic Hazards

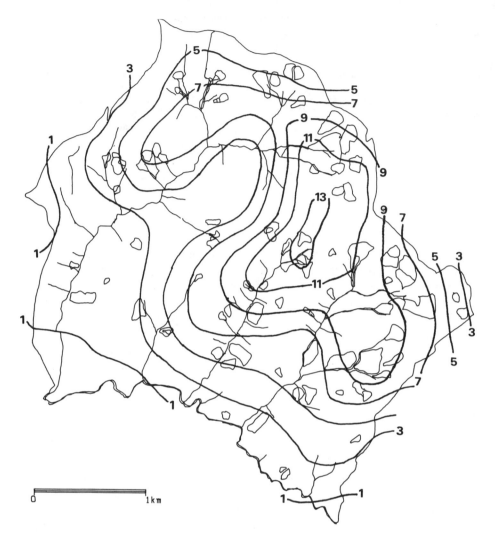

FIGURE 5.3 Isopleth map representing the density of slope instability phenomena. Isopleths are drawn according to the method described in Campbell (1973). Counting circle area = 1/100 of the total area of the zone under investigation. Numbers on the curves give the percentage of area within the counting circle covered with landslide deposits. The 89 landslides and the main drainage lines are shown on the map

A "forward stepwise variable selection" is adopted to control the entry of variables in the statistical model. At each step one variable is entered into the model and a check is made to control whether the variables already included are still meaningful; those ones that are not meaningful are removed.

The degree of significance is tested using Fischer's F-ratio: variables with F-ratio >6 are entered into the model step by step starting from the one with the highest F-ratio; variables with F-ratio <2 are selectively removed from the model.

According to this procedure, 16 of the 19 variables are included in the model, as shown in Table 5.2. In the same table the coefficient a_i is listed for each of the meaningful variables, together with statistics of the multiple regression. Predicted values of the independent variables are plotted versus observed values in Figure 5.5.

A correlation matrix between the variables is shown in Table 5.3. No strong correlation is evident between couples of variables (the maximum value of the correlation coefficient is 0·53). Therefore we prefer to keep the variables separate rather than grouping them together.

5.7 HAZARD ZONATION

Once the correlation coefficients are computed, they can be used as "weights" or "ratings" for the automatic hazard zonation with the GIS (Carrara et al., 1985). The values of the partial correlation coefficients represent the relative influence between variables and between parameters. For practical purposes, weights are taken as integers by multiplying the regression coefficients by 100. The list of weights is shown in Table 5.4.

For "lithology" the less critical unit is represented by "pebbles, gravel and sands". There is an apparent anomaly since "sands" are about three times more unstable than "clays". But this reflects the actual situation in the field. In fact the unit Pag is actually made up of stiff, overconsolidated clays in which the instability phenomena are limited to

1. Landslide area

2. Lithology zonation

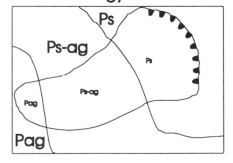

3. Slope gradient zonation

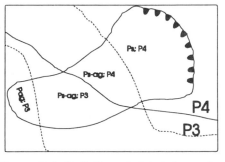

4. Land use zonation

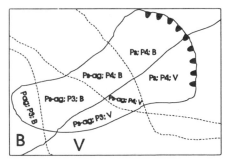

FIGURE 5.4   Definition of plots to be used as data records for variables. Labels as in Table 5.1

TABLE 5.2   Result of the stepwise variable selection and list of the coefficients and statistics of the multiple regression (N.C. = not considered; number of samples = 233)

Variable	Coefficient	Standard error	T-std
Coeff.	$a_0 = 0\cdot01$	$0\cdot01$	$1\cdot07$
P1	N.C.	N.C.	N.C.
$x_1 = $ P2	$a_1 = 0\cdot03$	$0\cdot02$	$1\cdot39$
$x_2 = $ P3	$a_2 = 0\cdot07$	$0\cdot03$	$2\cdot57$
$x_3 = $ P4	$a_3 = 0\cdot09$	$0\cdot03$	$2\cdot88$
$x_4 = $ P5	$a_4 = 0\cdot15$	$0\cdot05$	$2\cdot74$
Q	N.C.	N.C.	N.C.
$x_5 = $ dt	$a_5 = 0\cdot16$	$0\cdot06$	$2\cdot73$
$x_6 = $ Pegs	$a_6 = 0\cdot02$	$0\cdot01$	$1\cdot96$
$x_7 = $ Ps	$a_7 = 0\cdot20$	$0\cdot08$	$2\cdot79$
$x_8 = $ Psag	$a_8 = 0\cdot15$	$0\cdot03$	$2\cdot50$
$x_9 = $ Pag	$a_9 = 0\cdot07$	$0\cdot03$	$2\cdot40$
U	N.C.	N.C.	N.C.
$x_{10} = $ B	$a_{10} = 0\cdot04$	$0\cdot06$	$2\cdot36$
$x_{11} = $ C	$a_{11} = 0\cdot15$	$0\cdot02$	$2\cdot76$
$x_{12} = $ I	$a_{12} = 0\cdot14$	$0\cdot02$	$2\cdot77$
$x_{13} = $ SA	$a_{13} = 0\cdot13$	$0\cdot07$	$2\cdot45$
$x_{14} = $ PAS	$a_{14} = 0\cdot02$	$0\cdot01$	$1\cdot89$
$x_{15} = $ S	$a_{15} = 0\cdot18$	$0\cdot03$	$2\cdot80$
$x_{16} = $ V	$a_{16} = 0\cdot18$	$0\cdot04$	$2\cdot78$
R-sq.	$0\cdot98$	R-squared	$0\cdot43$
Adj. R-sq.	$0\cdot98$	Adjusted R-squared	$0\cdot39$
S.E. regression	$0\cdot05$	Standard error of regression	$0\cdot49$
Durbin-Watson stat.	$165434\cdot49$	Durbin-Watson statistic	$96469\cdot72$
Sum. resid. sq.		Sum of residuals squared	
F-stat.		Fischer's F statistic	

movements of the surficial debris cover; the unit Ps is made up of sand with silt and clay partings; landslides develop on these planes of weakness and usually involve quite large volumes of material; therefore landslide hazard is higher on the heterogeneous "sands" than in the "homogeneous" clays. For "slope angle" the partial regression coefficients closely reflect the steepening of slopes.

For "land-use" the results show that slope instability phenomena affect mainly slopes under anthropogenically modified land use. Rangelands, woods and poplar tree zones have not been subject to human influence, hence their coefficients are quite low. High coefficients are present for olive groves, mixed arable, arable and vineyards; these high values are caused mainly by wrong agricultural practices which cause a strong degradation of slopes. Brush zones are unstable simply because brush tends to develop over the landslide masses.

An index for the relative hazard zonation can be obtained by adding up the weights of the variables (GNGFG, 1987) for each of the 9000 pixels of the digital terrain model; for each pixel the number of variables is reduced to three, one for each of the thematic parameters under consideration.

The most critical combination of variables, with respect to slope instability, is represented by slopes with gradient $>25\%$ (class P5), on sands (class Ps), with arable

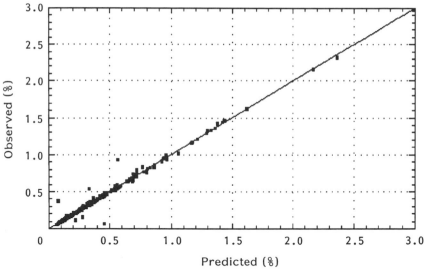

FIGURE 5.5   Observed values of the ratio (expressed as a percentage) between the area of each plot and the total area involved in landslides, versus predicted values of the same quantity from multiple regression

land or vineyards (classes S and V); the sum of the single weights for this combination gives a maximum total rating of 53. The hazard indices can be scaled to 100 with respect to this figure.

In establishing hazard classes based on intervals of this scaled index, it does not seem appropriate to fix arbitrary boundaries which cannot be meaningful for the actual field situation. Hence the choice of boundaries is based on the actual combination between variables, as shown in Table 5.5.

Once the classes are defined, it is possible to draw the hazard map shown in Figure 5.6. A comparison between this map and the isopleth map demonstrates the remaining uncertainties associated with the statistical model.

5.8   CONCLUSIONS

The method described in this paper consists of an automatic procedure for landslide hazard assessment which is based, as far as possible, on objective data. The method can be summarized in the following steps.

(a) Parameter selection: selection of thematic parameters influencing slope stability which are meaningful for the specific conditions of the site and for the scale taken into consideration. In the case study three parameters are chosen: lithology, land-use and slope gradient.

(b) Digital thematic mapping: mapping of the chosen thematic parameters carried out by considering different classes for each of them.

(c) Landslide inventory and mapping: landslides are mapped at a 1:2500 scale by photointerpretation and an accurate field check; the data are then included in a GIS.

TABLE 5.3 Correlation matrix

	B	C	I	PAS	S	SA	V	dt	Pag	Pegs	Ps	Psag	P2	P3	P4	P5
B	1.00															
C	-0.10	1.00														
I	-0.070	-0.078	1.00													
PAS	-0.098	-0.11	-0.075	1.00												
S	-0.035	-0.040	-0.027	-0.038	1.00											
SA	-0.11	-0.12	-0.081	-0.11	-0.041	1.00										
V	-0.12	-0.13	-0.089	-0.13	-0.045	-0.14	1.00									
dt	-0.035	-0.050	0.40	-0.048	-0.017	-0.026	0.029	1.00								
Pag	-0.037	-0.073	-0.023	-0.068	0.076	0.36	-0.085	-0.056	1.00							
Peg	-0.067	0.12	-0.046	-0.036	-0.026	-0.050	-0.0093	-0.032	-0.085	1.00						
Ps	0.33	0.083	-0.078	0.29	-0.058	-0.073	0.39	-0.073	-0.19	-0.11	1.00					
Psag	-0.063	0.16	0.070	0.039	0.53	0.17	-0.11	-0.068	-0.18	-0.10	-0.23	1.00				
P2	-0.056	-0.017	-0.0014	-0.047	-0.0087	0.29	0.0040	-0.030	0.039	-0.044	-0.085	0.25	1.00			
P3	-0.051	0.0039	0.062	0.035	0.50	0.39	0.026	0.094	0.17	-0.025	0.17	0.39	0.11	1.00		
P4	-0.064	-0.075	0.064	0.22	-0.042	0.018	0.35	0.0034	0.044	-0.046	0.28	0.0024	-0.11	-0.20	1.00	
P5	0.45	0.26	-0.041	0.17	-0.059	-0.098	0.072	-0.051	-0.13	0.0000	0.44	0.066	-0.10	-0.19	-0.11	1.00

TABLE 5.4 Weights of variables

Variable	Weight = coefficient × 100
Pegs	2
Pag	7
Psag	15
dt	16
Ps	20
P2	3
P3	7
P4	9
P5	15
PAS	2
B	4
SA	13
C	14
I	14
S	18
V	18

TABLE 5.5 Combinations of variables considered for the definition of hazard boundaries

Lithology	Slope	Land use	Total rating	Scaled rating
Pegs = 2	P2 = 3	PAS = 2	7	15%
Pag = 7	P3 = 7	B = 4	18	35%
Psag = 15	P4 = 9	SA = 13	37	70%
dt = 16	P5 = 15	C & I = 14	45	85%
Ps = 20	P5 = 15	S & V = 18	53	100%

(d) Definition of data records and variable selection: the definition of territorial variables is performed by means of a zonation of landslide areas according to the classes of the three parameters. Each landslide area is divided into several homogeneous plots, each of which constitutes a data record. Each class represents a variable, expressed in a dimensionless way, as the ratio between the area of the plot and the total area of the class. The dependent variable is chosen as equal to the ratio between the area of the plot and the total landslide area.

(e) Multivariate analysis: stepwise variable selection for a multiple linear regression. Regression coefficients are given for each variable that is meaningful for the statistical model.

(f) Hazard weights assessment: for each of the chosen variables a hazard weight can be obtained directly from the regression coefficient (for practical purposes multiplied by 100). Hazard weights are scaled to 100%.

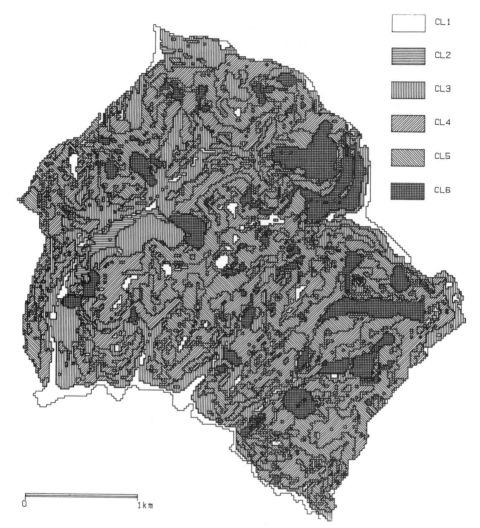

FIGURE 5.6 Hazard map expressed as expected percentage of landslide area with respect to the total landslide area in the zone under examination. CL1 = 0–14%; CL2 = 15–34%; CL3 = 35–69%; CL4 = 70–84%; CL5 = 85–99%; CL6 = 100%

(g) Hazard mapping: automatic overlying of thematic parameters performed by adding up the three weights of the variables for each pixel of the digital terrain model. In this way it is possible to obtain an instability index which gives at any point the expected percentage of landslide area with respect to the total landslide area in the considered zone.

(h) Verification of the model: comparison between hazard map and landslide distribution map. A visual examination of the two maps shows that the actual landslide distribution does not entirely reflect the zones with the higher values of the hazard index. Regions with high values of the index, in which landslides are not present, represent zones with the highest probability of future slope movements, since the combination of lithological, morphological and land-use parameters is assumed to be similar to the combination which determined instability conditions at different locations in the past.

Application of the methodology to the test site of Certaldo gives a good correlation coefficient for the multiple regression of 16 variables, which define lithological, morphological and land-use conditions. The hazard map provides a useful tool for the spatial detection of critical combinations of parameters influencing slope instability.

ACKNOWLEDGEMENTS

The research work presented in this paper is partially funded by MURST 60% "Modelling, Dynamics and Triggering of Slope Instability Processes: application of Geographical Information Systems" and GNDCI "Forecast and Prevention of High Risk Slope Movements". The GIS software used in the analysis is GEOSYS produced by GEOSYSTEMS, Florence.

REFERENCES

Campbell, R.H. 1973. *Isopleth Map of Landslide Deposits, Poit Dume Quadrangle, Los Angeles County California.* US Geological Survey Miscellaneous Map MF-535.

Carrara, A. 1983. Multivariate methods for landslide hazard evaluation. *Mathematical Geology*, **15**(3).

Carrara, A., Catalano, E., Sorriso-Valvo, M., Reali, C. and Osso, I. 1978. Digital terrain analysis for land evaluation. *Geologia Applicata e Idrogeologia, Bari*, **13**, 69–127.

Carrara, A., Agnesi, V., Macaluso, T., Monteleone, S., Pipitone, G., Reali, C. and Sorriso-Valvo, M. 1985. Modelli matematici per la valutazione della pericolosit connessa con i fenomeni di instabilita' dei versanti. *Geologia Applicata e Idrogeologia, Bari*, **10**(2) I, 63–91.

de Graff, J.V. 1978. Regional landslide evaluation: two Utah examples. *Enviromental Geology*, **2**(4), 203–214.

de Graff, J.V. and Canuti, P. 1988. Using isopleth mapping to evaluate landslide activity in relation to agricultural practices. *IAEG Bulletin*, **38**, 61–71.

Einstein, H.H. 1988. Landslide risk assessment procedure. In Bonnard, C. (ed.), *Landslides*, Proceedings of 5th International Symposium on Landslides, July 1988, Lausanne 2, 1075–1090.

GNGFG–Gruppo Nazionale Geografia Fisica e Geomorfologia 1987. Cartografia della pericolosità connessa ai fenomeni di instabilità dei versanti. *Bollettino Società Geologica Italiana*, **106**, 199–221.

Hartlén, J. and Viberg, L. 1988. General report: evaluation of landslide hazard. In Bonnard, C. (ed.), *Landslides*, Proceedings of 5th International Symposium Landslides, July 1988, Lausanne 2, 1037–1058.

Sestini, G. 1970. Postgeosynclinal deposition. *Sedimentary Geology*, **4**, 445–479.

Varnes, D.J. et al. 1984. *Landslide Hazard Zonation — A Review of Principles and Practice.* International Association of Engineering Geology Commission on Landslides, UNESCO Paris.

6

Geomorphic Risk Zonation Related to June 1991 Eruptions of Mt Pinatubo, Luzon, Philippines

JAN J. NOSSIN

International Institute for Aerospace Survey and Earth Sciences (ITC), The Netherlands

AND

RICARTE S. JAVELOSA

Bureau of Mines and Geosciences, Philippines

ABSTRACT

The geomorphic hazards, both volcanic and non-volcanic, associated with the June 1991 eruptions of Mt Pinatubo, Luzon, Philippines, are identified and analysed with the aid of satellite imagery and field survey. Geomorphic hazard domains are determined in terms of propensity to affect geomorphic stability, perceived vulnerability and priority of georesource function. A composite risk zonation index, incorporating geomorphic mapping, geomorphic risk analysis and georesource priority, is then calculated. Three risk zones are established and, supplemented with the site-specific geomorphic mapping, provide valuable input to regional planning.

6.1 BACKGROUND

Mt. Pinatubo is part of the Luzon arc in the southern continuation of Zambales Range. It has awoken from 600 years of inactivity (PHILVOLCS, 1991). Its paroxysmal and cataclysmic eruptions in June 1991 are cited by Pallister et al. (1992) to have been triggered by an injection of basaltic magma at the base of the magma chamber. According to Defant et al. (1991), volcanism throughout the Luzon arc is associated with the eastward subduction of the South China Sea floor along the Manila Trench.

Emphasis is placed on a practical way to ascertain the geomorphic instability threatening the floodplains of Santo Tomas and Bucao in Zambales; Gumain, Porac, Potrero and Abacan in Pampanga; and Sacobia-Bamban and O'Donnell in Tarlac (Figure

---

Geomorphic Hazards. Edited by O. Slaymaker.

6.1). Principally, this paper aims to identify and to interpret geoenvironmental and geomorphic changes imposed both by volcanic and non-volcanic incidents which might be consequential to hazard and risk zonation.

6.2 CATACLYSMIC INCIDENTS

The eruptive activity of Mt. Pinatubo in June 1991 (Hoblitt et al., 1991; Daag et al., 1991) marks the advent of volcanic upheaval in this part of the Philippine Mobile Belt. Large-scale destruction occurred both on the west and east flanks. The incidents of cataclysmic destruction can be grouped practically into two major geomorphic process suites: volcanic and non-volcanic.

6.2.1 Volcanic incidents

The June 1991 eruption of Mt. Pinatubo unleashed three major destructive volcanic incidents, namely airfall tephra, pyroclastic flow and lahar.

6.2.1.1 Airfall tephra

An hourly observation of Mt. Pinatubo eruptions on 15 June 1991 by satellite was carried out by Koyaguchi (1991). A giant disc-shaped eruption cloud covering an area of 60 000 km^2 appeared in the satellite images at 14:40 Philippine time. The cloud expanded radially against the wind of 20 m s^{-1} and swelled to an area exceeding 120 000 km^2 within an hour. Our field survey established the timing of the initiation of airfall tephra by heavy fine ashfall at about 15:00.

Koyaguchi (1991) suggested that the outer part of the ash cloud at 14:40 was chiefly composed of fine ash alone. He further pointed out that the infra-red images at 14:40 and 15:40 indicated a radial expansion of hot material in the ash cloud suggesting a juvenile supply by Plinian activity.

Heavy airfall tephra from the 1991 June eruption of Mt Pinatubo was deposited towards the west-southwest (Figure 6.2). It consisted of at least three units (Figure 6.3). At the bottom, unit 1 occurred dominantly with lithic and pumice-rich coarse ash deposits. This unit was restricted in the southwest, where an isopach of 30 cm and less prevailed, reflecting the effect of typhoon Yunya. It attained an average thickness of 1·0 cm. Pumice clasts revealed an average size of 400 μm.

Immediately above unit 1 were well-laminated and partly vesiculated very fine ash deposits (unit 2). Unit 2 varied between 70 and 50 μm in size. Average thickness was 1·5 cm. Some of these were also observed in some parts of the southeast and northeast sectors of the volcano.

Unit 3 occurred as the uppermost member of the airfall tephra. It was the most widespread and can be correlated to the catastrophic eruption of Mt Pinatubo on 15 June. It attained an average thickness of 13·5 cm. Unit 3 manifested an upward-fining sequence. It appeared with an average size of 300 μm at the bottom and graded gradually

71

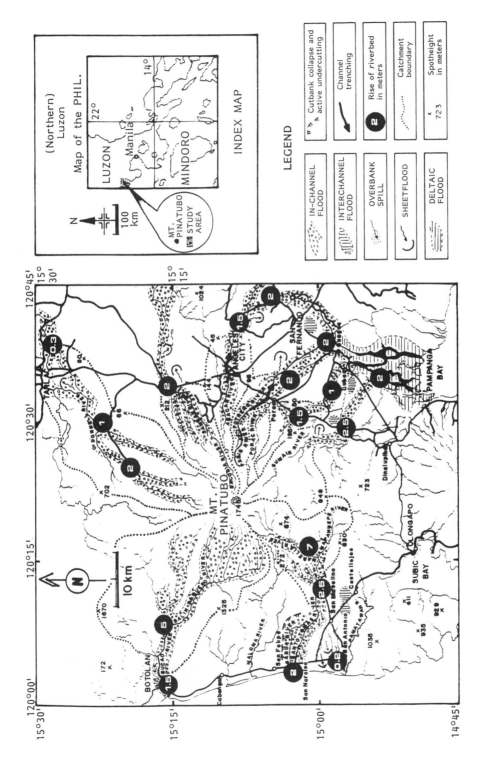

FIGURE 6.1 Flood hazard map related to the 1991 eruptions of Mt Pinatubo

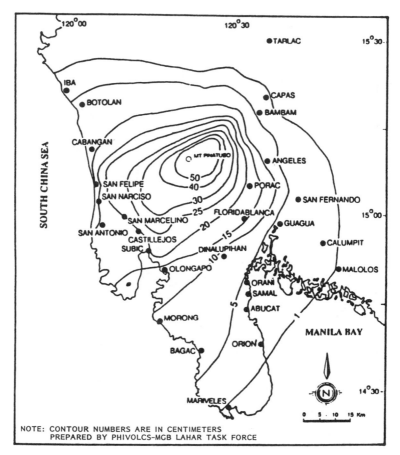

FIGURE 6.2   Isopach map of airfall tephra during the 12–15 June 1991 eruptions of Mt Pinatubo

to an average of 200 μm at the top. Much of this was composed of 40% crystals, 30% pumice and 30% others (e.g. lithic).

6.2.1.2   Pyroclastic flow

Interpretations on SPOT (XS) images of 1991 and 1988 indicate that the pyroclastic slopes are the product of two volcanic density-current processes (Carey, 1991): (i) accretionary blast surges; and (ii) flowage depositional transport. According to Sparks (1976) a density current may initially be fully turbulent (i.e. surge), but it can transform into a current with complex mode (i.e. flow) owing to changing particle concentration during transport process.

On the immediate slopes of Mt Pinatubo, the pyroclastic flows appear to have resulted from episodic multiple events. The episodicity is indicated by the existence of two types of pyroclastic flows: (i) a pre-1991 event; and (ii) the 1991 event. Their boundaries are featured by trimlines (Figure 6.4).

The youngest pre-1991 pyroclastic flow deposits are dated about $460 \leq 30$ a BP (Newhall et al., 1991). These are dominantly pumiceous in the upper watershed of Sacobia and Marella rivers. Another pre-1991 eruption from the northwest flank produced a lithic-rich pyroclastic flow deposit largely towards Bucao River and partly towards Santo Tomas River.

On the other hand, the pyroclastic flow deposits of the 1991 event are mostly pumiceous, from 1 to 30 m thick and extend as much as 20 km from the vent largely towards the west. A large portion of these deposits follows currently active volcanic flowlines and gullies radiating from the vent of Mt Pinatubo.

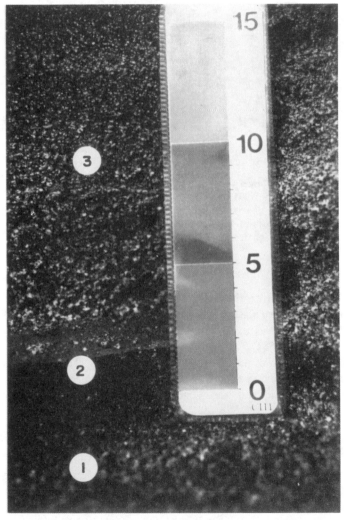

FIGURE 6.3 Pictorial profile of ashfall tephra deposited after the 15 June 1991 eruptions of Mt Pinatubo, showing three compositional units

FIGURE 6.4 Morphogenetic interpretation of active pyroclastic field on SPOT-XS image (December 1991) related to the 1991 eruptions of Mt Pinatubo. 1, Pre-eruption pyroclastic flows; 2, 1991 pyroclastic flows (a, blast surge removal zone; b, flowage depositional zone); 3, active lahar channel-fills; 4, major passes and flowlines; 5, volcanic rim of Mt Pinatubo after the 1991 eruptions; 6, pre-eruption volcanic rim based on SPOT-XS image (April 1988); 7, trimline; 8, volcanic outlier

The pyroclastic flow from the 1991 event of Mt Pinatubo is characterized by a combination of accretionary blast surges and flowage transport. A remarkable view of the blast surges is interpreted as a "ground surge removal zone". Best observed on aerial photographs and stereo-SPOT images, this zone is manifested by the stripping of vegetation and regolith from the older pyroclastic deposits. The boundary between the ground surge removal zone and the flowage transport zone of the 1991 event and that where saprolitic/regolithic soil and vegetation stumps remain is basically termed "trimline".

6.2.1.3 Lahar

Mudflows often accompany eruptions. In order to avoid confusion with those of semi-arid regions, Cotton (1944) suggested that volcanic mudflows be designated as "lahars", a name of Javanese origin. Lajoie (1984) and Walker (1984) elaborated that lahars are subaerial or subaqueous debris-flow deposits composed essentially of volcanic fragments. In this study lahar connotes a single hydrologic event, which may change in state from debris flow to hyperconcentrated streamflow or vice versa on a dominantly volcanic-evolved landscape (Rodolfo, 1989).

Surrounding Mt Pinatubo, lahars were caused primarily by remobilization of unstable pyroclastic flow deposits (Umbal et al., 1991). Along Santo Tomas River, the remobilization was observed to have been triggered by rain with intensity between $0 \cdot 12$ and $0 \cdot 36$ mm min^{-1} and duration between 20 and 185 min (PLHTF, 1991). The remobilization of pyroclastic flow deposits into lahar fills up major drainage lines emanating from the vent of Mt Pinatubo. Towards the west, passage of lahars has completely transformed the riverbeds of Bucao and Santo Tomas into lahar channels. On the east flanks of Mt Pinatubo, lahar fills perched and metamorphosed the main drainage line of O'Donnell, Bamban, Potrero, Abacan, Porac and Gumain (Figure 6.1).

Lahars are complex materials (Arguden and Rodolfo, 1990), composed of various admixtures of sediments with a wide variety of grain sizes. They flow in loose sludge-like form under the influence of gravity. However, the June 1991 lahars from Mt Pinatubo appeared so water-rich that they transformed initially from hyperconcentrated streamflow to hyperconcentrated floodflow.

The lahars related to the 1991 June eruption of Mt Pinatubo proceeded in series of waves and pulses. Based on observations in the vicinity of Santo Tomas River Basin on 13 August, they started as hot hyperconcentrated streamflow through Marella River. They had a temperature between 33 and 40°C and a flow velocity between $3 \cdot 9$ and $4 \cdot 3$ m s^{-1}. The flow was characterized with surges and antidunes varying between $0 \cdot 5$ and $1 \cdot 0$ m high followed by pulses of debris flows and lateral erosion with a speed of $0 \cdot 7$ m min^{-1}. Two surges occurred per minute during the first three hour period of the lahar event.

The above situation caused the initial damming and transformation of Mapanuepe River into a lake (Figure 6.4). Later, the hot hyperconcentrated streamflow lahars accelerated spasmodically to a maximum of $6 \cdot 0$ m s^{-1} causing the collapse of Santa Fe bridge, which is about 7 km downstream of the Marella — Santo Tomas junction, and the burial of Barrio Alosiis along Santo Tomas River, which is approximately 20 km downstream from the same junction. During the remaining days of August the Santo Tomas River was under a laharic regime essentially dominated by hot hyperconcentrated flows.

Clearly, the transportation of sediments under a laharic regime does not take place on the scale of individual grains of sand and stone (i.e. individual transportation), but as a form of collective transportation in which sand, gravel, cobbles and boulders flow and aggregate together. The collective transportation (Figure 6.5) is characterized by the fact that the volcaniclastics accumulate with boulders and cobble-dominated obstacle clusters at the front or "head" when the lahar stops.

Considering that lahar, by definition, behaves as a debris flow (Lajoie, 1984), we find it valid to consider laharic instability in terms of apparent shear strength (k) for debris flow as proposed by Johnson and Rodine (1984): $k = (T)(d)(\sin \alpha)$, where k = shear strength, T = estimated thickness of 1991 lahar deposits, d = unit weight and α = surface slope of 1991 lahar deposits. This formula assumes that during the laharic regime, the debris collectively slides over the surface of earlier riverbeds.

Results in Table 6.1 show the passage of lahars along Bucao, Santo Tomas, Abacan and Potrero rivers, with strength varying between $62 \cdot 5$ and $408 \cdot 7$ kg m^{-2} in comparison to the passage of lahars along Porac and Gumain rivers where shear strengths are estimated between 56·2 and 94·7 kg m^{-2}. This provides an explanation of why the vicinities of Bucao, Santo Tomas, Potrero and Abacan rivers suffered most during the laharic regime of Mt Pinatubo in 1991. At the moment, however, much of the laharic debris still persists, waiting to be remobilized and retransported downstream; this seems to characterize an incident of "arrested lahar fills".

6.2.2   Non-volcanic incidents

The aftermath of volcanic incidents leaves the surroundings of Mt Pinatubo with dynamic and unstable geomorphic conditions. Aside from an impending cold laharic regime, other post-eruption and non-volcanic incidents appear to continue endangering affected areas. Particularly eminent are floods, channel erosion and siltation (Figure 6.1).

A. FLOWING DOWN FORM

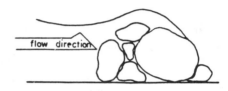

B. INDIVIDUAL AND COLLECTIVE TRANSPORTATION

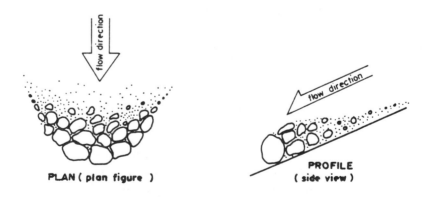

C. ARRANGEMENT OF SEDIMENT AT STANDSTILL

FIGURE 6.5   Schematic sediment delivery system of the 1991 Mt Pinatubo lahar

TABLE 6.1 Properties of laharic debris caused by the 1991 eruptions of Mt Pinatubo ($T =$ estimated thickness of laharic deposits; d = unit weight; α = surface inclination of laharic deposits; k = estimated shear strength of the 1991 laharic debris)

River	Obstruction site no.	T (m)	d (g cm^{-3})	sin α	k (kg m^{-2})
Abacan	1	4·0	1·43	0·07	399·4
	2	2·0	1·48	0·09	266·1
	3	1·0	1·40	0·09	126·0
Potrero	4	3·0	1·46	0·07	306·1
	5	2·7	1·46	0·04	157·2
	6	2·5	1·25	0·02	62·5
Porac	7	2·0	1·34	0·03	80·1
	8	3·0	1·09	0·02	65·41
Gumain	9	3·0	0·94	0·02	56·2
	10	1·3	1·46	0·05	94·7
	11	2·0	1·47	0·03	87·9
Santo Tomas	12	5·0	1·24	0·05	309·5
	13	3·0	1·05	0·05	157·2
	14	3·0	1·28	0·03	114·7
Bucao	15	6·0	1·24	0·05	371·1
	16	3·0	1·18	0·03	106·0
	17	2·0	1·36	0·15	408·7

6.2.2.1 Flood

Lahar fills and transport of ashfall debris from the highlands block major drainage channels. In most cases, this raises riverbeds and causes flooding of extensive low-lying areas surrounding Mt Pinatubo. Figure 6.1 indicates that major drainage channels along the western vicinity of Mt Pinatubo raised their riverbeds by between 0·2 and 7·0 m, which is generally much higher than on the east side, where riverbeds rose by between 0·3 and 2·5 m. A maximum rise of 7·0 m is noted along the junction between Marella and Santo Tomas rivers, where an active fault-related lineament crossed. Such a rise has further aggravated the transformation of Mapanuepe River into a lake.

As the heavy rains brought by tropical storm Diding and typhoon Yunya poured over Central Luzon during the 14−15 June eruptions, flooding activity began and continued for weeks. There were five modes of this activity, namely in-channel, interchannel, overbank spill, sheetflood and deltaic flood.

Among the floods, the in-channel and overbank spills were catastrophic owing to their association with the laharic activity. A mixture of mud and water flooding appeared diagnostic. These floods caused cutbank erosion and caterpillar-like movements of the mud/water mixture in the affected channels. Many of these triggered the collapse of concrete bridges. Along Potrero and Abacan rivers, in-channel floods were associated with channel trenching (Figure 6.1).

TABLE 6.2   Post-lahar measurements along the major drainage lines affected by the 1991 eruptions of Mt Pinatubo (as of December 1991; w = channel width; d = channel depth; v = flow velocity; Q = flow discharge)

River	Obstruction site no.	w (m)	d (m)	v (m s^{-1})	Q (cm s^{-1})
Abacan	1	260	0·1	0·42	10·9
	2	150	0·1	0·66	9·9
	3	500	0·25	0·50	62·5
Potrero	4	100	0·2	0·66	13·2
	5	290	0·3	1·43	124·4
	6	200	0·1	0·91	18·2
Porac	7	50	0·5	1·0	25·0
	8	80	0·5	0·33	13·0
Gumain	9	700	0·5	1·0	350·0
	10	1000	0·3	0·6	180·0
	11	700	0·3	0·43	90·3
Santo Tomas	12	1200	0·2	1·11	266·4
	13	1300	0·3	1·0	390·0
	14	1400	0·6	1·43	1201·0
Bucao	15	1300	0·5	0·91	591·5
	16	1000	0·5	0·7	350·0
	17	1500	0·2	1·0	300·0

On the other hand, interchannel and sheet floods occurred in areas where enormous ashfall tephra clogged the vestiges of distributary channels and floodplain depressions (e.g. backswamps). In the marginal areas of Pampanga Bay, where fine laharic debris choked river mouths and tidal inlets, the incidence of deltaic floods was common.

6.2.2.2 Siltation

This involves estimation of sediment/water mixture mobility over time in conjunction with the instantaneous and site-specific streamflow observations after the passage of lahars. Initially, measurement of surface velocities was made from the travel time of floats over a known distance. Multiplying these by the estimated cross-sections of the actual laharic channelbed gave us an instantaneous measure of sediment/water mixture discharge in cubic metres per second.

Results in Table 6.2 show that the high discharge of sediment/water mixture in the post-lahar channels emanating from the eastern flank of Mt Pinatubo is surprisingly dominated by Gumain (the highest, 350 m^3 s^{-1}) and Potrero (the second highest, 124·4 m^3 s^{-1}). The prominence of Potrero post-lahar channel in the eastern part of Mt Pinatubo involves catastrophic lateral-medial erosion as suggested by a large increase in the post-lahar channel width specifically at site 5. A similar situation is manifested in Gumain River at site 10.

TABLE 6.3   Post-lahar sediment and transport characteristics related to the 1991 eruptions of Mt Pinatubo (as of December 1991)

River	Obstruction site no.	Sediment		Mean size (mm)
		(ppm)	(t d^{-1})	
Abacan	1	5132	4386	0·230
	2	4180	3245	0·273
	3	9894	48482	0·250
Potrero	4	33257	34418	0·59
	5	27914	272254	0·59
	6	41896	71198	0·50
Porac	7	222	435	0·46
	8	909	941	0·297
Gumain	9	2902	79634	1·15
	10	2826	39882	0·137
	11	2525	17876	0·163
Santo Tomas	12	1963	41000	0·375
	13	4105	125519	0·325
	14	6995	658662	0·375
Bucao	15	1625	75359	0·475
	16	941	25882	0·375
	17	4722	111065	0·40

Siltation has essentially retarded the mobility of sediment/water mixture along the post-lahar channels. A large portion of the transported sediments, which are derived from the post-lahar channel itself, moves as intermittent suspended load. Although suspended sediment is easy to describe and to sample (i.e. using an improvised single-stage bottle sampler), its character usually changes as velocity increases (Dury, 1969).

Suspended-sediment concentration was determined by filtering the sediment/water mixture, with sediment concentration expressed as dry weight (mg) per unit volume (litre) of the mixture (mg l^{-1} is equivalent to ppm by weight). Results in Table 6.3 show non-uniformity in sediment concentration which varies from 222·0 to 41 896 ppm.

Now, given sample measures of suspended sediment (concentration per unit volume of water/sediment mixture), rates of instantaneous stream silting (tons per day, t d^{-1}) related to the post-laharic regime can be obtained using the concentration−discharge product. Results may be related to short-term discharge magnitude and low-energy flows during the time of measurement.

A comparison of results in Table 6.3 displays a strong relationship between suspended-sediment concentration and rates of post-lahar stream siltation. The post-lahar behaviour of Potrero River appears somewhat chaotic: the rate of siltation through site 4 drastically increases from 34 418 to 272 254 t d^{-1} towards site 5 and decreases to 71 198 t d^{-1} towards site 6. The pattern is at variance with the downstream trend of sediment concentration, where it decreases towards site 5 and increases towards site 6.

It appears that the post-lahar stream velocity and discharge have shown direct influence on the rate of siltation, which is in turn conditioned by general relief. Such a relief is

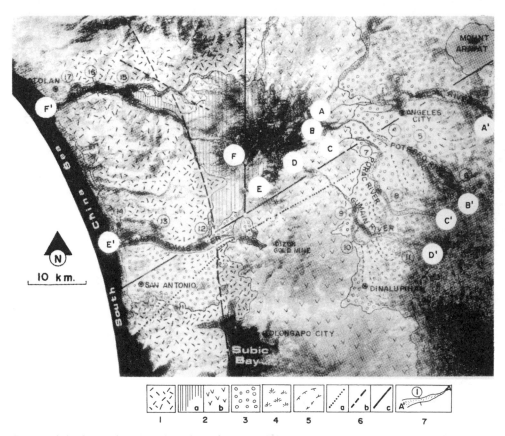

FIGURE 6.6 Geoenvironmental setting after the 1991 eruptions of Mt Pinatubo. 1, Ophiolitic region; 2, volcanic region (a, sloping active pyroclastic fields; b, hilly to mountainous non-active volcanic complex); 3, fluvial region; 4, coastal region; 5, inactive distributary channel/floodplain; 6, neotectonic zone (a, lineament 1; b, lineament 2; c, lineament 3); 7, the 1991 lahar route shown with transect lines for longitudinal profiles (in letters) and observed cross-sections (in numbers)

relatively higher in the vicinity of Potrero River in comparison to the other rivers along the eastern side of Mt Pinatubo (Javelosa and Domingo, 1992).

6.3 CHANNELIZATION

We shall draw attention to the geomorphic instability of affected drainage routes (Figure 6.6) which are now in the process of active channelization and abrupt gradational transformation caused by both the volcanic and non-volcanic incidents. For purposes of comparison, this investigation considers six major drainage routes for the gradational projections.

6.3.1 Pre-1991 eruption profile

The profiles are drawn roughly along the axis of the valley on the basis of the highest elevation of alluvial terrace fragments (i.e. Late Quaternary in age) above an adjacent riverbed. The longitudinal profiles give a fair representation of elevations and gradients of pre-1991 eruption aggradational limits.

On the eastern slopes of Mt Pinatubo, the upstream ends of pre-eruption aggradation limits along Abacan (A−A′), Potrero (B−B′), Porac (C−C′) and Gumain (D−D′) have reached an elevation of 80, 150, 100 and 200 m above their contemporary floodplains, respectively. The elevation decreases gradually to 2·0 m along the downstream ends of Abacan and Potrero, and 10·0 m along the downstream ends of Porac and Gumain. Obviously, the gradients of pre-1991 eruption limits are steeper than the equivalent riverbed profiles.

Compared to Potrero, Gumain and Porac, the pre-eruption aggradation limit associated with Abacan River (Figure 6.7.1) generally trends towards lower gradient at elevations close to its riverbed. This convergence usually occurs in an environment of progressive incision, probably in response to active differential uplift.

On the western flank of Mt Pinatubo, the equivalent aggradation limit along Santo Tomas River (Figure 6.7.5), which is at 120 m at the upstream end, is comparatively lower than that of Bucao River (Figure 6.7.6), where the pre-1991 eruption aggradation limit at the upstream end is approximately 150 m above the contemporary riverbed. The pre-1991 eruption aggradation limits of both rivers progressively decrease to 3 m and 5 m, respectively, closer to the riverbed. Both were therefore actively incising even before the aggradations of lahar fills caused by the 1991 eruptions of Mt Pinatubo.

6.3.2 Post-1991 eruption (as of December 1991)

The aggradation caused by lahar fills manifests three distinct morphologies, namely (1) lobate in reference to the overall planform of the lahar fill; (2) lateral; and (3) medial with reference to a channel that extends sourcewards from points near the snout, as schematized in Figure 6.8. In sites 2 and 4, along Abacan (Figure 6.7.1) and Potrero rivers (Figure 6.7.2), respectively, the deposition of lahar fills raises an aggradational mode of medial debris flow from 2 to 4 m above former water level. Their passage deeply scoured and incised the central pier of the bridges, causing these bridges to collapse.

In Figure 6.7.4, the situation is quite different along the upstream reaches of Gumain River (e.g. site 9) where the passage of medial lahar fills obviously widens and bifurcates into an in-stream gully system. The gully system undercuts and overtops the relatively low banks in this part of Gumain River, transforming into broad lobes towards site 10.

Further down the lahar channel systems of Potrero, Abacan and Santo Tomas rivers, the main bulk of lahar fill aggraded by lateral accretion. Decrease in the depth of incision is viewed to be one of the principal causes. Normally, as the depth of incision decreases, the passage of high-energy flows (e.g. lahar) widens the channel and bifurcates into distributary channel-fills distally (Johnson and Rodine, 1984). Such a situation has stimulated catastrophic overbank spills and mud-flooding along Santo Tomas and Potrero rivers.

Passing through the mid-reach of Potrero River (site 5), the left arm of the lateral lahar fill devastated almost the entire town of Bacolor in Pampanga. The same happened towards the lower reaches of Santo Tomas River, where the left arm of the lateral lahar fills flooded a large portion of Barangay Alosiis in San Narciso, Zambales, with volcanic debris.

Geomorphic Hazards

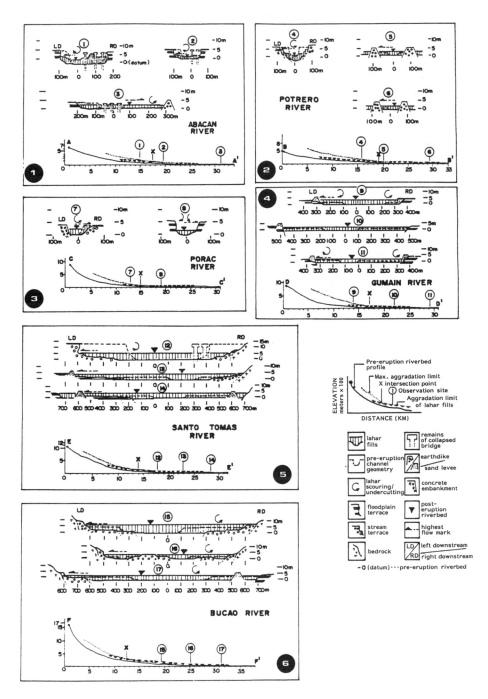

FIGURE 6.7 Longitudinal and cross-sectional profiles of major drainage lines affected by the June 1991 eruptions of Mt Pinatubo

An interesting morphodynamic feature of laharic incidents is found along Porac River. The lateral accretion of lahar fill in site 7 overtopped the right embankment forming a lateral ridge or "levee". Lateral ridges are usually formed by debris "slugs" (Johnson and Rodine, 1984; Johnson and Rahn, 1970). These ridges buried residential houses with more than 1·0 m depth of volcaniclastics.

A combination of lobate and medial lahar fills seems to dominate the western footslopes of Mt Pinatubo. Here, their combination is widely spread and thickly entrenched to a maximum of 7 m above the former bed.

Passing through site 12 in Santo Tomas River, the combination of lobate and medial lahar fills completely wiped out the bridge linking Barrio San Rafael and Santa Fe. Also upstream of site 15 along Bucao River, the combination devastated the entire villages of Yangil and Poonbato. Initiation by the "firehose effect" (Fryxell and Horberg, 1943), which was provided coincidentally by the passage of local tropical depression Diding and typhoon Yunya, aggravated the destructive impact of lahars in this part of Mt Pinatubo.

6.3.3 Net aggradation or degradation

The examples of aggradation and degradation described in this study emphasize that a one-dimensional lahar routing is more than sufficient to stimulate drastic channel changes. Specifically, lahar-imposed scour-and-fill processes (e.g. Breussers and Raudkivi, 1991) are mechanisms observed to induce rapid channel gradational transformation in the area at present.

Those channel cross-sections narrower than the mean reach width (e.g. sites 2 and 4) tended to lose sediment (scour). These channel cross-sections are translated to characterize a "degradation stage", where: (i) bank retreat and pop-out failures are

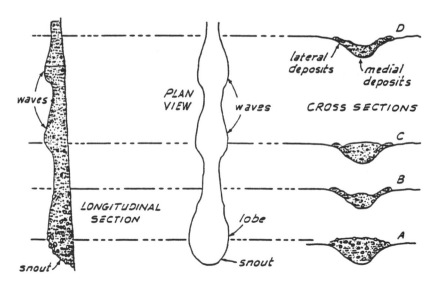

FIGURE 6.8 Schematized representations of a moving debris flow (after Johnson and Rodine, 1984)

TABLE 6.4 Estimates and assumed minimum risk period of lahar threat based on the calculated rate of water/sediment mobility (t d^{-1} of Table 6.3) along the drainage lines affected by the 1991 eruptions of Mt Pinatubo

River	Total volume of 1991 ejectamenta (m^3)	Total volume of laharic transport in 1991 (m^3)	Sediments still revertible into laharic transport (m^3)	Risk period (years)
Abacan	50	16·5	47·97	3
Potrero	50	25·0	36·0	2
Porac	50	5·0	62·0	10
Gumain	150	32·0	152·0	6
Santo Tomas	143	52·0	100·0	3
Bucao	250	63·0	260·0	7

prevalent; and (ii) the critical threshold for transport of the basal bank is exceeded at approximately bankfull regimes.

Conversely, cross-sections wider than the mean reach width and particularly those within regulated channels (e.g. sites 5, 6, 7 and 10) tended to accumulate sediment (fill) at discharge greater than bankfull. These sections are currently witnessing an "aggradation stage", where hydraulic sorting and dispersal of sediment tend to be catastrophic during the passage of lahars.

Differential dispersal of sediment (Figure 6.8) from a point source of lahar occurs both longitudinally (i.e. medial lahar) and laterally (i.e. lateral-lobe lahar). The latter, however, is particularly important in the construction of counter-measures and confinement of the main flow-line. Essentially, the dispersal of laharic sediments operates under live-bed conditions at present. The present aggradational situations in Potrero, Abacan and Gumain lahar channels are precarious, especially for urban areas.

In any case, the former, pre-eruption channel dimension of Abacan indicates that a narrower and relatively deeper form improves sediment transport efficiency under imposed flow conditions. Narrower and deeper channels with higher channel gradients allow rapid transmission of laharic debris further downstream.

Estimates of the rate of sediment mixture mobility in tons per day along with other parameters (e.g. volume of ejecta) allow us to project the "site-specific risk period" for an impending cold lahar destruction to occur. In Table 6.4 it is presumed that destructive lahars will remain a major threat for a period of at least two years in the Potrero area and for at least three years in the vicinity of the Santo Tomas and Abacan rivers. It will take at least six years for Gumain River, seven years for Bucao River and ten years for Porac River to regain "normality".

6.4 RISK PERCEPTION

Compared to the more dramatic and instant effects of the 1990 July earthquake, lahar and river flooding in particular remain, in pecuniary terms at least, the most consistently menacing and damaging. Despite little loss of life, the destruction of property, damage to georesources and the dislocation of families have triggered various reactions on the part of both government and general public regarding the ability to predict where and when inundation imposed by lahars will occur and how extensive its effects will be.

Risk domains can be assessed pragmatically by the application of a site geomorphic survey with optimum use of remote-sensing images. There is a lack of geomorphic studies and related mapping techniques in the affected area to cope with the problem of "composite-risk zonation". To provide a means of approximating risks, on-site geomorphic information is of practical importance, because it strengthens our risk perception of the tectonically active setting and the highly dynamic surrounding of Mt Pinatubo.

Although each "cataclysmic event" has its own uniqueness, for the most part, they are not random phenomena. They differ from truly random occurrences because cataclysms similar to geological events (Mann and Hunter, 1988) rarely, if ever, constitute an infinitely long sequence from which theoretically correct probabilities could be determined.

With the subjective and very limited historical information on the geoenvironmental repercussions related to the catastrophic activities of Mt Pinatubo, the "concept of possibility" (Kim, 1988; Anderson, 1988) appears appropriate. This concept becomes applicable since it does not require stringent demands on information and factoral contents. It allows an expert's opinion, which depends upon the expert's own understanding of an event or process, his/her experience and abilities and that relationship which he/she perceives as existing between the particular geomorphic situation of concern and other geoenvironmental elements that are known.

In the context of risk analysis, we shall consider the pragmatic order-of-magnitude estimates (Hunter, 1983) that are assigned subjectively. Through the application of related matrices, we shall identify and perceive a ranked triangular structure based on three domains (Figure 6.9), namely geomorphic hazard, vulnerability and georesources.

6.4.1 Geomorphic hazard domain

Geomorphic hazard is defined by Schumm (1988) as any landform change, natural or otherwise, that adversely affects the geomorphic stability of a place. There are basically two ways to identify geomorphic hazards and to assess their potential effect. The first is a historical approach that utilizes existing information on geomorphic history to recognize change. The second is more specific and relies on the recognition of the geomorphic dynamics and instability from current site-specific conditions.

In many areas surrounding Mt Pinatubo, there is insufficient historical information available to permit an approximation of the relative intensity of lahar, mudflow and flood hazards. In particular, the historic river-survey data as well as gauging-station records are too limited and geomorphically fragmented to provide useful historical information.

Since landform configuration plays an important role in the spatial distribution of geomorphic hazards, geomorphic information is the logical starting point for hazard evaluation. The information is initially efficient and effective alongside an optimum use of remote-sensing images due to the good visibility of landforms and associated terrain features in the immediate vicinity of Mt Pinatubo.

In order to increase survey efficiency, it was found necessary to consider the degree of geomorphic instability (Panizza, 1987). This is provided by information from the site analysis of the causes and effects of cataclysmic incidents and gradational tendencies.

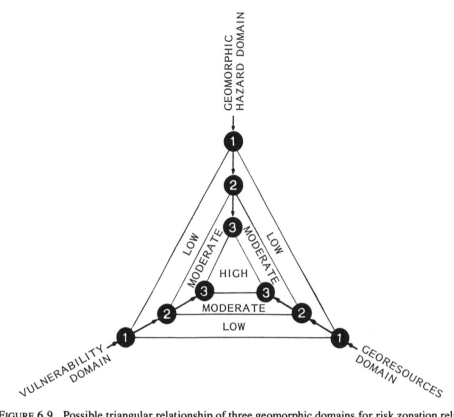

FIGURE 6.9   Possible triangular relationship of three geomorphic domains for risk zonation related
to the 1991 eruptions of Mt Pinatubo

TABLE 6.5   Numerical equivalents and ranking of geomorphic hazards

Landform types	Geomorphic hazards	Numerical equivalent	Rank
Active volcanic fields	Lahars	3	High
	Pyroclastic flows	2	Moderate
Post-lahar channels	River flooding	1	Low

Related to the 1991 eruptions of Mt Pinatubo, there are two potentially sensitive
landforms with a high degree of geomorphic instability and propensity for catastrophic
change, namely active volcanic fields (Figure 6.4) and post-lahar channels (Figure 6.7).
However, owing to the devastating repercussions both during eruptive and non-eruptive
activities of Mt Pinatubo, lahars are given priority in Table 6.5 and are given the highest
rank, with a numerical equivalent of 3.

As the available data are not sufficient to treat individual modes of flood hazards, simplification becomes a necessity. For practical purposes, all modes are grouped under one geomorphic hazard domain in this study — river flooding. Noting its strong affiliation to the effects of lahars, river flooding in Table 6.5 is ranked the lowest, with a numerical equivalent of 1. In effect, river flooding in the study area will generally be felt every time lahars and mud-floods occur.

6.4.2 Vulnerability domain

Recognition of risk must pass through the analysis of property and infrastructures existing in a certain area. The analysis must take into consideration what is more or less "vulnerable" to a certain geomorphic hazard. We shall consider the definition of vulnerability established by UNDRO (1979), which is the degree of loss to a given element or set of elements at risk resulting from the occurrence of natural phenomena. In this study, it is expressed on a cost-scale from 1 (low cost) to 3 (high cost).

In a densely populated area, like for instance Angeles City, a simple channel erosion or deposition could represent a "high risk". Thus, risk zonation must proceed with an on-site investigation of exposure to geomorphic instability (vulnerability).

Massive lahars and river flooding caused extensive damage to structures and public facilities. Many of these facilities were schools, public buildings, public markets, hospitals, bridges, housing, etc. Based on the damage report (DPWH, 1991), the areas of Zambales and Pampanga suffered most (Figure 6.10), in the order of $3 \cdot 2$ and $2 \cdot 5$ billion (Philippine) pesos, respectively. Owing to time constraint and to many building structures and infrastructures suffering major damage and/or collapse, not all facilities could be inspected.

Results of our random field investigation suggested that the severity and cost of damage at specific sites varied from 100 000 to 2 000 000 pesos per hectare. However, there was a high frequency of damage between approximately 1 000 000 and 500 000 pesos per hectare. Thus, we consider these values as the appropriate vulnerability scale for the site-severity of damage. This means that above 1 000 000 pesos per hectare is considered high cost with a vulnerability numerical equivalent of 3, and below 500 000 pesos per hectare is considered low cost with a vulnerability numerical equivalent of 1 (Table 6.6).

6.4.3 Georesource domain

Recognition of risk must also be carried out in relation to georesource functions of the affected environment. Georesources include not only urban areas but also other land-use/land-cover types. Essentially, there are three categories of georesource elements at risk from activities related to the 1991 eruptions of Mt Pinatubo, namely settlement/urbanization, agricultural land, and woodland/grassland.

Table 6.7 shows the numerical equivalents used in the estimation of georesources at risk from the eruptive activities of Mt Pinatubo. Owing to the importance of human life, the georesource component of land, where there is settlement or urbanization must always be assigned the highest priority, with a numerical equivalent value of 3.

6.5 RISK ZONATION

Given the numerical equivalent and ranking of geomorphic hazards, degree of vulnerability, and georesources at risk, their possible "triangular" relationship becomes

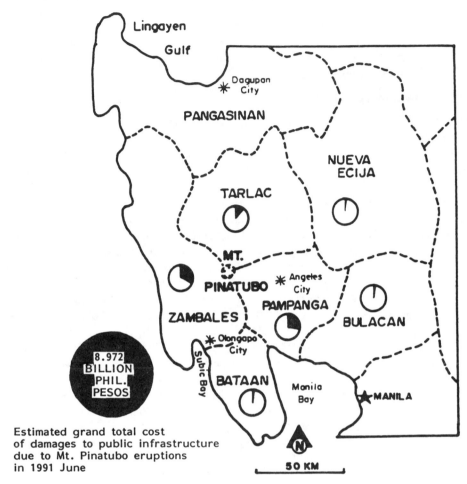

Estimated grand total cost
of damages to public infrastructure
due to Mt. Pinatubo eruptions
in 1991 June

FIGURE 6.10 Percentile distribution map showing the estimated cost of damages caused by the June 1991 eruptions of Mt Pinatubo (source: DPWH, 1991). Zambales 35%; Pampanga 28%; Tarlac 10%; Bataan 3.3%; Bulacan 1%; Nueva Ecija 0.3%

quantifiable. At each observation site, this relationship is numerically approximated, as cited in Table 6.8. By a simple "matrix-and-point" score method, an individual site at risk is scored.

Essentially, the efficiency of the scoring is governed by the synthesis of several methods (Figure 6.11) introduced by Verstappen (1989), Panizza (1987) and UNDRO (1979). Information and scoring in Table 6.8 proceed as follows:

1. Sum of the site-numerical values of geomorphic hazard and degree of vulnerability; this provides an approximation of the specific geomorphic risk or the probability that adverse socioeconomic impacts of a particular geomorphic phenomenon reflecting geomorphic instability will exceed a determined range of severity.

TABLE 6.6 Vulnerability scale and ranking of
damages caused by the 1991 Mt Pinatubo eruptions

Estimate of severity and cost of damage per hectare (Philippine pesos)	Vulnerability scale	
	Numerical equivalent	Rank
1 000 000	3	High cost
500 000 – 1 000 000	2	Moderate cost
500 000	1	Low cost

TABLE 6.7 Numerical equivalents and ranking of georesources at risk
from the eruptions of Mt Pinatubo

Georesources	Numerical equivalent	Rank
Settlement/urbanization	3	High priority
Agricultural land	2	Moderate priority
Woodland/grassland	1	Low priority

TABLE 6.8 Matrix-and-point score chart. High risk area has 12 to 18
points; moderate risk area = 8 to 12; Low risk area = 2 to 6

Geomorphic hazard domain	Vulnerability domain	Georesources domain		
		3	2	1
3	3	18	12	6
2	2	12	8	4
1	1	6	4	2

2. Product of the site-numerical value of georesource element at risk and the result from step 1; synthesized from the concept of UNDRO (1979) this provides an approximation of the overall geoenvironmental stability of the area in relation to the degree and level of socioeconomic organization present.

Figure 6.12 shows the classification and rank of three "risk zones" related to the eruptive activities of Mt Pinatubo. Each risk zone appears numerically distinct in terms of geomorphic hazards and stability.

6.5.1 Class A

Areas within this class are considered to be high risk zones. Based on field investigation results, these areas showed high incidence of lahars. The incidence of lahars is associated with drastic changes in channel morphologies. The most prominent of these changes is channel shifting by avulsion. In places such as sites 7, 10, 13 and 14, channel shifting causes very damaging overbank spills. Bank erosion can be a very significant geomorphic hazard within Class A, even for moderate to large non-lahar flood flows. This geomorphic situation is evident particularly in areas where active channel widening dominates (e.g. Potrero, Abacan, Gumain and Bucao rivers). The incidence of lahars within Class A has caused severe and costly damage to land, properties and infrastructures which, if combined, would exceed 1 000 000 pesos per hectare. The severity of the damage is extensive and devastating (e.g. vicinities of Bacolor in Pampanga and Alosiis in Zambales).

In terms of composite risk zonation by simple on-site matrix-and-point approximation, Class A has a maximum score of 18 (i.e. $(3+3) \times 3 = 18$). Urban and settlement areas often score this high.

6.5.2 Class B

Areas where impacts of geomorphic hazards are principally moderate in pecuniary terms fall within Class B. Inclusion of risk areas in this class expresses site-specific criteria which include: (1) high to moderate incidence of pyroclastic flows, lahars and river

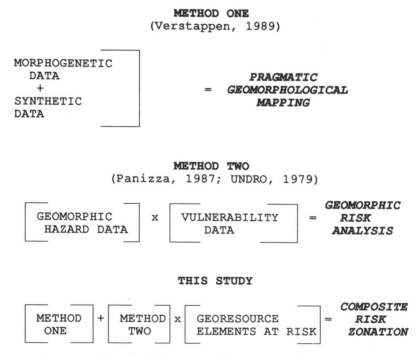

FIGURE 6.11   Procedure for risk zonation related to the 1991 eruptions of Mt Pinatubo

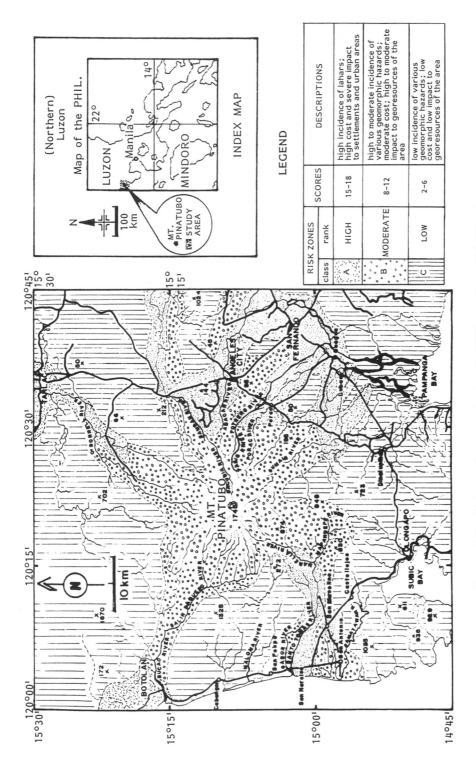

FIGURE 6.12   Risk zonation map related to the 1991 eruptions of Mt Pinatubo

flooding; (2) vulnerability and cost of damages caused by the passage of lahar estimated to be in the order of 500 000 to 1 000 000 pesos per hectare; and (3) high to moderate impact to the socioeconomic fabric of local communities.

The Class B risk zone appears in Figure 6.12 with relatively high incidence of pyroclastic flows, because of the current proximity of this zone to the immediate footslopes of Mt Pinatubo. It should be noted, however, that the high incidence of this particular geomorphic hazard mostly affects forest and agricultural lands and has less and moderate impact on urban areas. This geomorphic situation primarily constitutes Class B with a risk score between 8 and 12.

6.5.3   Class C

The Class C risk zone is characterized by areas with low incidence of geomorphic hazards related to 1991 eruptions of Mt Pinatubo. This risk zone is dominated by local geomorphic instabilities on the slopes and in the mountainous regions. Remarkable among these instabilities is concentrated overland flow. In some places along the western region of Mt Pinatubo, many of the concentrated overland flows transform into mudslides.

The geomorphic instability in Class C risk zone was essentially activated by enormous ashfall during the eruptive activities of Mt Pinatubo in June 1991. The ashfall which immediately descended on the surrounding lands, from a few centimetres to *c.* 60 cm in thickness, caused the partial or total collapse of structures including schools, housing, buildings and public facilities. In concurrence with typhoon Yunya and tropical storm Diding, which prevailed towards the west-northwest direction, the ashfall initiated massive concentrated sheetfloods, mudslides and river flooding causing further damage to infrastructure facilities including roads and bridges.

River flooding, which serves as the primary domain of geomorphic hazard in Class C risk zone, is expected to continue to be a source of damage over the next ten years and until the drainage conditions readjust and stabilize. Compared to lahar, river flooding causes minimal damages and low-cost impact to the overall socioeconomic organization of the area. On this count, the rank of risk areas within Class C is designated low with scores between 2 and 6.

6.6   DISCUSSION AND CONCLUSION

Information in Figure 6.12 indicates that a simple "triangular" approach and on-site matrix-and-point approximations prove to be effective for a rapid and pragmatic type of composite risk zonation. It should be noted that observed sites with low risk scores were partly affected by destruction from lahars and mudflows. Therefore, this study on composite risk zonation directs prime attention to the mitigation and management of the geoenvironments and observed sites with eminently high risk scores.

The type of laharic activity surrounding Mt Pinatubo appears to be capable of causing total devastation. The vulnerability is therefore 100%. Basically, this makes the site-specific geomorphic risk directly proportional to the geomorphic hazards, notably lahars.

Though the singularity of lahars and pyroclastic flows remains as a major obstacle to an accurate zonation of current geomorphic hazards surrounding Mt Pinatubo, river flooding seems to show dynamic behaviour. For risk mitigation of this dynamic behaviour, the present instantaneous observations on site geomorphic instability must be supplemented with long-term investigations of affected river and sediment discharge and stream geometry.

With full use of all that imagery and photo-interpretation have to offer, the application of a site geomorphic survey is concluded to be superior in regions with very limited terrain data. Its superiority is greatly appreciated in this paper: during the eruptive events of Mt Pinatubo in 1991 it allowed rapid provision of site-specific geomorphic information and quick geomorphic risk zonation. SPOT stereoscopy is a powerful tool in the context of natural hazard evaluation, where the differences between pre- and post-geomorphic events and the distinction between rapid and slow geomorphic processes are discernible. Nossin (1989) rightly stresses that an important asset of SPOT is its repetitive coverage.

Related to the 1991 eruptions of Mt Pinatubo, there are some fundamental difficulties in risk zonation with multidomains. A primary one is boundary definition. The discussion leads to the application of a simple triangular relationship and on-site matrix-and-point approximations which ensure an effective composite risk zonation. The risk perception based on this relationship emphasizes that geomorphic hazard zonation and vulnerability analysis for catastrophic events cannot be considered separately and independently from the georesource elements. Accordingly, their relationship has to be approximated on the specific site at risk. Although the matrix relationship will have uncertainties, it appears sufficiently informative to be helpful in rapid risk perception and zonation. It allows a quick identification of point data-sets or clusters useful for future automated mapping and site-specific monitoring.

In other words, the elaboration of "spatial geomorphology" in this paper enters into the context of regional planning which includes sociofunctional and spatio-organizational aspects, criteria for defence and protection of the quality of natural and human environments against natural hazards. This shows the necessity of integration of site geomorphic criteria in spatial plans for naturally hazardous areas, such as the current geoenvironment of Mt Pinatubo.

REFERENCES

Anderson, L. 1988. *The Theory of Possibility and Fuzzy Sets: New Ideas for Risk Analysis and Decision-making*. Doc D-8: 1988, Swedish Council for Building Research, Stockholm.

Arguden, A. T. and Rodolfo, K. S. 1990. Sedimentologic and dynamic differences between hot and cold laharic debris flows of Mayon volcano, Phil. *Geological Society of America Bulletin*, **102**, 865–876.

Breussers, H. N. C. and Raudkivi, A. J. 1991. *Scouring*. International Association for Hydraulic Research, Hydraulic Structures Design Manual, 2, 143 pp.

Carey, S. N. 1991. Transport and deposition of tephra by pyroclastic flows and surges. In Fisher, R. V. and Smith, G. A. (eds), *Sedimentation in Volcanic Settings*. SEPM, Tulsa, Special Publication 45, 39–57.

Cotton, C. A. 1944. *Volcanoes as Landscape Forms*. Whitcombe and Tombs, Wellington, 416 pp.

Daag, A. S., Tubianosa, B. S. and Newhall, C. G. 1991. Monitoring of sulfur dioxide emissions at Pinatubo volcano, Central Luzon, Phil. *4th GEOCON 1991, Abstract*, Geological Society of the Philippines, 10.

Defant, M. J., Jacques, D., Maury, R. C., Ripley, E. M. and Feigenson, M. D. 1991. An example of island-arc petrogenesis: geochemistry and petrology of the southern Luzon arc, Philippines. *Journal of Petrology*, **32**(3), 455–500.

Department of Public Works and Highways, Phil (DPWH). 1991. *Assessment of Damages to Infrastructures Caused by the June 1991 Eruptions of Mt. Pinatubo*. Unpublished Internal Report, September 1991.

Dury, G. 1969. Hydraulic geometry. In Chorley, R. J. (ed.), *Introduction to Fluvial Processes*. Methuen, London, 146–155.

Fryxell, F. M. and Horberg, L. 1943. Alpine mudflows in Grand Teton National Park, Wyoming. *Geological Society of America Bulletin*, **54**, 457–472.

Hoblitt, R. P., Wolfe, E. W., Lockhart, A. B., Ewert, J. E., Murray, T. L., Harlow, D. H., Mori, J., Daag, A. S. and Tubianosa, B. S. 1991. 1991 eruptive behaviour of Mount Pinatubo. *4th GEOCON 1991, Abstract*, Geological Society of the Philippines, 9.

Hunter, R. L. 1983. *Preliminary Scenario for the Release of Radioactive Waste from a Hypothetical Repository in Basalt of Columbia Plateau*. NUREG/CR-3353, SAND83-1342, Sandia National Laboratories, Albuquerque, 75 pp.

Javelosa, R. S. and Domingo, E. 1992. *Behaviour and Hazard Consequences of Mt. Pinatubo Lahars*. Unpublished technical report, Mines and Geosciences Bureau, Quezon City, Philippines, 40 pp.

Johnson, A. M. and Rahn, P. H. 1970. Mobilization of debris flows. *Zeitschrift für Geomorphologie*, Supplementband **9**, 168–186.

Johnson, A. M. and Rodine, J. R. 1984. Debris flows. In Brunsden, D. and Prior, D. (eds), *Slope Instability*. John Wiley, Chichester, 257–357.

Kim, K. 1988. *Risk Perception in Urban Planning and Management*. UNESCO, Paris.

Koyaguchi, T. 1991. Origin of the giant eruption cloud of Pinatubo, June 15, 1991. *4th GEOCON 1991, Abstract*, Geological Society of the Philippines, 10.

Lajoie, J. 1984. Volcaniclastic rocks. In Walker, R. G. (ed.), *Facies Models*, 2nd edn, Geoscience Canada Reprint Series-I, 39–52.

Mann, J. C. and Hunter, R. L. 1988. Probabilities of geologic events and processes in natural hazards. *Zeitschrift für Geomorphologie*, Neue Folge, Supplementband **67**, 39–52.

Newhall, C. G. et al. 1991. History and hazards of Mt. Pinatubo, Philippines. *4th GEOCON 1991, Abstract*, Geological Society of the Philippines, 8–9.

Nossin, J. J. 1989. Aerospace survey of natural hazards: the new possibilities. *ITC Journal*, **3/4**, 183–188.

Pallister, J. S., Hoblitt, R. P. and Reyes, A. G. 1992. A basalt trigger for the 1991 eruptions of Pinatubo volcano. *Nature*, **356** (6368), 426–428.

Panizza, M. 1987. Geomorphological hazard assessment and analysis of geomorphological risk. In Gardiner, V. (ed.), *International Geomorphology Part-I*. British Geomorphological Research Group, John Wiley, Chichester, 225–229.

Philippine Volcanology and Seismology Institute (PHILVOLCS) 1991. *Mt. Pinatubo: Wakes from 600 Years Slumber*. PHILVOLCS Brochure 9 Oct. 1991, 27 pp.

Pinatubo Lahar Hazard Task Force (PLHTF) 1991. *An Update on the Zambales Lahar Situation: The Southwest Monsoonal Rains of 13–26 August*. Unpublished report, Mines and Geosciences Bureau, Quezon City, Philippines.

Rodolfo, K. S. 1989. Origin and early evolution of lahar at Mabinit, Mayon Volcano, Philippines. *Geological Society of America Bulletin*, **101**, 414–426.

Schumm, S. A. 1988. Geomorphic hazards — problems of prediction. *Zeitschrift für Geomorphologie*, Neue Folge, Supplementband **67**, 17–24.

Sparks, R. S. J. 1976. Grainsize variations in ignimbrites and implications for the transport of pyroclastic flows. *Sedimentology*, **23**, 147–188.

Umbal, J. V. et al. 1991. Damming and breaching of the Mapanuepe River, Zambales,Phil.: A case study of the Aug. 24–26 and Sept. 13–21, 1991 events. *4th GEOCON 1991, Abstract*. Geological Society of the Philippines, 15.

United Nations Disaster Relief Coordinator (UNDRO) 1979. *Natural Disasters and Vulnerability Analysis*. Report of expert group meeting, Geneva, 9–12 July, 49 pp.

Verstappen, Th. H. 1989. Satellite remote sensing, geomorphological survey and natural hazard zoning: some new development at ITC, The Netherlands. *Supplemento di Geografica Fisica e Dinamica Quateruaria*, **II**, 103–107.

Walker, R. 1984 (ed.). *Facies models*. 2nd edn, Geoscience Canada Reprint Series-I, 317 pp.

7

Prevention of Disasters Caused by Debris Flows at Unzen Volcano, Japan

Masaru Iwamoto

Department of Civil Engineering, Nisho-Nippon Institute of Technology, Fukuoka, Japan

ABSTRACT

Unzen volcano began regular activity again in 1989 after quiescence of 197 years. Magma formed lava domes and pyroclastic flows occurred frequently as a result of dome collapse. Then, the mountain area was severely damaged by pyroclastic flows, surge deposits and ash fall. Vegetation cover, surface soil properties and gradient were changed so that debris flows occurred during short intense rainfall episodes.

Based on the relationship between site condition and rainfall, the author made a mechanical model for the occurrence of debris flow, and predicted the standard amount of rainfall for warning and evacuation from debris disasters. The risk of debris flow becomes extremely high when rainfall intensity exceeds 7 mm h^{-1}. The disaster prevention division could therefore make a plan for warning and evacuation from debris flows.

Precautionary evacuation plans are arranged as follows: the first stage results from rainfall of 10 mm h^{-1} or 5 mm/10 min; the second stage from 20 mm h^{-1}; and the third stage from 30 mm h^{-1}. The information is immediately transmitted to municipal government, fire station, police and mass media by telephone, fax, radio, TV, etc. As a result, residents can quickly take refuge in shelter houses.

7.1 INTRODUCTION

Japan is an arc of islands (Figure 7.1) located at the boundary zone between the Pacific, Philippine and Eurasian plates. There are about 250 volcanoes around the islands, and 77 of them are still active. According to records of the past 40 years, eruptions and earthquakes have occurred at 12 volcanoes every year. Thus, 18 volcanoes are regularly observed by the Japan Meteorological Agency and several universities.

In 1989, Unzen volcano became active after being quiescent for 197 years. Magma formed lava domes at the summit and pyroclastic flows occurred frequently when the lava domes collapsed. Then, the mountain area was severely damaged by pyroclastic flows, surge deposits and ash fall. Consequently, 43 persons died in pyroclastic flows on 3 June 1991. Debris flows often occurred during heavy rainfall. These volcanic hazards caused serious social problems in Japan because the refugees had to stay in public shelters for

Geomorphic Hazards. Edited by O. Slaymaker.

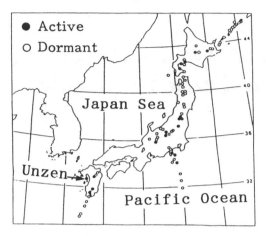

FIGURE 7.1   Distribution of volcanoes in Japan

more than two years. Eruptions are still very common and so these volcanic hazards may happen around Unzen mountain at any time.

This paper reports on the mechanism of debris flows due to topographic changes, and warning and evacuation systems for debris flow disasters.

7.2   CHARACTERISTICS OF UNZEN VOLCANO

7.2.1   Site conditions

Unzen volcano is located in the Unzen graben, on western Kyushu Island. It is a composite volcano, characterized by many dacitic domes, and the basement is early Pleistocene sediment of the Kuchinotsu Group. The piedmont deposits consist of various kinds of pyroclastic rock, and are covered with terrace and fan deposits and recent alluvium. According to topographic observation, there are three faults with N−S strike and eastward inclination in this zone (Figure 7.2).

7.2.2   History of volcanic hazards

Table 7.1 summarizes the historical records concerning volcanic hazards in the Unzen area. The disaster of 1792 was triggered by a large earthquake at the foot of Unzen volcano. As a result, Mayu-yama dacitic lava dome ($Z = 819$ m), (Z = elevation), on one of the Unzen volcanoes, suddenly collapsed and about 15 000 persons died in the resulting landslide and tidal waves. This is the worst disaster in the history of volcanic hazards in Japan (Ohta, 1969).

7.3   VOLCANIC ACTIVITY DURING 1990−1992

7.3.1   Earthquake

An earthquake swarm (main shock, M 5.7, M = Mercalli scale magnitude of earthquake) occurred in 1984. From the data observed at several seismic stations, the focal mechanism of these earthquakes changed with each event. The tension axes had a common direction; the Unzen graben is spreading slightly in the N−S direction at a rate of $2-3$ mm a^{-1}, but this event did not cause a disaster (Shimizu et al., 1988) (Figure 7.2).

7.3.2 Eruption

Unzen volcano began activity again in November 1990. A new crater appeared at the summit in February 1991, and caused ash fall around the summit area (deposit depth $D = 1 \cdot 5$ m). Subsequently, lava domes were gradually formed at the rate of $0 \cdot 3 \times 10^6$ m^3 day^{-1}. Since then, many lava domes have been formed, and the lava domes and pyroclastic deposits had a volume of about 150×10^6 m^3 by the end of 1992, as shown in Figures 7.3 and 7.4 (Japan Meteorological Agency, 1992).

7.3.3 Pyroclastic flow

The first pyroclastic flow was generated by the collapse and fall of a lava dome on 24 May 1991. It was a highly mobilized turbulent flow consisting of hot, vesiculated, juvenile fragments derived from basement formations (Figure 7.5). The flow spread laterally from the source, and rapidly crossed over topographic ridges more than $500-1000$ m in height, with a maximum velocity of 100 m s^{-1}. Consequently, 43 persons were killed by a debris flow on 3 June 1991. Since then, pyroclastic flows have occurred frequently just after the collapse of lava domes.

7.3.4 Debris flow

Pyroclastic flows successively fill the local undulating topography, resulting in a pyroclastic plateau. In this situation, debris flows occur frequently during short, heavy rainfall episodes. Figure 7.6 shows the distribution map of debris flow and pyroclastic

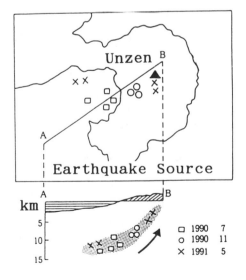

FIGURE 7.2 Characteristics of Unzen

TABLE 7.1　History of volcanic activity in the Unzen area

Year	Phenomenon	Damage
860	Eruption	—
1663	Eruption	Furuyake lava flow
1664	Earthquake	Debris flow 30 persons died
1791	Earthquake	—
1792	Eruption	Shinyake lava flow
	Earthquake	Mayu-yama landslide and tidal wave 15 000 persons died
1922	Earthquake	Debris flow 27 persons injured
1989	Earthquake	—
1990	Eruption	—
1991	Eruption	Lava dome, pyroclastic and debris flows 43 persons died

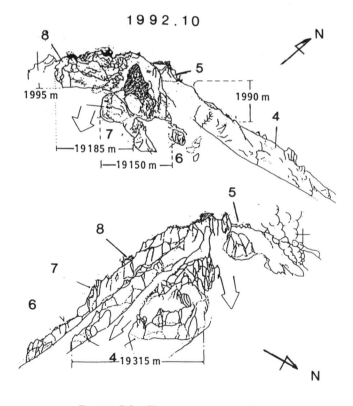

FIGURE 7.3　Changes to the lava domes

flow. From the figure it is clear that debris flows run further than pyroclastic flows and severely damage downstream areas (Figure 7.7).

7.3.5 Damages

Table 7.2 summarizes the volcanic activity and total damage during 1990−1992 (Shimabara City, 1992). According to the latest information in 1993, such damage continues to increase due to volcanic activity. A large new lava dome appeared at the northern summit in June 1993, which may cause a disaster in the near future (Takahashi, 1992).

7.4 TOPOGRAPHIC CHANGE AND DISASTERS

After the eruption, the riverbed profile of the Mizunashi River was changed by frequent pyroclastic flows and debris flows. Figure 7.8 shows the riverbed changes during 1990−1992. Pyroclastic flows began near the summit ($\theta = 30°$, $L = 8$ km), ran through the steep valley ($30° < \theta < 10°$, $L = 7−5$ km) and were deposited near the confluence ($\theta = 4°$, $L = 3$ km) on the average.

Debris flows began on the upper fan ($\theta = 20°$, $L = 7$ km), ran through the confluence and lower fan ($10° < \theta < 4°$, $L = 2−4$ km), and left swollen or flat debris-flow lobes near the mouth of the river ($\theta = 1°$, $L = 1−0$ km).

The main differences between these flows result from their mechanisms. Pyroclastic flow is a highly mobilized turbulent flow consisting of hot gas and lithic fragments derived from magma. The occurrence of debris flows depends on both the short, heavy rainfall episodes and the availability of riverbed sediments. The sediments are regularly supplied from pyroclastic flows and gully erosion. The upstream banks are remarkably dissected by rainfall.

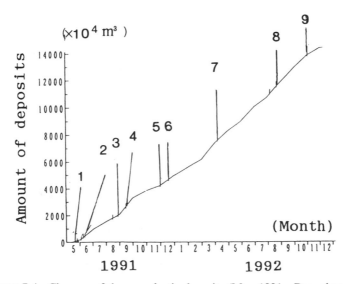

FIGURE 7.4   Changes of the pyroclastic deposits (May 1991−December 1992)

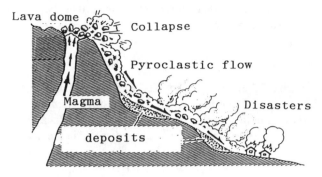

FIGURE 7.5 Mechanism of pyroclastic flow

The typical pattern of topographic changes on Unzen volcano may be summarized as follows.

1. Volcano erupts and volcanic ash is deposited on the summit area.
2. Lava domes are formed by the magma supply.
3. Pyroclastic flows subsequently occur as a result of dome collapse.
4. Sediments are deposited on the fans in the middle and upstream reach of Mizunashi valley.
5. Gully erosion occurs in the upstream banks and these sediments are deposited on the middle stream fans.
6. Topography is changed with each event, but the river gradient is gradually modified by the constant sedimentation.

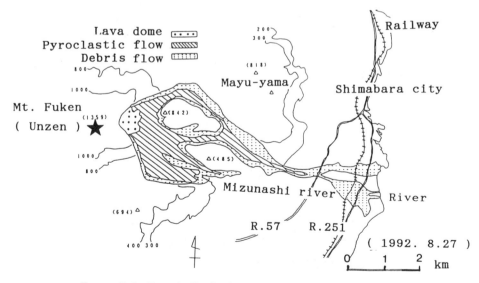

FIGURE 7.6 Deposit distribution by pyroclastic and debris flow

FIGURE 7.7 Disaster due to pyroclastic and debris flows

7. As a result, debris flows begin to occur in heavy rainstorms and run further downstream.

7.5 PREDICTION OF DEBRIS FLOW

7.5.1 Model of debris flow

According to the statistical analysis of debris flow in many places under various site conditions, the occurrence of debris flow is closely related to rainfall characteristics, such

TABLE 7.2   Volcanic activity and damage
(1990–1992)

No. of earthquakes	41 302
No. of pyroclastic flows	4581
No. of debris flows	25
No. of fatalities	43
No. of refugees	7609
No. of damaged houses	783
Cost of damage	10 billion US$

as the amount, intensity and duration. Especially in volcanic areas, heavy rainfall in a short period of time is the key to debris flows because of the rapid occurrence of surface flow.

Based on this fact and on field observations which show that debris flow occurs at the same time as the surface flow first appears on the slope, a formula for defining the criterion for occurrence of debris flow was defined as follows (Iwamoto and Hirano, 1982).

The equations of continuity and motion of water before the occurrence of surface flow are:

$$v = k \frac{\partial (x \sin \theta - H)}{\partial x} \tag{1}$$

$$\lambda \frac{\partial H}{\partial t} + \frac{\partial (vH)}{\partial x} = r \cos \theta \tag{2}$$

When the slope is steep, $\partial H / \partial x$ in the transport term is negligibly small compared with $\sin \theta$. Furthermore, assuming that the diffusion term is much smaller than the transport term, these equations can be solved by means of a characteristic curve:

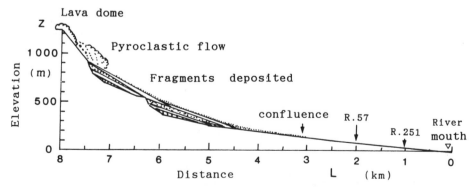

FIGURE 7.8   Slope changes due to pyroclastic flows (Mizunashi River, November 1991)

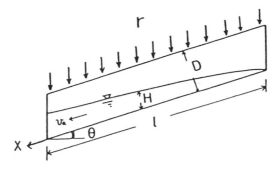

FIGURE 7.9   Model of debris flow occurrence

$$x = k \sin \theta \, (t - t_o)/\lambda$$

and

$$\int_{t_o}^{t_s} r \cos \theta \, dt = \lambda H$$

When the depth of seepage flow exceeds the depth of bed material, surface flow will occur. Therefore, the criterion for the occurrence of surface flow is given by:

$$1 \geq kT \sin \theta / \lambda$$

and

$$\int_{t_o}^{t} r(t_s - \tau) \cos \theta \, d\tau \geq \lambda D, \ (T = t_s - t_o)$$

From the above equations, the condition for debris flow is defined by the following equation (Hirano and Iwamoto, 1991):

$$\int_{t_o}^{t} r(t_s - \tau) \, d\tau \geq \frac{Dk}{l} \tan \theta$$

(3)

where k = hydraulic conductivity, H = flow depth, λ = void ratio, D = depth of deposited material, θ = slope angle, l = slope length, r = rainfall intensity, T = time of concentration, v = velocity, x = coordinate taken in the downstream direction, t = time, t_o = beginning time of rainfall, t_s = end time of rainfall and τ = differential time (Figure 7.9).

7.5.2   Critical accumulated rainfall and concentration time

By using equation 3 the critical accumulated rainfall can be defined as a single criterion. However, the criteria for occurrence of debris flow were actually divided into two zones, occurrence and non-occurrence, with some boundary area zones resulting from site differences, such as slope length, depth, angle and rainfall. Then, the criterion was defined as the nearest point between the upper limit of non-occurrence and the lower limit of occurrence zones, as shown in Figure 7.10. In the figure, whenever the accumulated rainfall R exceeds the level of R_{TC} at time T_C, the potential risk of debris flow is very high. Therefore, "the standard amount of rainfall" for debris flow can be defined in terms of the criterion of accumulated rainfall, R_{TC} (R_{TC} = critical rainfall, T_C = concentration time).

Rainfall data during 1991–1992 were analysed in relation to the occurrence and non-occurrence of debris flows at the Mizunashi River (Figure 7.11). In the figure, the rainfall data could be divided into two zones, occurrence and non-occurrence of debris flow, especially in the first period of time. As a result, it is indicated that the occurrence of debris flow is possible when the accumulated rainfall within 1 h exceeds 7 mm, and rainfall in excess of 15 mm certainly causes a debris flow.

7.6 COUNTERPLANS FOR VOLCANIC HAZARD

In the face of volcanic hazards, one of the most significant countermeasures is to establish a mass communication system to broadcast warnings. In order to promote such a system, the following measures are effective against debris disasters.

7.6.1 Disaster prevention communication network

From the data analysis, both the mechanism and possible occurrence of debris flow could be estimated. Then, several kinds of monitors, such as wire-sensor, raingauge, water-level gauge, camera, VCR and seismograph were arranged in the field to obtain precise data forecasting the disaster. Figure 7.12 shows some of these systems transferring visual data for the Ministry of Public Construction. Other data are also transferred to the disaster prevention divisions of both city and prefecture, as shown in Figure 7.13. Information on the occurrence of debris flow could be safely observed by using these data

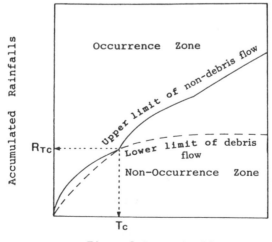

FIGURE 7.10 Schematic graph to predict occurrence of debris flow

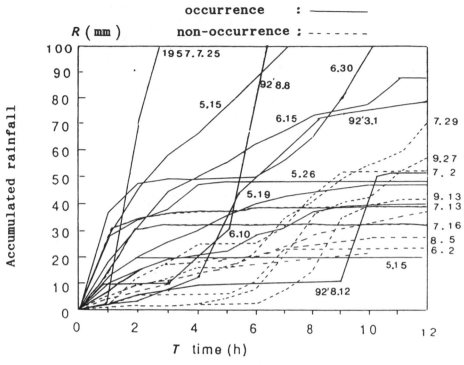

FIGURE 7.11   Relationships between accumulated precipitation and time of concentration $(R-T)$

and rapidly transferred to the disaster prevention division. The information is then systematically transferred to the individual sections and residents as shown in Figure 7.13.

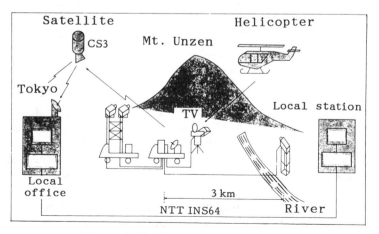

FIGURE 7.12   Visual data transfer system

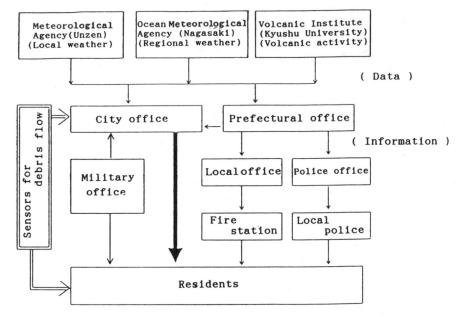

FIGURE 7.13   Precautionary evacuation plans

TABLE 7.3   Precautionary evacuation plans

Precautionary stage	Rainfall			Preparation
	(mm/10 min)	(mm h^{-1})	Σr (mm)	
1	5	10	>20	Today's working shift
2	10	20	>40	Headquarters and today's shift
3	15	30	>50	All staff

7.6.2   Precautionary evacuation measures

The headquarters of the disaster prevention division made a plan for debris flow countermeasures using the new concept of rainfall warning guidelines as shown in Table 7.3. This information is immediately transmitted to municipal government, fire station, police, mass media, residents and other concerned bodies by the use of mass communication systems, such as telephone, fax, radio, TV, loud-speaker, etc. (Figures 7.12 and 7.13).

Furthermore, the disaster prevention division checked and rearranged the warning and evacuation areas and shelter houses at each event, because reasonable safety plans are necessary for refuge shelters for more than one or two years. Figures 7.14 and 7.15 show the changes to the warning and evacuation areas and shelter houses during these two years.

7.6.3 Evaluation of precautionary evacuation system

Shimabara fire station implemented the warning and evacuation systems shown in Table 7.3 and Figure 7.13. Table 7.4 summarizes the changes to shelter places, their distances from refuge houses and travel times. Of course, when evacuating, weak persons, such as the aged, children and the sick, should be rescued first. In the table, the travel times were actually measured by car with an average speed of 50 km h^{-1} including the time lost due to curves and hills. The times in 1992 were about half those in 1991. In addition, citizens formed voluntary self-help group networks that support the official works and are integrated with it.

7.6.4 Prevention works

In the Unzen area, it is difficult to construct protective facilities because the volcano is still very active. Several temporary works have been constructed to maintain life-line systems and human life. These include railway, road, river dykes, shelter houses and schools.

At present, the most significant countermeasure is required to make a masterplan and rebuild a living environment. In order to promote this plan, volcano hazard assessment, such as hazard risk mapping due to earthquake, lava and debris flow, and urban safety measures (water, sanitation, transportation, energy and communication systems) should be achieved first. Furthermore, when supporting these assessments, a special law for natural disasters should be established because the present law is only for an urgent and temporary countermeasure and does not have a permanent effect. For example, a

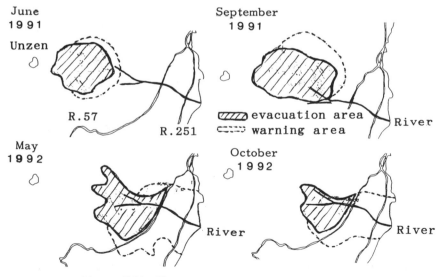

FIGURE 7.14 Changes to warning and evacuation systems

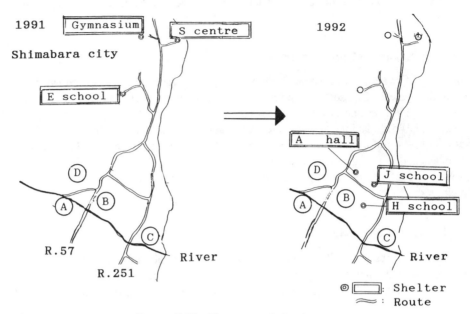

FIGURE 7.15   Changes to shelter houses

TABLE 7.4   Comparison of evacuation times

Block	1991			1992		
	Shelter	Distance (km)	Travel time (min)	Shelter	Distance (km)	Travel time (min)
A	E school	2·4	5	A hall	1·5	4
B	E school	2·3	5	A hall	1·3	3
C	S centre	5·7	14	H school	2·4	8
D	Gymnasium	3·4	9	J school	1·2	3
	Average	—	8·3	Average	—	4·5

municipality does not have the authority and revenue to make and carry out a reconstructive masterplan in Japan.

7.7   IMPLICATIONS

Since Unzen volcano began to erupt again in 1990, the resulting disasters have increased with each event. However, the occurrence of debris flow can be predicted and so precautionary evacuation systems have been developed. However, protective works are not regularly installed yet because of the dangerous site conditions (Figure 7.16).

Therefore, the following counterplans should be performed to rebuild a new city with a safe and comfortable living environment.

1. A Disaster Prevention Institute should be established to analyse the data observed in real time.
2. Hazard risk maps and precautionary evacuation systems should be developed to prevent new disasters.
3. Prevention works should be planned systematically from the viewpoint of watershed management around the mountain, river and seaside.
4. A new masterplan to rebuild a city with disaster precautions should be made through land-use evaluation.
5. For example, reclamation projects for agriculture, fishery and businesses must be discussed and promoted through cooperation between the residents, municipal corporations, and government.

FIGURE 7.16 Temporary debris flow reservoir

Volcano hazard assessment is very important in Japan, and should be considered in a long-range plan to maintain and rebuild a safe environment for human life. Assessment is expensive, long term, problematic and controversial. However, it is the only responsible action in volcanic zones.

REFERENCES

Hirano, M. and Iwamoto, M. 1991. Study on the concept of standard rainfall for warning and evacuation from debris disaster. *Proceedings of Disaster Reduction Symposium (Kyoto)*. Japan Society of Civil Engineers, 87–96.

Iwamoto, M. and Hirano, M. 1982. A study on the mechanism of the occurrence of debris flow. *Journal of Japan Forest Society*, **64**(2), 48–55.

Japan Meteorological Agency 1992. *Observation Records at Unzen: monthly data, 1989—1992* (in Japanese).

Ohta, K. 1969. *Study on the Collapse in the Mayuyama*. Report of Shimabara Volcanic Institute, Kyushu University, No. 5, 6—35 (in Japanese with English abstract).

Shimabara City 1992. *Report on the Disasters Due to Unzen Volcano*, 1989—1992 (in Japanese).

Shimizu, H. et al. 1988. Seismic activity and tectonic stress in the Unzen volcanic region. *Abstract of Volcanic Conference, Kagoshima Prefecture, Japan*. 177—178.

Takahashi, K. 1992. *Report on the Mt. Fuken Disaster in 1991-92*. Faculty of Civil Engineering, Nagasaki University, 1—215 (in Japanese).

8

Water Erosion in the Cape Verde Islands: Factors, Characteristics and Methods of Control

D. DE BRUM FERREIRA

Centro de Estudos Geográficos, Universidade de Lisboa

ABSTRACT

In the Cape Verde Islands, 90% of all the annual precipitation occurs from July to October, but these rains have a high temporal and spatial variability. The annual amount results from a few days or hours of intensive rains with high erosivity. Since 1968, a severe drought has disorganized the altitudinal distribution of vegetation and agriculture. The unprotected soils become more vulnerable to erosion. But the climatic degradation is not the main cause of advancing desertification in the islands. The increasing population, the systematic ploughing of soil just before the summer rainfalls, even on steep slopes for rainfed corn, the cutting down of trees and shrubs and the herding of goats lead to the intensification of erosion and to the initiation of rills and gullies in the unconsolidated volcanic materials. Severe soil erosion is associated with gully incision and mass movements from steepened slopes. This results in loss of soil fertility, impacts on channels and on stream uses. During the last 15 years, with the help of international organizations, emergency steps have been taken to restore the vegetal cover of the denuded hillslopes, to control the river flooding and to increase underground water supply. The first results are encouraging but complete realization of the long-term measures requires the combined effort of all the population, mobilization of technology and international aid.

8.1 INTRODUCTION

Located in the eastern tropical Atlantic Ocean, less than 500 km from Dakar and some 2500 km south of the Azores, the Cape Verde archipelago consists of nine major inhabited islands of volcanic origin, several of which are very mountainous. From its geographic location it is an oceanic extension of the Sahelian arid and semiarid climatic zone of Africa.

8.2 RAINFALL CHARACTERISTICS

More than 90% of the annual rainfall falls between July and October. The rainfall is extremely variable from one year to the next; it falls in a very small number of days or

Geomorphic Hazards. Edited by O. Slaymaker.
© 1996 by John Wiley & Sons Ltd

even hours, under the influence of local convection cells of disturbances which are associated with the northernmost extension of the intertropical convergence zone and of tropical cyclones. The heavy rainfall events (>50 mm d^{-1}), common on the most mountainous islands, are those which establish the pattern of the rainfall regime. On average, the storms do not last more than $6-8$ h but their hourly intensities are still poorly known as rainfall recorders are few and are not always located in the most useful places. At Praia airport, on a volcanic plateau at the edge of the sea in the arid zone of the southeast of the island of Santiago, the average hourly rainfall intensity with a recurrence interval of 10 years is 140 mm. Twice in 100 years the hourly intensity has exceeded 200 mm and the 100 year recurrence interval intensity is 240 mm h^{-1}. At the centre of the same island, the intensities are certainly higher. At S. Jorge dos Orgaos, for example, in the upper basin of the Ribeira Seca, hourly intensities of more than 200 mm h^{-1} have a return period of 25 years, resulting generally from the movement of convective depressions over the mountainous massif in September and October. These intensities are always recorded at a site; much heavier intensities may well occur at sites only a few kilometres away but where no rain gauges are located.

The rain is awaited impatiently every year by the inhabitants of Cape Verde, because it is the rain that renews the groundwater and ensures the success of the agricultural season. The same rain is also feared because its intensity causes destructive erosion on the slopes and the irreplaceable loss of crops; it is the cause of sudden floods which are extremely dangerous in the narrow steep valleys.

8.3   THE CURRENT SITUATION

Like the other countries of the Sahel, the Cape Verde archipelago has not escaped the long and intense drought since 1968 which continues at present with only rare exceptions. The drought crisis has led to an average of two-thirds of the annual rainfall as compared with $1949-1958$, a relative variability that is even greater in the high plateaux, a concentration in the months of August and September, a smaller number of days with agriculturally useful rain and a reduction in high-intensity rains (Ferreira, 1987). Since 1968, the summer water balance has become less appropriate for the cultivation of corn and beans, the staple food of Cape Verde islanders and the principal resource of the mountainous islands (Santo Antao, Santiago and Fogo) which provide more than 95% of the cultivatable land and employ almost 70% of the population.

Because irregular and often violent rains, concentrated in a small number of days, have always been a characteristic of the climate of the Cape Verde Islands, they now present a higher erosivity as a result of the persistence of drought for more than 25 years. To demonstrate this apparent paradox and the efforts being made to improve the situation, the southern island of Santiago will be used as a case study (Figure 8.1). This is the largest of the islands, one of the most mountainous, the most agriculturally productive, producing more than 50% of the harvest of the archipelago, and the most populous (145 957 inhabitants in 1980, with a density of 147 km^{-2}).

8.4   IMPACT OF THE CLIMATIC CRISIS

The agroclimatic altitudinal zonation of land use and landscapes for the island of Santiago representative of the period before 1968, as shown in Figure 8.2, has been completely

FIGURE 8.1 Morphological map of the island of Santiago (Ferreira, 1987). 1, mountain massifs; 2, slightly dissected plateaux; 3, deeply dissected plateaux; 4, canyons; 5, spot heights in metres; 6, meteorological station

rearranged. Today, the arid region covers those regions previously defined as semiarid. The subhumid zone has retreated to the heads of the eastern valleys and the ridge tops of the Pico da Antonia and the Serra da Malagueta. The only evidence of the old humid zone is a covering of strato-cumulus from the boreal tradewind which occasionally covers the highest summits (Ferreira, 1992).

The same soil cultivation as before 1968 is no longer possible. Pasture land is extremely degraded. The southern volcanic plateau, used exclusively for fodder until

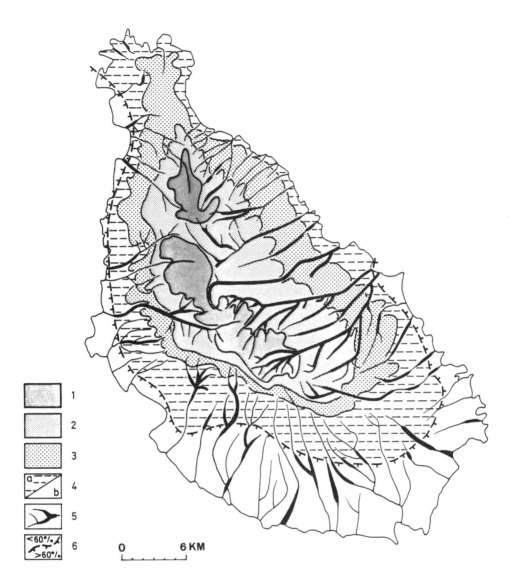

FIGURE 8.2 Agroclimatic zonation of Santiago before the current drought crisis. 1, humid zone
(rainfed agriculture, high pasture, rainfall from July to November > 400 mm with a frequency of
1 year in 2, frequent fog); 2, subhumid zone (rainfed agriculture, rainfall from July to November
> 400 mm with a frequency of 4 years in 10; frequently cloudy); 3, semiarid zone (rainfed
agriculture risky, pasture, sisal; rainfall from July to November < 400 mm in 8 years out of 10);
4, arid zone (a, pasture with good potential for development; rainfall from July to November >
200 mm, 50% of the time; b, pasture lands with water deficit; forage species renewal difficult; rain
from July to November < 200 mm in 80% of cases); 5, irrigation agriculture in rainy years; 6, the
60% coefficient of variation isoline for total rainfall from July to November (after Ferreira, 1987.
The agricultural zonation from Teixeira and Granvaux Barbosa, 1958)

1967 has turned into deflation regs. Traditional agriculture, based on corn, which supported a high population on the central plateau of Assomada and in all the eastern valleys up to 350 m a.s.l., has been destroyed. If, before 1968, cultivation was already hazardous because one in four years gave inadequate yield, today a normal harvest is exceptional. Almost all the country's need for corn is provided by international aid; this is the only way that famine has been avoided. Meanwhile, the Cape Verde islanders continue to sow their corn each year, making several attempts during the rainy season, even if the results are problematical.

The majority of the cultivated land is now on the wettest high plateaux, at the bottom of the valley or on the slopes, even the steepest ones. Even slopes above 80% are regularly cultivated. As part of the subhumid zone, the heads of the eastern valleys are now being agriculturally developed. The work must be done with a hoe because of the slope and the scantiness of the plots (0·2 ha per capita). The work of preparing the soil is done before the first rains, in June or July. The slopes are made completely bare, even the steepest ones and left without standard soil conservation measures. The surface layer of the soil is scraped to encourage infiltration. The seed beds are often dry and are separated by about 1 m, sometimes in association with vegetables. Each year, 15 000−20 000 ha are sown on Santiago.

In addition to these traditional agricultural practices it should be added that almost all the herbaceous and tree vegetation has been destroyed by drought, illegal cutting and goats, of which there were 66 000 head in 1980. The island of Santiago, like the other islands, can no longer provide the necessities of wood for heating or for cooking fuel.

Since 1968 the soil has become quite unproductive outside irrigated valley bottoms but, in order to confront the rapid demographic growth, the clearing of land and corn cultivation has continued in the subhumid zone. Between 1970 and 1980, the population grew at a rate of more than 2% per year. Also, in spite of substantial emigration, the population doubled from 1950 to 1980 and Santiago, the richest island agriculturally, multiplied by 2·5 because of migration from the other islands of Cape Verde.

The indiscriminate use of the land has opened the way for desertification. Intensely cultivated in spite of unsuitable climatic conditions, agricultural islands like Santiago have lost their ability to protect themselves against accelerated erosion by water. Drought conditions prevail but the occasional intense rainstorms in August and September, even though less numerous, have a destructive impact by encouraging surface runoff and initiating intense erosion of agricultural soils and the loose pyroclastic materials. They also increase the sudden torrential flows with increased transport capacity.

8.5 THE CHARACTERISTICS OF EROSION BY WATER

The effects of water erosion are negligible other than during high flows. Thus, the transport of sediment, which may be as important on the slopes as in the thalweg, has a seasonal character paralleling the short rainy season. On the interfluves and on gentle slopes, where the vegetation cover is low or absent and the soil is dry at the beginning of summer, general sheetflow occurs as soon as the rainfall becomes heavy. This sheetflow is responsible for movement of fines over the surface until the first rains stop. If they are not followed rapidly by a new rainy spell, this fine layer of silt and clay hardens with the drying out of the soil and is changed into a crust which develops cracks. A similar

FIGURE 8.3   View of the Ribeira Seca basin above Poilâo (photo: Ferreira, 13/12/1992)

process, during the later rainfall events, encourages the growth of rills which concentrate surface runoff. It is in this way that even on gentle slopes shallower but dense gullying develops.

As the gradient increases, and because of the extreme heterogeneity of the lithology of the substrate and the random distribution of the most intense rainfall, deep gullies grow rapidly and develop more deeply upslope, making detailed topographic maps useless after several years (Figure 8.3). Runoff conditions vary from one basin to the next. Other than the slope, the lithology of the substrate is the most discriminating factor.

The network of gullies in the large receiving basins from the eastern valleys thus becomes more dense and more extensive during each rainy season. They dissect the thick accumulations of shattered and altered cinders, scoria and lava and play an important role as the local pathway for material removed from the slopes. Many factors explain the erosion and quantity of sediments transported: morphometry of the channels, heterogeneity of lithology, slope gradient and slope form, soil use, intensity of rainy event sequence and even the precise timing of the intense precipitation event in the rainy season. It is those years when the heavy rains occur at the beginning of the rainy season which are the most hazardous for soil erosion.

8.6   MEASUREMENT OF SEDIMENT TRANSPORT AND EROSION

The study of landform evolution and surficial formations correlated with rainfall measurements for each rainy season would be a simple method to describe the processes and measure the rate of erosion and identify the regional zonation. Little attention has been paid to this research methodology. The reason is that the fight against erosion has been integrated into programmes under the Ministry of Rural Development and entrusted primarily to agronomists and hydrologists.

Materials transported as bedload, blocks, pebbles and gravels are visible everywhere and the evidence of erosion by water on the slopes is widespread. The river thalwegs also contain highly heterogeneous accumulations of sediment. Along the main channels especially downstream from the large canyons, the allochthonous materials are much more important than the autochthonous ones and aggrade the stream beds, forming flat floodplains. These sediment accumulation areas in the watersheds carry an increasing proportion of fines in suspension in a downstream direction. It is only at the time of the most intense rainfall episodes that the slopes of the major valleys feed colluvial talus that restricts the alluvial bed laterally. The base of these slopes is regularly stripped by flood flows (Figure 8.4).

When independence of the Cape Verde Islands was declared in 1975, the agricultural situation had become unsustainable. The authorities initiated an agroecological rehabilitation programme. A fight against desertification, supported by international agencies and the countries of the European Economic Community, has changed the archipelago into an experimental laboratory to investigate ways of fighting water and wind erosion and to develop soil and water conservation. The Ministry of Rural Development has formed a unit with special responsibility for collecting information on the volume of material removed from the slopes and retained in the basins constructed in the drainage network of the main watersheds (Figure 8.5). Retention dams are transverse dykes whose dimensions are fixed according to the size and long profile of the thalweg (2 – 10 m in height and 10 – 300 m in length). They allow the retention of a specific volume of sediments that can be measured. The siting of these dams is normally carried out at a break of slope in the valley such that there are good conditions for sediment accumulation upstream allowing the economic construction of an agriculturally productive aggraded surface.

On Santiago, corrective works have been completed on 15 watersheds corresponding mostly with those which had the greatest economic potential in the eastern part of the island exposed to the trade winds. The results for the period 1975 – 1990 are shown in Table 8.1. They show, on the one hand, the effort made since independence in construction of dams, absorbing most of the unemployed work force and, on the other hand, the magnitude of the volume of material removed from the slopes. The figures quoted are relative to the volume of sediments transported and deposited during the flood and to the volume of fine sediment discharged on the recession limb. The total transported in suspension during the flood cannot be calculated from these data.

This means that the figures are inadequate to calculate the specific denudation and erosion of the basins. The tonnage transported is a function of the speed with which the water reached its flood peak and the damage caused in the valleys. The fine material transported in suspension poses technical problems with respect to what was not measured and its calculation was not routinely carried out for each flood. However, it would be very useful to know this figure in relation to the removal of thin soils and the loss of fertility of the agricultural soils.

On Santiago, the basin of the Ribeira Seca has benefited most from the corrective work since 1975; 1873 dams hold a total volume of 929 067 m^3. The material caught behind these dams, after removal of the coarsest boulders weighing several hundred kilograms, has already permitted the re-establishment of agriculture over 77 ha. In this basin, the average rate of sedimentation for the period 1975–1990 was estimated at $8 \cdot 7$ m³ ha⁻¹ a⁻¹. The highest rate of sedimentation was recorded in the basin of the Ribeira dos Picos, which is intensely cultivated in its upstream part. The calculation of the volume of sediments behind 1414 dams constructed since 1975 gave an average rate of $10 \cdot 3$ m³ ha⁻¹ a⁻¹. The area of arable land recovered in this basin is currently 67 ha. Based on the specific weight of 1 m³ of sediment as $1 \cdot 6$ t, the Ribeira Seca loses an average annual total of 1400 t km⁻², and the Ribeira dos Picos loses 1650 t km⁻².

This is a gross calculation of the specific denudation of the two basins and is certainly an underestimate. For the basin of the Ribeira Brava on the island of S. Nicolau, Olivry (1989) quotes values of suspended sediment discharge observed during the flood of

FIGURE 8.4 Surface water erosion features in the valley of the Ribeira dos Engenhos (photo: Ferreira, 31/12/1992). Note the importance of gullying in the unvegetated unconsolidated sediments on the steep slopes and the efforts to control erosion by construction of a dense network of terracettes with a view to reafforestation

FIGURE 8.5 Transverse dykes in the valley bottom of the Ribeira Seca downstream from Poilâo. This kind of dyke not only reduces the impact of floodwaters but retains sediments. When the coarsest particles have been removed, new agricultural land is created (photo: Ferreira, 15/12/1992)

26 September 1978; 75 000 m^3 of fine sediment were removed, corresponding to 11·2 mm of soil denudation in this one event. The specific denudation of the basin of the Ribeira Brava for that year would have been 14 500 t km^{-2}. During the period 1978–1983, Olivry (1989) calculated the mean annual specific denudation at 4300 t km^{-2}. In effect, this kind of average is difficult to interpret when a single hydrometeorological event can itself account for the erosion over a long period.

Indeed, the average figures of Table 8.1 conceal the speed of filling-in of the settling ponds, which is very high for the most intense rainfall episodes. Between 1975 and 1990 on the island of Santiago, there were no more than 10 intense rainy periods responsible for most of the volume caught. This is because the rainy periods that lead to runoff are fewer each year. In certain years, there is no runoff. Runoff in the valleys is always short-lived, lasting from a few hours to a few days, most often between August and October. The runoff intensity is very variable depending on the rainfall intensity and the trajectory of the rainstorm across the basin. It is when the storms are concentrated in the middle of the basin or downstream that the flows are most powerful.

The rainfall period of September 1984 is a useful illustration. The collecting basins constructed between 1978 and 1980 on the islands of Santiago and Santo Antao were entirely filled up after the heavy rains of 16 and 17 September 1984 caused by cyclone Fran (Figure 8.6). More than half of the annual rainfall fell during 17 consecutive hours on 16 and 17 September. More than 400 mm fell on the central mountains of Santiago; what is even more remarkable is that these totals were recorded during winds of 50 to

Geomorphic Hazards

TABLE 8.1 A measure of sediment transport on the island of Santiago: sediment accumulated in stilling basins between 1975 and 1989 (Sabino, 1990)

Basin	Surface (ha)	Number of dykes	Accumulated volume (m³ × 1000)	Average volume per dyke (m³)	Average rate (m³ ha⁻¹ a⁻¹)
Seca	7103	1873	927·0	492·3	8·7
Picos	5477	1414	850·0	601·0	10·3
Principal	3694	353	40·5	114·7	0·7
Santa Cruz	3673	1059	366·6	346·2	6·7
S. Domingos	3043	307	94·2	306·8	2·1
Flamengos	3010	260	131·4	505·4	2·9
Grande	1459	41	20·1	493·0	0·9
S. Miguel	1386	570	114·1	200·2	5·5
Tarrafal	1361	40	25·8	645·0	1·3
Boa Entrada	1279	414	65·0	157·0	3·4
Cumbe	1274	47	8·7	185·0	0·5
Salto	1218	361	101·0	280·0	5·5
Mangue	996	101	24·0	237·6	1·6
Prata	305	285	37·2	130·4	8·1

100 km h⁻¹. The return period of such a rainfall event was estimated at about 30 years. The maximum hourly rainfall intensity at S. Jorge dos Orgaos was 200 mm h⁻¹. This rain generated floods in all the valleys, but in the eastern part of the island floods were extremely rapid and exceptionally high. The specific discharge of Ribeira Seca at S. Jorge dos Orgaos at the flood peak was estimated at 22 m³ s⁻¹ km⁻² (INIA, 1989). Thousands of tonnes of material were removed from the slopes, burying roads and hydraulic structures. The force of the water in the managed valleys destroyed more than 900 dams on Santiago, remobilizing some of the material caught during earlier floods.

It was nevertheless the island of Santo Antao which was most affected, with more than 500 mm of rain in 12 h. The alluvial bed of the Ribeira do Chao das Pedras was filled by 6 m of sediments, 400 dams were destroyed, 160 ha of arable land restored in the settling basins was buried or remobilized and 2000 agricultural properties were damaged.

We have calculated the Wischmeier factor R for erosivity of the rain in the upper basin of the Ribeira Seca (from the recording rain gauge at S. Jorge dos Orgaos) for the rainfall event of 16 September 1984. The value obtained was 610 MJ cm ha⁻¹ h⁻¹. This represents more than 90% of the rainfall erosivity for the whole of 1984 and is double the mean R value calculated by Faurès and Morais (1988) for the period 1981–1987.

8.7 METHODS OF FIGHTING EROSION BY WATER

Measures for fighting erosion by water have been integrated into an ecological rehabilitation project for the whole country. To protect the soil against accelerated erosion implies reducing the direct impact on bare soil, reducing the speed of surface runoff and stabilizing the slopes. Also, towards the end of the 1970s the priorities shifted towards protection and restoration of vegetation cover, and the correction of slopes and torrent beds. These restoration works mobilized an important work force during the dry

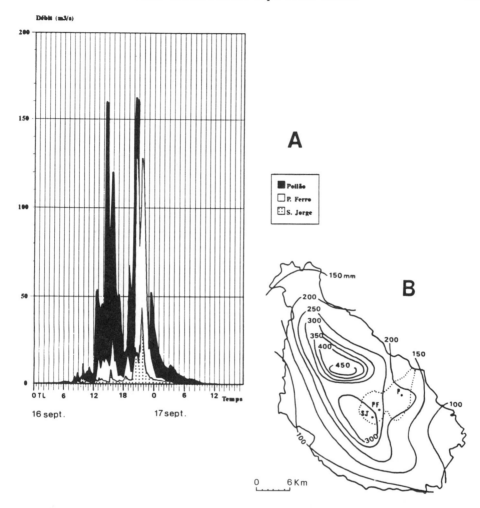

FIGURE 8.6 Rainfall and discharge event of 16−17 September 1984 on the island of Santiago: A, discharge hydrographs from the Ribeira Seca basin (data from INIA, 1989); B, spatial distribution of total rainfall (Ferreira, 1988); the limits of the Ribeira Seca basin indicated by dotted line

season each year. The ultimate goal is to maintain agriculture, which is still the main occupation of the Cape Verde Islands, and rural development even in climatically adverse conditions.

On the slopes, terraces and terracettes, separated by walls, have been constructed along the contours where slopes exceed 20%. Their size (5 to 15 m) varies according to the rate of infiltration of the water and the frequency of daily precipitation of high intensity. These structures are associated with tree plantations for forage (*Acacia holosenicea*; *Parkinsonia aculeata*; *Prosopis juliflora*; *Atriplex*) or rainfed agriculture, for which the water supply is significantly improved on the managed slopes. In the 1980s, many of the walls supporting the terraces needed frequent repairs in order to prevent them from becoming the cause of gullying. They have been replaced by sisal, euphorbes and

Angolan pea (*Cajanus cajan*) plantations that stabilize the slopes naturally. On the steepest slopes, the cultivation of *Cajanus cajan* has been encouraged to replace corn so as to minimize erosion at the start of the rainy season. These works have been accompanied by construction of diversion canals to improve gully drainage towards the nearest thalwegs.

On the steepest slopes that are too denuded to support rainfed agriculture, individual circular or half-moon shaped terracettes have been constructed by the thousand (Figures 8.4 and 8.7). In each of them a tree will be planted at the start of the rainy season. Table 8.2 shows the extent of the soil conservation works, built each year in the dry season, in several basins on Santiago.

Programmes of land preparation and planting have been regularly announced each year since independence. Some figures from 1989 are quoted here as an example and they give an idea of the extent of the effort. That year, 2800 km of benches, one million terracettes and 30 000 small dams were built, and 2 800 000 holes for tree planting were prepared. By 8 August, the date of the first rains of the year, two million trees had been planted on the islands of Santiago, Fogo, Brava, Maio and Santo Antao, equivalent to the restoration of 5400 ha (Ministère du Développement Rural, 1990).

This reforestation has benefited two different ecological zones. On the one hand, the mountainous core of the islands has had an increase in forest cover and afforestation has taken place at the heads of the valleys. The object is to create a forest cover (eucalyptus, Canary pines, cypress) sufficiently dense and continuous to hold the unstable soils on

FIGURE 8.7 Detailed set-up on a slope in the valley of the Ribeira de Sâo Francisco, in the southeast of the island of Santiago (photo: Ferreira, 5/12/1992). Individual terracettes before trees have been planted. The density and arrangement of the terracettes depends on the slope of the land and the sensitivity of the superficial materials to gullying

TABLE 8.2 Soil conservation works completed in drainage basins on the island of Santiago between 1980 and 1983 (Sabino, 1984)

Basin	Year	Total length of constructed embankments (m)	Area of restored slope (ha)	Number of trees planted
Santa Cruz	1980	1802	0·9	8202
	1981	10948	16·8	6000
	1982	12200	18·7	16662
	1983	26608	17·74	59193
Saltos	1980	3040	2·4	800
	1981	10038	7·7	—
	1982	24877	18·7	4500
	1983	11233	7·5	—
Flamengos	1980	—	—	1700
	1981	8816	5·1	12682
	1982	5776	4·5	5900
	1983	15025	10·0	—
S. Miguel	1980	1050	0·8	4993
	1981	5834	6·0	—
	1982	5243	4·8	6600
	1983	9227	6·2	14500
Total	1980 – 1983	142898	127·64	141732

steep slopes and stop the growth of gullies, and increase water infiltration. On the other hand, the lower, extremely denuded arid and semiarid regions were the object of special attention, especially on Santiago, where they cover 20% of the island. The first stage of the vegetative recolonization was to plant woody species known to be resistant to drought to provide a microclimate that would provide protection against the wind. On the southern plateaux, 6000 ha were planted with American acacias, *Parkinsonia* and *Prosopis* spp. One stratum of gramineae was planted after the achievement of a sufficiently dense forest cover. They appeared to be able to survive in the shade of the trees provided that they were utilized rationally and given protection from hungry goats.

8.8 CONCLUSION

The present drought crisis is no more than a minor part of the degradation occurring in the Cape Verde Islands. The process of desertification and the associated accelerated erosion by water are primarily of anthropogenic origin. The proof of this is that it was enough for a minimal programme of agroecological rehabilitation in the islands, applied at farm level, and a mobilization of the population around the major problem of erosion to improve the situation over a period of 15 years. The project is ambitious and long-term especially in the present socioeconomic conditions, but it already appears to be giving results. The tendency to continual degradation of the islands is perhaps reversible. Less fine material and soil is lost to the sea during heavy rains, arable land has increased, floods are better controlled, slopes are better protected from gullying and trees are growing again. At the same time, traditional agricultural practices and the ancient cultivation of corn, linked to a well-established nutritional pattern, have not been displaced. The other, no less important aspect of the fight is the scale of international aid, both technical and financial. The financial cost of corrective measures remains to be determined. The Republic of Cape Verde has limited national resources. More than 70% of the budget comes from varieties of aid; financial means to sustain the fight against erosion come from outside (France, Belgium, Germany, Italy, Switzerland, European Economic Community, FAO, USAID, PNUD, UNICEF, etc.). This is the dilemma of the Cape Verde government. Rehabilitation of the islands is only possible if the fight is intensified. But the traditional donors to the Cape Verde Republic are currently providing more aid to the ex-Soviet bloc countries and there is a risk that there will be insufficient money to continue the work initiated. Seeing the very encouraging results achieved in the short term it would be ironic if it were necessary to reduce the effort, especially when the viability of Cape Verde depends on it.

REFERENCES

da Silva Teixeira, A. and Granvaux Barbosa, L. A. 1958. *A Agricultura do Arquipélago de Cabo Verde*. Memória da Junta de Investigaçao do Ultramar, 2nd series, no. 2, Lisboa, 178 pp.

de Brum Ferreira, D. 1987. La crise climatique actuelle dans l'archipel du Cap Vert. Quelques aspects du problèmes dans l'ile de Santiago. *Finisterra*, **XXIII**(43), 113–152.

de Brum Ferreira, D. 1988. Les vicissitudes des cultures pluviales en 1984 dans l'ile de Santiago (Cap Vert). *Climats et Climatologie, Volume d'Hommage offert au Professeur Pierre Pagney*. Dijon, 99–105.

de Brum Ferreira, D. 1992. L'oscillation climatique actuelle dans l'ile de Santiago et la mobilité des paysages. *Comunication, 5 Colloque de l'Association Internationale de Climatologie*. Dijon, 16–18 Sept. 1992.

Faurès, J. and Morais, J. T. 1988. Apliçao da equaçao universal de perda de solos de Wischmeier à bacia hidrográfica de S. Jorge. In Kloosterboer, E. (ed.), *Actas do Iº Seminário Nacional de Conservaçao de solos e água, Sto Antao, 9–12 Nov. 1987*. Projecto de Cooperaçao bilateral Cabo-Verde/Holanda, MDR, Praia, 103–113.

INIA. 1989. *Hidrologia de superfície (1984–1988)*. Programa AGRHYMET, Praia.

Ministère du Développement Rural. 1990. *Bulletin Trimestriel du Ministère du Développement Rural*, no. 3.

Olivry, J. C. 1989. *Hydrologie de l'archipel du Cap Vert. Etude de l'Ile de Sao Nicolau*. Etudes et Thèses, ORSTOM, 311 pp.

Sabino, A. A. 1984. *Conservaçao do solo e água em Cabo Verde. Relatório*. Ministério de Desenvolvimento Rural, Praia, 130 pp.

Sabino, A. A. 1990. *As infraestruturas hidraúlicas de conservaçao do solo e da água e a quantificaçao dos impactes. Caso de estudo na área do 'Watershed development Project'*. INIA, Praia, 55 pp.

9

Experimental Activities for Soil Erosion Evaluation and Modelling

P. BALLERINI, C. BECHINI AND S. MORETTI

Earth Science Department, University of Florence

ABSTRACT

Coordinated research on terrain analysis has been performed by several research institutes during the MAC-Europe multisensor campaign on the Montespertoli test site in Italy. In this paper the experimental activity, mainly devoted to soil applications and hydrogeology, is summarized. The objective of obtaining geomorphological information (e.g. soil erosion processes), and of assimilating data from microwave remote sensing into hydrological models is explained through examples of model outputs.

9.1 INTRODUCTION

The aim of this research is to investigate the different stages of transport and redeposition of material on watershed slopes by means of hydrological models and the role of SAR (synthetic aperture radar) data as a surrogate for field measurement programmes.

The research will include two fundamental points: extraction of hydrological parameters from field experiment data and validation of erosion models in which SAR data can be introduced (Figure 9.1).

Problems related to erosion are extensive in central Italy and remote sensing techniques can be a useful method for monitoring hydrological parameters in large watersheds, with the use of new sensors, therefore allowing the analysis of erosion data (Chiarantini et al., 1990). The research activity, which is being carried out in the framework of the SIR (shuttle imaging radar)-C/SAR-X experiment, and in particular the Multisensor Airborne Campaign (MAC '91), aims at an understanding of the information that we can extract from multifrequency SAR images to be used in hydrology and, in particular, in estimating soil erosion (Bechini et al., 1991).

MAC '91 was a comprehensive remote sensing campaign carried out in June–July 1991 on several sites in Europe, based on two NASA/JPL (jet propulsion laboratory) aircraft equipped with microwave and optical sensors. Some results, which were worked

Geomorphic Hazards. Edited by O. Slaymaker.
© 1996 by John Wiley & Sons Ltd

126   *Geomorphic Hazards*

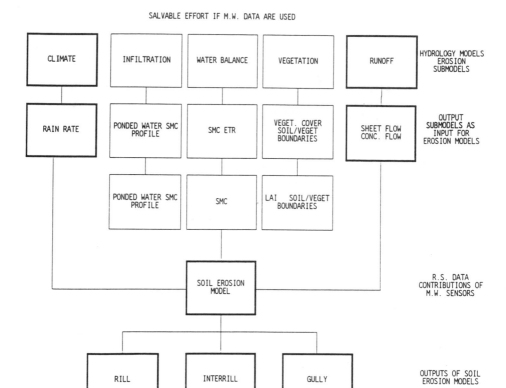

FIGURE 9.1   Flow chart showing the potential value of remotely sensed (RS) data using microwave (MW) sensors. The boxes with lighter outlines indicate the effort in field instrumentation that can be saved if microwave data are used. (SMC = soil moisture content; LAI = leaf area index)

out using hydrological models to reconstruct different stages of transport and deposition of material on the watershed slopes, have been compared to experimental data obtained by means of a rain simulator.

Geological characteristics of the site are well known (Canuti et al., 1979, 1986); moreover, during each flight, ground truth was measured and much ground data were collected on selected fields and areas. The ground measurements included soil moisture, soil surface roughness, soil bulk density, texture, soil temperature, organic matter, crop type and distribution. Other geophysical measurements were performed to characterize dielectric properties of the soil and, in particular, geoelectrical measurements, ground penetrating radar stratigraphy and measurements of the resistivity. Furthermore, a digital terrain model was used to support digital images and morphological data.

The sampling strategies have been differentiated for three specific areas: an agricultural area along the Pesa River, the Virginio Basin, and a small catchment (a subbasin of the Virginio) where field measurements were performed intensively. In the latter area, this work has been done both to obtain a map of the relevant parameters and to identify areas with relevant soil loss and concentration of erosion. Using a field rain simulator, we analyse the effects of different rainfall in this area with respect to infiltration capacity, runoff and soil detachment, to study the relationships between the dynamics of infiltration — determined as the difference between the amount of rainfall and the measured amount of runoff — on the soil erosion.

9.2 TEST SITE DESCRIPTION

The site chosen for testing the methodology applied in this work is the Pesa River Basin, located on the Tyrrhenian side of the northern Apennine in Tuscany, 30 km south of Florence (Figure 9.2).

This basin is representative of lithological, climatic, vegetational and land-use conditions common to wider agricultural areas in Tuscany (central Italy). The site is a representative area of those Tyrrhenian—Apennine slopes where bedrock is made up of Plio-Pleistocene marine and fluvio-lacustrine soft sediments which are affected intensively by geomorphological processes of erosion and mass movements. The Pesa Basin is a prevalently agricultural area in which the current principal activity involves vineyards and olive growing; these activities, especially regarding wine production, have also been the principal cause of hillside remodelling. In fact the hillsides, where the vineyards are prevalently located, have been extensively remodelled over the last 20 years to make the vineyards themselves more accessible to mechanical farm equipment.

This transformation has obviously brought some advantages to productivity; however, in many cases it has reduced slope stability and made soil erosion processes, directly affected by this management, more widely present in the area.

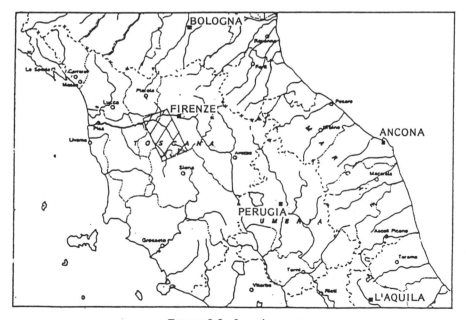

FIGURE 9.2 Location map

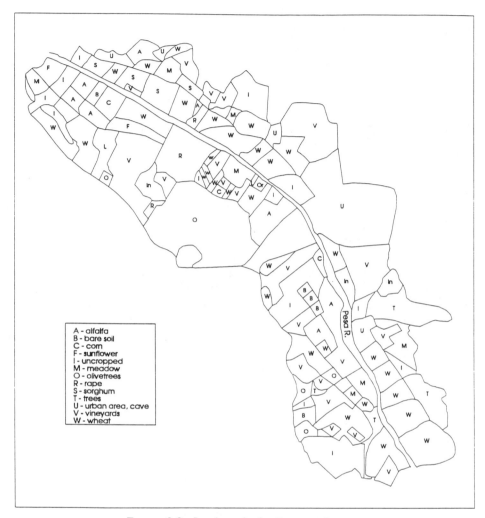

FIGURE 9.3   Land use in the Pesa sample area

In the flatlands the principal land use is wheat, corn and sunflower, and the sowing bed
is generally prepared at the end of summer.

The typically Mediterranean climate is characterized by an arid period during summer
and high rainfall intensities in autumn, decreasing in winter.

Two small areas have been selected from the entire region for more specific
experiments and intensive field measurements: an agricultural area along the Pesa River
(Figure 9.3), characterized by square agricultural fields of different crops, and a subbasin
of the Virginio River (Figure 9.4), where an experimental station for bed and suspended-
sediment load discharge is located; the latter was also chosen for hydrological purposes.
The agricultural site is a flat area where soil properties and remote sensing data can be
compared, disregarding the problem of surface slope which greatly affects SAR image

interpretation. Here, three plots of bare soil have been specifically tilled with different surface roughness, to act both as extended targets for calibration and to allow analysis of roughness effects on SAR polarimetric response.

9.3 METHODOLOGY

To study erosion processes and to analyse the effects of different rainfall with respect to infiltration capacity, runoff and soil detachment, a field rain simulator was used. Infiltration was determined as the difference between the amount of rainfall and the measured amount of runoff (Canuti et al., 1985). The simulations have been performed on the Pesa area, and others are still in progress to retrieve data on the Virginio Basin as well. The rain simulator is a portable instrument with variable rain intensity. It is made up of a sprayer which oscillates with variable period (Canuti et al. 1985). These operating conditions make it possible to change rainfall conditions during the experiment, to give better simulation of natural intensity distribution. However, for the present study, the rain has been maintained constant for an hour to avoid excessive variables.

The SAR data is used by means of two different approaches: qualitative and quantitative (Figure 9.5). The qualitative approach leads to a direct analysis of the images (photointerpretation) in order to obtain three kinds of thematic data by which it is possible to create thematic maps. The quantitative approach deals with the analysis of geophysical,

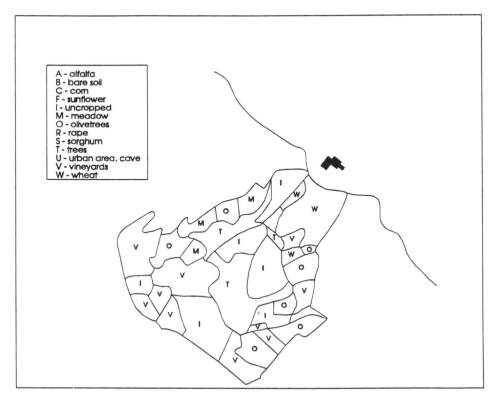

FIGURE 9.4   Land use in the Virginio subbasin sample area

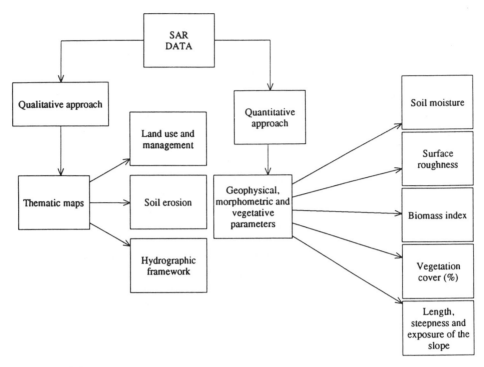

FIGURE 9.5   Flow chart of the methodology used showing the two different approaches

morphometric and vegetative parameters from which it is possible to derive all the data (soil moisture, roughness, biomass index, etc.) to be inserted in the procedure for analysing the soil erosion process along the slopes (Figure 9.1).

Regarding the second approach, the SAR data need to be both calibrated and corrected for the surface slope. In order to correct SAR data for the surface slope, a digital terrain model with a 5 m side has been prepared for the hilly areas using the contour lines of 1:5000 maps. The outputs of the digital terrain model are the exposition and the slope percentage, which is divided into five classes with different ranges (0−5; 6−10; 11−20; 21−30; >30). To calibrate the SAR polarimetric data, four trihedral corner reflectors (made by JPL) have been placed in the area.

A preliminary and qualitative analysis of three-frequency SAR images allowed the discrimination of several surface types and the identification of some geophysical characteristics. For the different bands it is possible to discriminate the following characteristics: for C-band — hydrographic network enhanced, low sensitivity to surface roughness and vegetation cover; for L-band — surface features well indicated, good performances in land use, soil roughness detection; for P-band — similar to L-band, urban areas enhanced.

All the information obtained has been analysed and the study has been focused on those areas in which the upland erosion processes are severe. A map of relative classes of soil erosion (Figure 9.6) has been made from the geomorphological survey of the area.

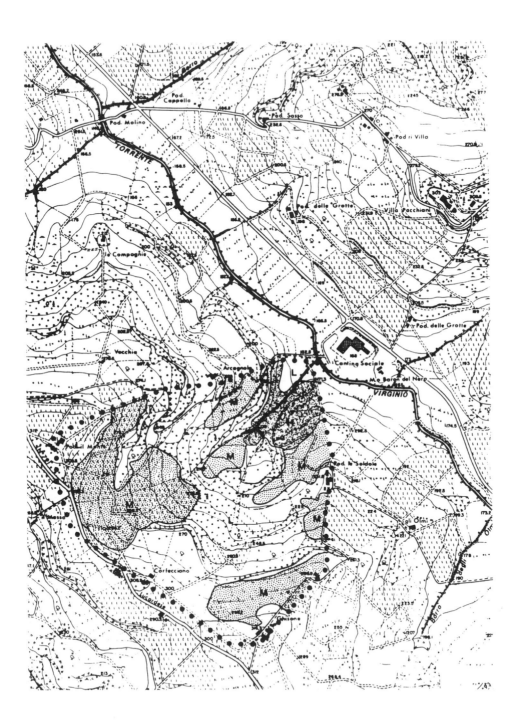

FIGURE 9.6 Map of relative classes of soil erosion: H = high; M = medium; L = low

9.4 HYDROLOGICAL RESULTS

Many models are available for the study of soil erosion problems (Engman et al., 1989); however, the most suitable model allowing the use of remote sensing data, and consequently of SAR data, seems to be the WEPP (Water Erosion Prediction Project) model. This model has recently been turned by USDA (Laflen, 1990) and is now available in the slope profile version. The WEPP model allows continuous monitoring both in time — it estimates the soil loss at any time interval — and in space — information from sensing data on the quantity of soil removed can be compared, disregarding the problem of surface slope which greatly affects SAR image interpretation. Here, three plots of bare soil have been specifically tilled with different surface roughness: smooth (height standard deviation (h.st.d.) 1·4 cm); medium rough (h.st.d. 2·2 cm); and rough (h.st.d. 3·1 cm).

Although the application of the WEPP model (Figure 9.7) has given results which must be confirmed through sufficient experimental repetition on the Virginio Basin, several applications of this model and relative rain simulation tests have been carried out during and after the MAC '91 campaign and are shown in this section.

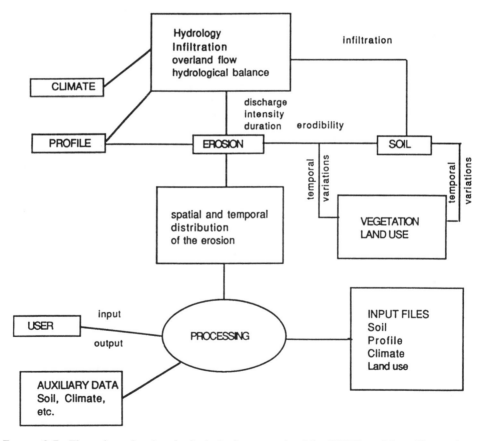

FIGURE 9.7 Flow chart showing the hydrologic approach of the WEPP model profile version

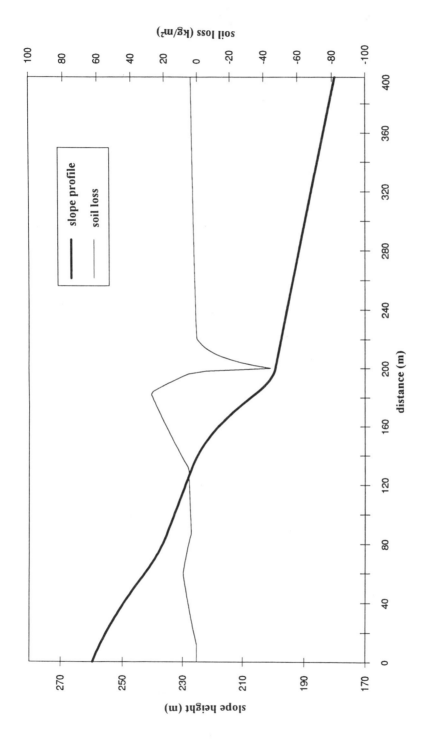

FIGURE 9.8 Diagram showing the WEPP output along a sample profile

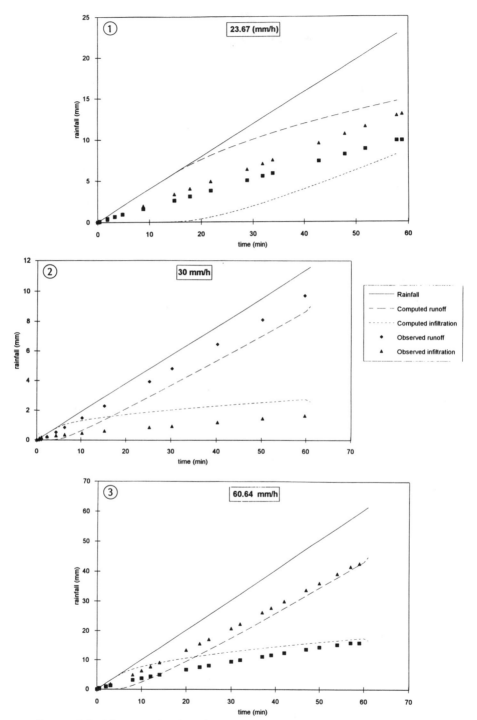

FIGURE 9.9   Diagrams showing observed and computed soil loss data at different
rainfall intensities

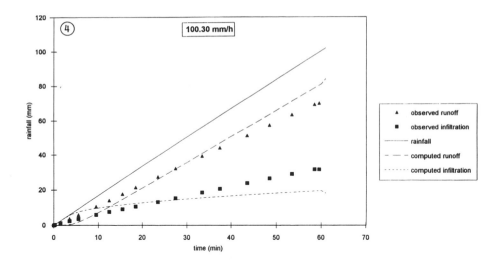

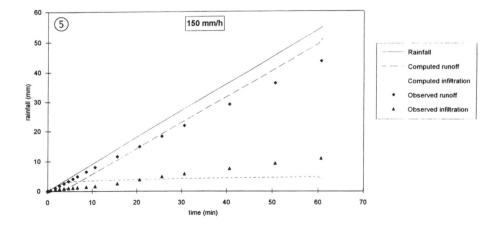

Observed And Computed Soil Loss Data

FIGURE 9.9 *continued*

Here, an example of WEPP application on a slope of the Virginio subbasin is performed, where intensive measurements of soil moisture content were carried out during the MAC-Europe campaign. During the experiment, herbaceous crops (alfalfa) growing on the slope at the beginning of the vegetative cycle were studied, and hillslope was characterized by a slight cover. From the lithological point of view the slope is composed of sandy-loam soils, with the presence of pebbles in correspondence to the higher portion of the slopes. Soils are clay-loamy (Virginiolo series) with a calcareous skeleton generally less than 10% in volume. The profile which characterizes these soils is Ap type, C, which is often influenced by relatively deep ploughing which reaches the sediments of the Pliocene substratum. Figure 9.8 represents the soil loss distribution along the slope; the part where erosion is negative indicates a local redeposition of eroded material in the superior portion; this is particularly evident at the bottom of the steeper part of the slope (210 m).

In order to verify the reliability of the data obtained with the model (Styczen and Nielsen, 1989), comparison has been made with direct measurements of infiltration and erosion carried out by means of a rain simulator.

Figure 9.9 shows the data obtained both by field experiments (observed soil loss data) and WEPP applications (computed soil loss data). A rather good correspondence is found for the extreme events (lower and higher rainfall intensity); however, the comparison of soil loss data obtained with the other rainfall intensities show several discrepancies with respect to the computed data. Consequently, further field tests must be performed in the experimental areas, both to obtain a good representation of rain simulations and to investigate the other soils.

The rather good correspondence for hydrological parameters, such as infiltration and overland flow, is clear on both observed and computed data, although for the lower intensity ($23 \cdot 6$ mm h^{-1}) there is some difference which can be explained by means of the test itself. In fact, the low intensities do not develop a high runoff and the accuracy of the measurements during the experiments can be influenced by the difficulty in correctly measuring low discharges.

9.5 FINAL REMARKS

The hydrological models give good results in the assessment of water infiltration and overland flow measurements, as shown by the comparison between field tests and computed data, even though the field and the computed soil loss results are not clearly related. Furthermore, the methodology employed gives an opportunity to introduce remote sensing data related to geophysical parameters (i.e. soil moisture) into the hydrological model.

Through the analysis of SAR data, even though only data from one flight and two incidence angles have been processed, several interesting results have been obtained. The sensitivity of SAR data to surface features has been confirmed. Different surface types can be discriminated using the appropriate frequency. In particular, the L-band is able to discriminate between different types of herbaceous crops and the C-band allows the identification of bare and vegetated soils.

As expected, the sensitivity to soil roughness is quite strong, mainly at the lowest frequencies. The correlation between the backscattering coefficient and soil moisture content has been investigated, and some sensitivity has been found at the P-band, although an incidence angle of 35° is not the best configuration.

ACKNOWLEDGEMENT

This work has been partially supported by ASI.

REFERENCES

Bechini, C., Canuti, P., Moretti, S., Paloscia, S. and Pampaloni, P. 1991. Microwave remote sensing for hydrological and agricultural monitoring. *Proceedings of 24th International Symposium on Remote Sensing of Environment*. Rio de Janeiro, Brasil.

Canuti, P., Garzonio, C. A. and Rodolfi, G. 1979. Applied geomorphological maps on photo-assemblage in areas of intense agricultural transformation, subject to mass movements. IGU Comm. on Geomor. Survey and Mapping, *Proceedings of 15 Meeting*. Modena, Studi di Geol. Appl. e Geol. Ambiente 9, Ist. Geol. e Paleont, Firenze.

Canuti, P., Moretti, S. and Zanchi, C. 1985. A rain simulator for quick field tests of infiltration and soil loss evaluation. *IV International Conference on Soil Conservation*. Maracay, Venezuela, 132–144.

Canuti, P., Focardi, P., Garzonio, C. A., Rodolfi, G. and Vannocci, P. 1986. Slope stability mapping in Tuscany, Italy. In Gardiner (ed.), *International Geomorphology*. John Wiley, Chichester, Part I, 231–240.

Chiarantini, L., Canuti, P., Coppo, P., Moretti, S., Luzzi, A., Paloscia, S. and Pampaloni, P. 1990. Microwave Remote Sensing measurements for hydrological studies and soil erosion forecasting. *Proceedings of X International Geosciences and Remote Sensing Symposium*. Washington, DC.

Engman, E. T., Kustas, W. P. and Wang, J. R. 1989. Remotely sensed soil moisture input to a hydrological model. *Proceedings IGARSS*. Vancouver, Canada, 2150–2153.

Laflen, J. M. 1990. *Water Erosion Prediction Project — Hillslope Profile Model*, 2nd edn. NSERL Report No. 4, National Soil Erosion Research Laboratory, USDA — Agricultural Research Service, West Lafayette.

Styczen, M. and Nielsen, S. A. 1989. A view of soil erosion theory, process-research and model building: possible interactions and future developments. *Quaderui Scienza del Suolo, Firenze*, CNR Vol. II.

10

LISEM — A Physically Based Model to Simulate Runoff and Soil Erosion in Catchments: Model Structure

A.P.J. DE ROO, C.G. WESSELING, N.H.D.T. CREMERS, M.A. VERZANDVOORT

Department of Physical Geography, Utrecht University

AND

C.J. RITSEMA, K. OOSTINDIE

Department of Soil Physical Transport Phenomena, The Winand Staring Centre

ABSTRACT

The Limburg Soil Erosion Model (LISEM) is described as a way of simulating hydrological and soil erosion processes during single rainfall events at catchment scale for winter rainfall events. Sensitivity analysis of the model shows that the initial matric pressure potential, the hydraulic conductivity of the soil and Manning's n are the most sensitive variables of the model. Planning and evaluation of various strategies for controlling pollution from intensively cropped areas can be assisted with the use of this model. Specifically, the siting of erosion control measures can be determined by comparing scenarios simulated by LISEM.

10.1 INTRODUCTION

Soil erosion and surface runoff have always been problems concomitant with intensive agricultural land use in hilly areas. These problems can be exacerbated by soil and geology, as is the case in the hill country of South-Limburg (The Netherlands), where soils developed on loess are especially vulnerable to surface runoff and soil erosion. Since people started clearing the forests, soil erosion processes and human reactions to them have created the characteristic landforms of dry valleys, incised ("hollow") roads and lynchets.

Geomorphic Hazards. Edited by O. Slaymaker.
© 1996 by John Wiley & Sons Ltd

Until recently, traditional land use practices could keep soil erosion and surface runoff at acceptable levels. During the last two decades, however, the expansion of urban areas, the increased area of sealed surfaces, the intensification of agriculture and increased arable agriculture have caused soil erosion and flooding to increase. Reallotment schemes have resulted in larger fields, causing surface runoff to be more erosive. Changes in land use also contribute to increasing erosion, total runoff and peak runoff. The area of grassland has decreased in favour of urban areas and, since 1975, in favour of arable land (De Roo, 1993b). Moreover, there has been a change in land use and in the kinds of crops grown in South-Limburg. Between 1960 and 1986, the kinds of crops which give rise to a higher erosion risk, such as maize and sugarbeet, have increased in South-Limburg, replacing cereals such as winter wheat. Runoff with a high sediment load causes obstructed waterways and choked-up sewage systems, causing damage to roads, gardens and houses.

Since 1980, awareness of soil erosion problems in South-Limburg has increased. Schouten et al. (1985) were among the first to report the causes and damaging effects of surface runoff and soil erosion. However, quantitative information on soil erosion rates and the effects of conservation strategies was not available. Local and provincial policy makers and parties concerned (both farmers' organizations and environmental groups) needed a quantitative evaluation of the extent and the magnitude of the soil erosion problems and the possible management strategies in South-Limburg on a regional basis. Therefore, field measurements were necessary. Also, quantitative simulation models of surface runoff and soil erosion, which can be used to evaluate alternative strategies for improved land management, not only in the monitored areas but also in ungauged catchments, are useful.

10.2 THE LISEM PROJECT

In 1991, a soil erosion project started in three catchments in the loess area of South-Limburg, funded by local, provincial and national authorities. The Departments of Physical Geography of the Universities of Utrecht and Amsterdam, and the Soil Physics Division of the Winand Staring Centre in Wageningen cooperated to develop and validate a new physically based hydrological and soil erosion model, which can be used for planning and conservation purposes: the Limburg Soil Erosion Model (LISEM).

In three catchments, discharge and sediment load at the outlet are measured continuously. Rainfall is measured at six locations to take into account both the spatial and temporal variability. Furthermore, in six subcatchments discharge and sediment load measurements are carried out. Also, at 12 sites in the catchments along four slope profiles, continuous soil suction measurements are done to assess both vertical and lateral transport of water in the soil. The soils in the catchments were mapped in detail to serve, amongst other purposes, as a basis for the soil hydrological submodel. Several times during the year, land use and soil cover, surface roughness parameters, soil porosity, soil moisture content, soil shear strength and aggregate stability are measured using advanced methods. Furthermore, to assess the effects of soil conservation measures, and to validate the simulations of conservation practices, the effects of tillage systems, grass strips with different widths and the influence of slope length are investigated on field plots under natural rainfall and/or by using rainfall simulators. In the laboratory, soil physical and soil chemical properties, such as soil texture, organic matter content, the water retention and hydraulic conductivity curves, and soil acidity are measured to support the model with data.

10.3 THE LISEM MODEL

The LISEM model is one of the first examples of a physically based model that is completely incorporated in a raster Geographical Information System (GIS). Incorporation means that no conversion routines are necessary, the model is completely expressed in terms of the GIS command structure. This approach was introduced by Van Deursen and Kwadijk (1990) and the principles were demonstrated in RHINEFLOW, a water balance model for the river Rhine (Van Deursen and Kwadijk, 1993). PC Raster (Van Deursen and Wesseling, 1992) is used as the GIS to prototype these ideas. Furthermore, the incorporation facilitates easy application in larger catchments, improves the user friendliness, and allows remotely sensed data from aeroplanes or satellites to be used, such as demonstrated by De Jong (1994). If required, the model can be linked easily with other GISs. The development and structure of the LISEM model is based on experiences with the ANSWERS model (Beasley et al., 1980; De Roo et al., 1989; De Roo, 1993a, b) and SWATRE (Belmans et al., 1983), but process descriptions are changed totally. The advantages of linking a model with a GIS have been described in De Roo et al. (1989) and De Roo (1993b). The main reason for using a GIS is that runoff and soil erosion processes vary spatially, so that cell sizes should be used that allow spatial variation to be taken into account. Also, the data for the large number of cells required are enormous and cannot easily be entered by hand, but can be obtained by using a GIS. Not all data are equally available, however. At present, most detailed information is available about the terrain form (Kirkby, 1985). To make the best possible use of distributed topographic data a catchment should be modelled by a digital elevation model (DEM). In many cases this DEM will have several thousands of elements, so that entering data by hand is no longer feasible. A DEM can be constructed by digitizing contour maps. The GIS can compute maps of altitude, slope and aspect, which are all input for the LISEM model. Because detailed field sampling of input variables is not feasible, a limited number of point observations of the soil etc., collected during field experiments, are often available. Geostatistical interpolation techniques, incorporated in the GIS, can be used to produce maps from these point observations. Using a method such as block kriging, point observations are interpolated to blocks of the same size as the elements used for simulation. When there are insufficient field measurements available, the distribution of a desired input variable can be derived from digitized soil or land use maps. A raster-based GIS is the ideal tool to serve needs and fulfil requirements associated with the DEM and the geostatistical interpolation techniques.

Further advantages of using a GIS are (1) the possibilities of rapidly producing modified input maps with different land use patterns or conservation measures to simulate alternative scenarios; (2) the ability to use very large catchments with many pixels, so the catchment can be simulated with more detail; and (3) the facility to display the results as maps. A series of maps can be produced showing the variation with time of spatial patterns of soil erosion, sedimentation and runoff over the catchment. These maps can be compared by subtraction to yield maps indicating how erosion or sedimentation might be affected by certain control measures within the catchment, or they can be viewed successively to create a video of the modelled process. Runoff can also be displayed as an overlay on the landform surface (digital elevation model).

Processes incorporated in the model, which are described below, are rainfall, interception, surface storage in microdepressions, infiltration, vertical movement of water in the soil, overland flow, channel flow, detachment by rainfall and throughfall, detachment by overland flow, and transport capacity of the flow. Also, the influence of tractor wheelings, small paved roads (smaller than the pixel size) and surface sealing on the hydrological and soil erosion processes is taken into account.

After rainfall begins, some is intercepted by the vegetation canopy until such time as the maximum interception storage capacity is met. Besides interception, direct throughfall and leaf drainage occur, which, together with overland flow from upslope areas, contribute to the amount of water available for infiltration. The water remaining after infiltration begins to accumulate on the surface in microdepressions. When a predefined amount of depressions is filled, overland flow begins. Overland flow rates are calculated using Manning's *n* and slope gradient, with a direction according to the aspect of the slope. When rainfall ceases, infiltration continues until depression storage water is no longer available.

Soil detachment and transport can both be caused by either raindrop impact or overland flow. Whether or not a detached soil particle moves, depends upon the sediment load in the flow and its capacity for sediment transport. When water and sediment reach an element with a channel, they are transported to the catchment outlet. Sedimentation within a channel appears when the transport capacity has been exceeded.

LISEM is written in a prototype GIS modelling language currently being developed at the Utrecht University. The language comprises all PC Raster commands as statements with exactly the same syntax as the command form of these statements. When compiled, an efficient run time mechanism eliminates redundant data transfer.

10.3.1 Rainfall

Data from multiple raingauges can be entered in an input data file. A map is used as input to define for each pixel which raingauge must be used. For every time increment during the simulation of a storm, the model generates a map with the spatial distribution of the rainfall intensity. Thus, the model allows for spatial and temporal variability of rainfall. In the future, this approach allows for the input of, for example, radar data indicating rainfall intensity patterns changing in space and time, which could be used to simulate a thunderstorm moving over a catchment.

10.3.2 Interception

Interception by crops and/or natural vegetation is simulated by calculating a maximum storage capacity, which is filled during rainfall. The maximum interception storage capacity is estimated using an equation developed by Von Hoyningen-Huene (1981):

$$SMAX = 0 \cdot 935 + 0 \cdot 498 LAI - 0 \cdot 00575 LAI^2 \tag{1}$$

where $SMAX$ = maximum storage capacity (mm) and LAI = leaf area index.

Cumulative interception during rainfall is simulated using an equation developed by Aston (1979), which is modified from Merriam (1960):

$$CINT = SMAX * \left[1 - e^{-(1-p) * \frac{PCUM}{SMAX}} \right] \qquad (2)$$

where $CINT$ = cumulative interception (mm), $PCUM$ = cumulative rainfall (mm) and p = correction factor $(1 - 0.046 LAI)$. This equation simulates throughfall before $SMAX$ is reached. The factor k, equal to $(1 - p)$, was introduced by Aston (1979) to incorporate the effect of slower interception when the vegetation is dense. Simultaneously, this factor incorporates the fact that only that part of the cumulative rainfall which falls on the vegetation ($PCUM \times PER$, where PER is the soil coverage by vegetation) can contribute to the interception storage. From the cumulative interception equation, interception rate is calculated by subtracting the $CINT$ at time $= (t - 1)$ from $CINT$ at time $= t$.

10.3.3 Infiltration and soil water transport

Infiltration and soil water transport in soils are simulated by a solution of the well known Richards equation, which combines the Darcy equation and the continuity equation:

$$\frac{\partial \theta}{\partial t} = \frac{\partial}{\partial z} K(h) \left(\frac{\partial h}{\partial z} + 1 \right) \qquad (3)$$

where K = the hydraulic conductivity (m s^{-1}); h = the pressure (matric) potential (m); θ = the volumetric water content (m^3 m^{-3}); z = the gravitational potential or height above a reference level (m); t = time (s).

Using the soil water capacity $C(h) = d\theta(h)/dh$ (the slope of the soil water retention curve $\theta(h)$), the unsaturated flow equation is derived:

$$C(h) \frac{\partial h}{\partial t} = \frac{\partial}{\partial z} K(h) \left(\frac{\partial h}{\partial z} + 1 \right) \qquad (4)$$

where C = the soil water capacity.

The Mualem/Van Genuchten equations (Mualem, 1976; Van Genuchten, 1980) are used to predict the soil water retention curves and the unsaturated hydraulic conductivity, which are needed to solve the equation above. In the catchments, soil profile types are defined, and for each characteristic soil horizon, the van Genuchten parameters are determined. Optionally, the measured $K-\theta-h$ relations can be used. The equations are solved by explicit linearization using the so-called Thomas (tridiagonal) algorithm (e.g. Remson et al., 1971). The submodel operates with a variable time increment depending on pressure head changes.

10.3.4 Storage in microdepressions

Storage in microdepressions is simulated by a set of equations developed by Onstad (1984) and Linden et al. (1988). The variable random roughness is used as a measure of microrelief. Surface storage in depressions is simulated by (Onstad, 1984):

$$RETMAX = 0 \cdot 112\,RR + 0 \cdot 031\,RR^2 - 0 \cdot 012\,RR \times S \qquad (5)$$

where $RETMAX$ = maximum depressional storage (cm); RR = random roughness (cm); S = slope gradient (%).

The rainfall excess (rainfall + overland flow − interception − infiltration) required to fill all depressions is calculated using the equation (Onstad, 1984):

$$RETRAIN = 0 \cdot 329\,RR + 0 \cdot 073\,RR^2 - 0 \cdot 018\,RR \times S \qquad (6)$$

where $RETRAIN$ = rainfall excess needed to fill depressions (cm).

Moore and Larson (1979) identified three possible stages during a rainfall event:

(a) microrelief storage occurring, no runoff;
(b) additional microrelief storage accompanied by runoff;
(c) runoff only with the microrelief storage.

To determine the transition from stage (a) to stage (b), the data of Onstad (1984) were analysed. From this analysis the following equation was developed, simulating the starting point of runoff:

$$DETSTART = RETMAX(0 \cdot 0527\,RR - 0 \cdot 0049\,S) \qquad (7)$$

where $DETSTART$ = rainfall excess needed to start runoff (cm).

Thus, during stage (a), all excess rainfall becomes depression storage. Then, from point $DETSTART$ to point $RETMAX$ both overland flow and further depressional storage occur, based on a linear filling of the depressions until $RETMAX$. After $RETMAX$, all excess rainfall becomes runoff. Thus, using these relationships the actual storage in depressions (RET) can be calculated.

Also, using the same input data, the maximum fraction of the surface covered with water can be calculated (Onstad, 1984):

$$FWAMAX = 0 \cdot 152\,RR - 0 \cdot 008\,RR^2 - 0 \cdot 008\,RR \times S \qquad (8)$$

where $FWAMAX$ = maximum fraction of the surface covered with water.

The actual fraction of surface covered with water is calculated using a relationship based on the work of Moore and Larson (1979) and Onstad (1984):

$$FWA = FWAMAX \left(\frac{RET}{RETMAX}\right)^{0 \cdot 6} \qquad (9)$$

where FWA = actual fraction of the surface covered with water.

Based on the findings of Linden et al. (1988), some depressions are (temporarily) isolated and do not contribute to overland flow. From their data it was determined that if the storage (RET) was less than 75% of the $RETMAX$, 20% of the depressions are isolated. If RET is between 75% and 100% of $RETMAX$ then the following equation was derived:

$$FWAISO = 0 \cdot 20 FWA \left[1 - \left(\frac{\frac{RET}{RETMAX} - 0.75}{0 \cdot 25} \right) \right] \qquad (10)$$

where $FWAISO$ = fraction of the isolated depressions.

10.3.5 Overland flow and channel flow

For the distributed overland and channel flow routing, a four-point finite-difference solution of the kinematic wave is used together with Manning's equation. Procedures of the numerical solution can be found in Chow et al. (1988) and Moore and Foster (1990).

10.3.6 Splash detachment

Splash detachment is simulated as a function of soil aggregate stability, rainfall kinetic energy and the depth of the surface water layer. This submodel is calibrated by field experiments (Cremers et al., submitted). The kinetic energy can arise from both direct throughfall and drainage from leaves. The following equation is used:

$$DETR = \left[\frac{2 \cdot 07}{AGGRSTAB} KE \exp(-1 \cdot 45 DEPTH) + 2 \cdot 20 \right] (P - I) \frac{(\mathrm{d}x)^2}{\mathrm{d}t} \qquad (11)$$

where $DETR$ = splash detachment (g s^{-1}); $AGGRSTAB$ = soil aggregate stability (median number of drops); KE = rainfall kinetic energy (J m^{-2}); $DEPTH$ = depth of the surface water layer (mm); P = rainfall (mm); I = interception (mm); dx = size of an element (m); dt = time increment (s).

10.3.7 Transport capacity

The transport capacity of overland flow is modelled as a function of unit stream power (Govers, 1990). For loess soils, the following equation, valid for $D50 = 50\chi$m is used:

$$TC = 0 \cdot 063 [S \times V - 0 \cdot 4]^{0 \cdot 56} \qquad (12)$$

where TC = volumetric transport capacity (cm^3 cm^{-3}); S = slope gradient (m m^{-1}); V = mean flow velocity (cm s^{-1}).

10.3.8 Rill and interrill erosion

Flow detachment and deposition are simulated using equations from the EUROSEM model (Morgan et al., 1992). These equations will be validated or calibrated to field measurements in Limburg.

Whenever the transporting capacity, calculated using equation 12, is less than the available sediment from splash, from upslope areas and from previous time steps, deposition occurs at the following rate (Morgan et al., 1992):

$$DEP = wv_\mathrm{s}[TC - C] \qquad (13)$$

where DEP = deposition rate (kg m^{-3}); w = width of the flow (m); v_s = settling velocity of the particles (m s^{-1}); TC = transport capacity (kg m^{-3}); C = sediment concentration in the flow (kg m^{-3}).

If the transporting capacity of the flow exceeds the sediment concentration in the flow, detachment by the flow takes places and is calculated using the following equation (Morgan et al., 1992):

$$DF = ywv_s[TC - C] \tag{14}$$

where DF = flow detachment rate (kg m^{-3}); y = efficiency coefficient.

The efficiency coefficient in equation 14 is determined by (Morgan et al., 1992; Rauws and Govers, 1988):

$$y = \frac{u_{gmin}}{u_{gcrit}} = \frac{1}{0 \cdot 89 + 0 \cdot 56\, COH} \tag{15}$$

where u_{gmin} = minimum value required for the critical grain shear velocity (cm s^{-1}); u_{gcrit} = critical grain shear velocity for rill initiation (cm s^{-1}); COH = cohesion of the soil at saturation (kPa).

10.4 VALIDATION OF LISEM

Distributed hydrological and soil erosion models can be validated by comparing measured and simulated values of discharge and sediment concentration at the catchment outlet. Also, overland flow patterns can be observed in the field and compared to the simulated patterns. Figure 10.1 shows the simulated overland flow pattern in one of the research catchments, which resembles the actual pattern. Furthermore, spatial soil erosion patterns can be evaluated using ^{137}Cs (De Roo, 1991; Quine and Walling, 1991). Thus, the distributed model is evaluated in a distributed way.

In the three research catchments in Limburg which are being monitored for the LISEM project, the following validation data are available and used:

— measurements of discharge and sediment load at three outlet gauging stations
— measurements of discharge and sediment load from six subcatchments within the main catchments
— measurements of the soil pressure head at 12 locations along four slope profiles at seven depths down to 150 cm
— 143 spatially distributed ^{137}Cs samples in one of the catchments
— data from rainfall simulation studies in the catchments or at the experimental farm Wijnandsrade (validation of splash detachment equations and flow and transport equations)
— runoff and sediment load data from several plots where soil conservation experiments have been carried out.

Necessary data are kept in the PC Raster GIS. The model results are compared with observed data (validation). Statistical criteria determine the "goodness of fit". The model user has to decide whether the results are satisfactory. If so, the simulations end and the "final results" are produced. If the validation is not satisfactory, there are several options:

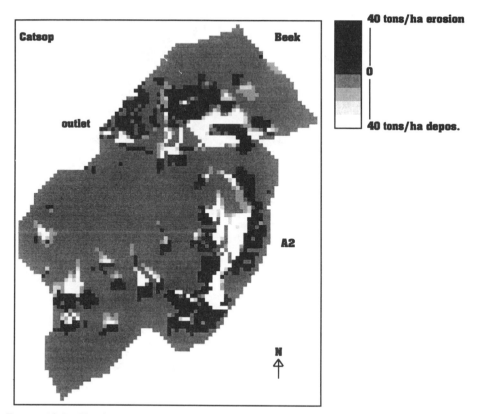

FIGURE 10.1   Simulated soil erosion in the Catsop research catchment with the LISEM model

—   modify the model
—   recalibrate the model
—   change the resolution (pixel size or simulation time step)
—   collect more data
—   collect better data (measurement errors)
—   collect different data (other variables).

This procedure is repeated until satisfactory results are obtained.

Sensitivity analysis of the model (De Roo et al., 1994) showed that the initial pressure potential, the hydraulic conductivity of the soil and the Manning's n are the most sensitive variables of the model, as is known from several other distributed hydrological and soil erosion models.

The model is not calibrated for the summer rainfall events. Several test simulations (calibrated runs) pointed out that calibration of single events yields better results, but using such a calibration data set on other events yields worse results. However, the model has been calibrated on initial pressure head in the upper soil layers for the winter events. Table 10.1 lists the hydrological validation results of LISEM. Figure 10.2 gives a runoff hydrograph for a rainfall event in one of the research catchments. This is one of the most

Geomorphic Hazards

TABLE 10.1 Validation (hydrological) results of the main events in three research areas in South-Limburg, The Netherlands

Date	Mean discharge		Peak discharge		McCuens coefficient
	Measured ($l\ s^{-1}$)	Simulated ($l\ s^{-1}$)	Measured ($l\ s^{-1}$)	Simulated ($l\ s^{-1}$)	
Catsop					
22-01-93	25·05	12·57	95·56	77·29	0·825
30-05-93	50·70	124·97	343·61	411·08	0·415
14-10-93	25·47	17·52	153·82	133·36*	0·929
St. Gillisstraat					
04-06-92	1·12	0·06	4·98	0·39	−0·949
24-08-92	2·03	0·05	4·23	0·12	0·022
11-01-93	10·91	14·88	34·45	88·02*	−0·027
12-01-93	52·76	5·88	127·36	30·02*	−0·025
14-11-93	18·36	12·89	96·38	145·86	0·423
31-12-93	212·32	53·67	700·00	300·75*	0·180
02-01-94	30·31	27·66	134·07	146·47*	0·305
03-01-94	22·11	8·41	164·43	63·21	0·029
Etzenrade					
05-07-92	56·88	90·88	337·00	383·11	0·255
28-08-92	3·00	0·00	3·00	0·00	—
25-10-92	22·40	9·02	121·00	106·39	0·679
17-11-92	38·35	42·84	164·00	406·24*	0·324
11-01-93	17·28	3·79	77·00	64·97	0·738
22-01-93	12·30	4·05	94·00	71·27	0·618
12-05-93	18·00	0·00	19·00	0·00	—
14-10-93	113·75	36·80	588·00	377·88	0·518
13-12-93	76·39	10·70	260·00	115·16*	0·410
30-12-93	31·45	13·52	284·00	300·74*	0·617

*Initial pressure potential data not available, but estimated.

successful simulations. It is obvious that there are worse examples. However, the figure shows that the model produces reasonable results. The soil erosion data set is smaller and more difficult to interpret.

It is clear that, although the model has several advantages over other models, the results are far from perfect. One reason for this is the lack in our theoretical understanding of the hydrological and soil erosion processes. It is clear from our data that summer and winter response to rainfall are quite different, which was also observed by Kwaad (1991). But even within the main seasons there are significantly different responses to rainfall due to tillage operations and biological activity. Therefore, calibrating the model for spring and summer events is not possible.

Another reason for the difference between observed and measured discharge and sediment loads is the lack of available input data for the model. Despite two and a half years of field and laboratory measurements by a minimum of five scientists, there are still gaps in our data and we still do not have enough! This is a well-known problem with this type of model, and one can question the further development of this type of modelling, especially if these models have to be used as planning tools. However, for scientists it is an important tool to test their knowledge about the landscape.

10.5 APPLICATIONS AND USE OF LISEM

One of the applications of LISEM is for planning and evaluating various strategies for controlling pollution from intensively cropped areas. Within the LISEM project, several possible scenarios are being evaluated (De Roo et al., 1994). The implementation of a few control measures is being seriously considered; using the model the best possible locations for the measures can be determined.

Maps of soil erosion and sedimentation for the various scenarios can be compared by subtraction. These simulations indicate where possible control measures would have the greatest positive and negative consequences. Planners can decide to combine the positive elements from several scenarios and leave out the negative elements and develop new scenarios. The advantage of using LISEM is that this operation can be done very quickly: combining maps in the PC Raster GIS which accompanies LISEM is a standard operation. The map database can easily be updated with new data (such as field and laboratory measurements), followed by new interpolations to produce maps.

10.6 CONCLUSIONS

LISEM is a powerful model which simulates hydrological and soil erosion processes during single rainfall events on a catchment scale. Using LISEM it is possible to calculate the effects of land use changes and to explore soil conservation scenarios. Driven by

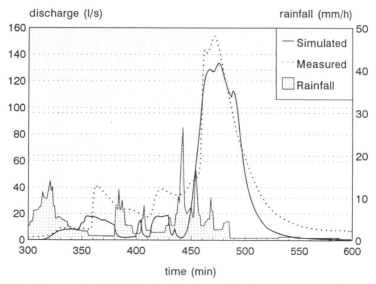

FIGURE 10.2 Measured and LISEM-simulated runoff in the Catsop research catchment on 14 October 1993

hypothetical storms of known probability of return, LISEM is a valuable tool for planning cost-effective measures to mitigate the effects of runoff and erosion. LISEM produces detailed maps of soil erosion and overland flow that are useful for planners. The integration of LISEM in a raster-based GIS, which holds the many data on the distribution of land attributes, is very useful.

Other advantages of LISEM are the use of physically based mathematical relationships, the ease with which newly developed relationships can be incorporated, the incorporation of information about the spatial variability of land characteristics, and the detailed spatially displayed output of the model which is useful for planners.

ACKNOWLEDGEMENTS

The Province of Limburg, the Waterboard "Roer en Overmaas", the Ministry of Agriculture and 14 municipalities of South-Limburg are gratefully acknowledged for funding a large part of the research which led to the development of the LISEM model.

In addition to the authors, several researchers have contributed to the project. H. Kolenbrander and R. Offermans of Utrecht University, J. J. B. Bronswijk and J. Stolte of the Winand Staring Centre Wageningen, and F. J. P. M. Kwaad, P. M. Van Dijk, A. C. Imeson and M. Van Der Zijp of the University of Amsterdam are all thanked for their contributions.

REFERENCES

Aston, A. R. 1979. Rainfall interception by eight small trees. *Journal of Hydrology*, **42**, 383–396.
Beasley, D. B., Huggins, L. F. and Monke, E. J. 1980. ANSWERS: A Model for Watershed Planning. *Transactions of the ASAE*, **23**(4), 938–944.
Belmans, C., Wesseling, J. G. and Feddes, R. A. 1983. Simulation model of the water balance of a cropped soil: SWATRE. *Journal of Hydrology*, **63**, 271–286.
Chow, V. T., Maidment, D. R. and Mays, L. W. 1988. *Applied Hydrology*. McGraw-Hill, New York, 572 pp.
Cremers, N. H. D. T., de Roo, A. P. J. and Van Der Zijp, M. (submitted). Validating a splash detachment equation with field measurements. *Earth Surface Processes and Landforms* (under review).
De Jong, S. M. 1994. Applications of reflective remote sensing for land degradation studies in a Mediterranean environment. *Netherlands Geographical Studies*, **177**.
De Roo, A. P. J. 1991. The use of ^{137}Cs as a tracer in an erosion study in South-Limburg (The Netherlands) and the influence of Chernobyl fallout. *Hydrological Processes*, **5**, 215–227.
De Roo, A. P. J. 1993a. Validation of the "ANSWERS" catchment model for runoff and soil erosion simulation in catchments in the Netherlands and the United Kingdom. In *Applications of Geographic Information Systems in Hydrology and Water Resources*. IAHS Publication No. 211, 465–474.
De Roo, A. P. J. 1993b. Modelling surface runoff and soil erosion in catchments using Geographical Information Systems; validity and applicability of the "ANSWERS" model in two catchments in the loess area of South Limburg (The Netherlands) and one in Devon (UK). *Netherlands Geographical Studies*, **157**, 295 pp.
De Roo, A. P. J., Hazelhoff, L. and Burrough, P. A. 1989. Soil erosion modelling using "ANSWERS" and Geographical Information Systems. *Earth Surface Processes and Landforms*, **14**, 517–532.
De Roo, A. P. J., van Dijk, P. M., Ritsema, C. J., Offermans, R. J. E., Cremers, N. H. D. T., Kwaad, F. P. J. M. and Stolte, J. 1994. *Soil Erosion Normalisation Projekt South Limburg, The Netherlands* (in Dutch), Utrecht University.

Govers, G. 1990. *Empirical Relationships on the Transporting Capacity of Overland Flow*. IAHS Publication No. 189, 45–63.

Kirkby, M. J. 1985. Hillslope hydrology. In Anderson, M. G. and Burt, T. P. (eds), *Hydrological Forecasting*, John Wiley, Chichester, UK.

Kwaad, F. J. P. M. 1991. Summer and winter regimes of runoff generation and soil erosion on cultivated loess soils (The Netherlands). *Earth Surface Processes and Landforms*, **16**, 653–662.

Linden, D. R., Van Doren Jr, D. M. and Allmaras, R. R. 1988. A model of the effects of tillage-induced soil surface roughness on erosion. *Proceedings of the 11th International Conference of the International Soil Tillage Research Organisation*, Edinburgh, Vol. 1, 373–378.

Merriam, R. A. 1960. A note on the interception loss equation. *Journal of Geophysical Research*, **65**, 3850–3851.

Moore, I. D. and Foster, G. R. 1990. Hydraulics and overland flow. In Anderson, M. G. and Burt T. P. (eds), *Process Studies in Hillslope Hydrology*. John Wiley, Chichester, 215–254.

Moore, I. D. and Larson, C. L. 1979. Estimating micro-relief surface storage from point data. *Transactions of the ASAE*, **20**(5), 1073–1077.

Morgan, R. P. C., Quinton, J. N. and Rickson, R. J. 1992. *EUROSEM Documentation Manual*. Version 1, June 1992, Silsoe College, Silsoe.

Mualem, Y. 1976. A new model for predicting the hydrologic conductivity of unsaturated porous media. *Water Resources Research*, **12**, 513–522.

Onstad, C. A. 1984. Depressional storage on tilled soil surfaces. *Transactions of the ASAE*, **27**, 729–732.

Quine, T. A. and Walling, D. E. 1991. Rates of soil erosion on arable fields in Britain: quantitative data from caesium-137 measurements. *Soil Use and Management*, **7**(4), 169–176.

Rauws, G. and Govers, G. 1988. Hydraulic and soil mechanical aspects of rill generation on agricultural soils. *Journal of Soil Science*, **39**, 111–124.

Remson, I., Hornberger, G. M. and Molz, F. J. 1971. *Numerical Methods in Subsurface Hydrology*. John Wiley, Chichester, 389 pp.

Schouten, C. J., Rang, M. C. and Huigen, P. M. J. 1985. Erosie en wateroverlast in Zuid-Limburg. *Landschap*, **2**, 118–132.

Van Duersen, W. P. A. and Kwadijk, J. C. J. 1990. Using the watershed tools for modelling the Rhine catchment. In J. Harts et al. (eds), *Proceedings EGIS '90*, 254–262. EGIS Foundation, Utrecht.

Van Deursen, W. P. A. and Wesseling, C. G. 1992. *The PC Raster Package*. Department of Physical Geography, Utrecht University.

Van Deursen, W. P. A. and Kwadijk, J. C. J. 1993. RHINEFLOW: an integrated GIS water balance model for the river Rhine. In *Applications of Geographic Information Systems in Hydrology and Water Resources*. IAHS Publication No. 211, 507–518.

Van Genuchten, M. Th. 1980. A closed-form equation for predicting the hydraulic conductivity of unsaturated soils. *Soil Science Society of America Journal*, **44**, 892–898.

Von Hoyningen Huene, J. 1981. *Die Interzeption des Niederschlags in Landwirtschaftlichen Pflanzenbestanden*. Arbeitsbericht Deutscher Verband für Wasserwirtschaft und Kulturbau, DVWK, Braunschweig, 63.

11

Gully Erosion and Thermoerosion on the Yamal Peninsula

A. Sidorchuk

State University of Moscow, Russia

ABSTRACT

The high (15−40 m) sand and loam marine terraces in the west-central part of the Yamal peninsula are deeply eroded by gullies. Gully network density is $1 \cdot 24$ km km^{-2}. There are four main processes which trigger natural gully erosion: (1) river channel migration and erosion of high banks; (2) massive ground-ice melting and cryoplanation; (3) cryogenic lake migration; (4) thaw slumps and active layer detachment failure (skinflow).

In zones of production and transportation facilities the human impact increases gully erosion potential due to: (1) technogenic damage of vegetation cover; (2) snow-water storage increase in upper parts of gully basins due to snow accumulation near constructions; (3) runoff coefficient increase on impermeable surfaces of the roads and buildings; (4) formation of local anthropogenic source of warm water.

The combination of high natural gully erosion potential and additional anthropogenic influence causes extremely intensive gully growth: up to $20-30$ m a^{-1} in loam and $150-200$ m a^{-1} in sands. A mathematical model of gully erosion was developed. This model was used for gully network growth prediction in Bovanenkovskoye gas-producing field under the influence of human interference. Calculations show that all drainage net thalwegs would be transformed by erosion. In more than 60% of thalwegs erosion depth would be more than $1 \cdot 0$ m. Some human-induced gullies would cross pipelines and roads and damage buildings and boreholes.

11.1 INTRODUCTION

Natural processes of gully erosion and thermoerosion are widespread in the arctic tundra of Russia. The main natural factors of erosion in this region are:

1. high river valley network density and associated relief amplitude up to $40-45$ m;
2. sufficient precipitation ($250-300$ mm a^{-1});
3. low soil permeability because of the permafrost and therefore high runoff coefficients (up to $0 \cdot 9 - 1 \cdot 0$);
4. high erodibility of thaw soils.

The main processes which trigger off natural gully erosion are:

Geomorphic Hazards. Edited by O. Slaymaker.
© 1996 by John Wiley & Sons Ltd

1. river channel migration and erosion of high river banks;
2. massive ground-ice melting;
3. erosion of the banks of cryogenic lakes and their migration;
4. thaw slumps and active layer detachment failure (skinflow).

All these factors lead to high natural gully network density in tundra regions. There are between six and 12 gullies per square kilometre with gully erosion volumes of more than 2×10^6 m³ km⁻² on the Yamal peninsula (Voskresenskiy and Zemchikhin, 1988).

Natural high gully erosion hazard has been greatly increased recently by human impact. In the regions of resource production and transportation facilities anthropogenic influence increases gully erosion potential due to:

1. technogenic deterioration of vegetation cover;
2. increased snow-water storage in upper parts of gully basins due to excessive snow accumulation near buildings and roads;
3. runoff coefficient increase on impermeable surfaces of the urbanized territories and roads;
4. local anthropogenic source of warm water;
5. gas and oil field and sand-pit operation, pipeline and ditch construction.

The combination of high natural gully erosion potential and additional human interference causes extremely intensive gully retrogressive growth: up to $20-30$ m a⁻¹ in loamy deposits and $150-200$ m a⁻¹ in sands. The old stable drainage lines are subjected to erosion and new gullies appear in previously gently sloping elongate depressions.

The period $1986-1992$ in the west-central Yamal peninsula was characterized by anomalously warm and wet summers with high activity of natural destructive processes. In the same period drilling and exploitation of the Bovanenkovskoye gas field was initiated and brought about the whole complex of accelerated erosion. The principal goal of our investigations in this period was to predict gully development under the influence of both natural and man-induced factors of erosion.

11.2 GENERAL DESCRIPTION OF THE FIELD AREA

The Yamal peninsula is situated at the northern part of the West Siberian plain and has an area of about 122 000 km². In the west-central part of Yamal the mean annual air temperature is $-8 \cdot 3$°C (weather station Marre Salye; measurements were begun in 1914). Mean January temperature is $-21 \cdot 8$°C (observed minimum -52°C) — it is the coldest month of the year. Mean temperature of August is $6 \cdot 7$°C (observed maximum 28°C) — the warmest month of the year. The air temperature is below 0°C for 223 days per year, hence the deep permafrost formation. Summer thaw layer thickness reaches its maximum ($0 \cdot 6 - 1 \cdot 2$ m) in August—September. Snow covers the territory from October till June. The thickness of snow cover does not exceed $0 \cdot 3 - 0 \cdot 4$ m on gentle slopes and flats at the beginning of the snowmelt period, but can exceed $3-5$ m in gullies and creek valleys and near steep river and lake banks. In most cases erosion forms are completely filled in by high-density snow. The depth of runoff for the period of snowmelt is $220-250$ mm.

Rainfall occurs generally in June—September; its total normal duration is 470 h and the maximum is up to 900 h in one season. The mean depth of rainfall for this period is 140 mm with observed maximum of 357 mm and minimum of 25 mm. Mean daily rainfall is 12 mm (an observed maximum is 40 mm) with mean 30 minutes intensity of $0 \cdot 8$ mm min^{-1} and up to 12 mm min^{-1}.

Gully erosion occurs mainly on marine terraces with heights 20—45 m above sea level. The high (30—45 m) terrace consists of loams and clays with massive cryogenic structure. It contains lenses and interlayers of ground ice up to 50 m thick and up to several kilometres wide. Steep slopes of this terrace are dissected by numerous natural bank gullies, usually 50—70 m long. Some of these gullies are up to 1—2 km long in the areas where ice content in eroded deposits is high. There is a network of long gentle depressions on the flat surface of terraces. Their density is $2 \cdot 3$ km km^{-2}. Natural and man-induced gullies can follow these depressions where vegetation cover deterioration takes place or volume of runoff increases.

The lower marine terrace (20—25 m above sea level) is composed of fine silty sand with ice wedges in the upper layers and massive ground ice in the lower layers. Natural gullies are more widespread on this surface and the main part of the drainage network is eroded due to high erodibility of fine sands.

The river floodplain is 3—5 m above the low water level. It is composed of silt and sand with peat layers. There are numerous river channels and chutes within the floodplain. Every year in May—June it is flooded to a depth of up to $1 \cdot 5 - 2 \cdot 0$ m. The accumulation rate of floodplain deposits is 1—2 mm a^{-1} in the central parts of the plain and up to 20—50 mm a^{-1} near river channels. The main river channels have a meandering pattern, the rate of bank erosion is usually $0 \cdot 3 - 0 \cdot 5$ m a^{-1} and up to 2—3 m a^{-1}. In some places intensive bank erosion of the high terrace causes new gullies.

Skinflows often occur during a wet summer following two or three years with hot summers. In such a situation, numerous laminations of ice are formed near the lower boundary of the thaw layer, and a heavy block of water-saturated surface deposits can slide to a distance up to some hundred metres for several hours. A newly exposed soil is subjected to intensive erosion and a new gully can be formed the next year after skinflow.

11.3 ANTHROPOGENIC GULLY EROSION ON THE WEST-CENTRAL YAMAL IN 1986—1992

Investigations conducted in 1986—1992 concentrated on three anthropogenic gullies (Figure 11.1). All these gullies formed in the territory of exploration camp KEH due to vegetation cover destruction and an increase of the meltwater supply. The skinflow in 1989 triggered this process.

11.3.1 Gully morphology

The gully 1 basin is 315 m long and its area is 36 000 m^2. The longitudinal profile of the initial slope had a convex form with the inclination in its upper part 3—4° and 12—13° in the lower part. The anthropogenic gully was formed at the site of a natural bank gully. The gully length in 1992 exceeded 200 m and its maximum depth reached $4 \cdot 5 - 5 \cdot 5$ m.

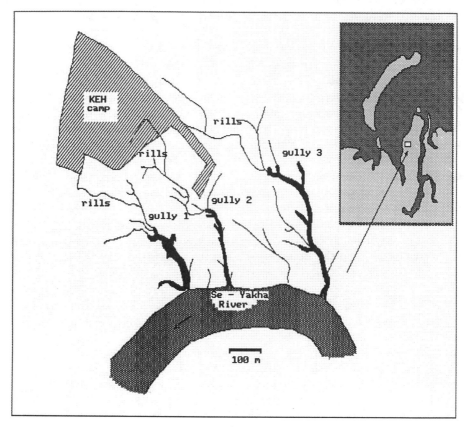

FIGURE 11.1 Anthropogenic gullies near KEH camp (west-central Yamal peninsula)

Its thalwegs had a convex longitudinal profile (Figure 11.2), cross-sections were V-shaped, with bank steepness up to 27°. The steep gully head was clear-cut. At the upper part of the watershed (area 10 100 m²) a system of rills with depth up to 0·5−0·6 m was formed.

The gully 2 basin is 410 m long and its area is 50 600 m². The initial basin slope is straight with the inclination in the upper part 2−3° and in the lower part 14−15°. An anthropogenic gully was also formed at the site of a short bank gully. In 1992 gully length was 210 m and its maximum depth exceeded 6·5 m. The longitudinal profile was convex (Figure 11.2), cross-sections were V-shaped, with bank steepness up to 33°. The gully head is not clearly defined and the erosional landform continues at the upper part of the watershed (area 28 300 m²) as a system of shallow rills.

The gully 3 basin is 680 m long and its area is 131 000 m². The basin slope is straight with the inclination in its upper part 1−2° and in its lower part 35°. The anthropogenic gully was formed at the site of a shallow natural gully. In 1992 the gully length exceeded 420 m and its maximum depth reached 6·0 m. The longitudinal profile was convex (Figure 11.2), cross-sections were trapezoidal with bank steepness up to 39°. The gully head is well defined. A dendritic rill system was formed in the upper part of the watershed (area 68 000 m^2).

11.3.2 Erosion and thermoerosion during the period of snowmelt

The processes of water and sediment transport in the gully basins are complex at the beginning of the snowmelt period. Snow cover on the urbanized watersheds is patchy while the non-urbanized basins are practically free of snow. A dendritic net of ephemeral meltwater flows is formed in the upper parts of the gully basins. The water and sediment from the basin area gather at the gully head, but the gully is full of snow at this period. The rate of snowmelt in the gully trench strongly depends on the quantity and temperature of meltwater supply from the upper part of the watershed and snow porosity. For example, in the first week of snowmelt (6− 10 June 1991), in the big natural gully with basin area of 30 ha the inside snowpack 3−5 m thick was completely cut by a meandering channel with vertical snowbanks. In gully 3 (basin area 10 ha) the flow was continuous, but several snow bridges remained in the lower part of the gully. In gully 2 only the upper segment of the trench was free of snowpack, and gully 1 was completely filled by snow. In these two gullies the water and sediment were filtering through snow cover.

In gully 1 about 83% of sediments, supplied to the gully head, remained in the snow at the beginning of the snowmelt period (on 7 June 1991 sediment input was $0 \cdot 18$ kg s^{-1} and output $0 \cdot 03$ kg s^{-1}). The gully was still full of snow on 19 June, and even at the end of July several snow bridges remained in the central segment of the gully. The main

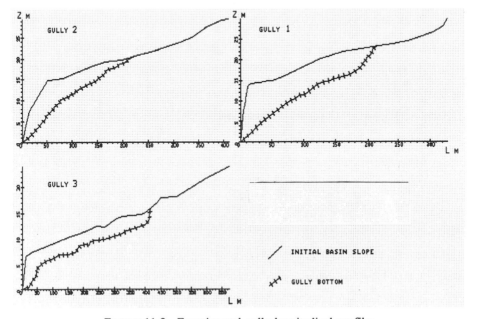

FIGURE 11.2 Experimental gully longitudinal profiles

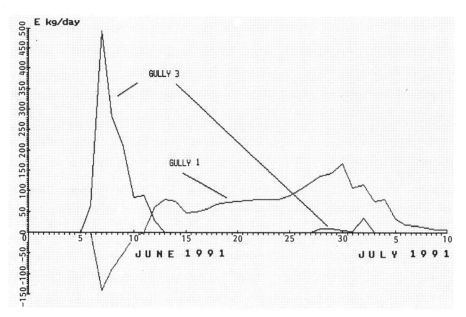

FIGURE 11.3   Erosion rate E in gullies 1 and 3 during the period of snowmelt

volume of water passed through the gully without erosion. Only at the end of the thaw period was active erosion of deposited sediments and gully walls and bottom observed (Figure 11.3). The sediment budget for the snowmelt period (6 June−4 July) was positive: sediment supply from the basin to the gully head was 25 m³, and output from the gully mouth was 110 m³.

In gully 3 a continuous stream flowed from the very beginning of the thaw period, and sediment transport was highly correlated with water discharge. The whole volume of erosion in the gully was 150 m³, mainly at the beginning of the snowmelt period (Figure 11.3).

The erosional behaviour of gully 2 had an intermediate pattern. At the beginning of the snowmelt period there was active erosion and thermoerosion on the watershed area and at the gully head. On 6− 13 June, 11 m³ of sediments were eroded from the basin slopes. At the head of the gully a deep (2·3 m) and narrow (0·4 m) trench was formed in frozen deposits. The porosity of gully snow pack was high, and the main part of sediments filtered through snow (on 7 June sediment input was 1·2 kg s⁻¹ and output was 1·0 kg s⁻¹). Snow melting in the gully was finished by 19 June and at the end of the thaw period (28 June− 3 July) the water discharge and erosion rate was negligible.

The average rate of thermoerosion in the gullies over the snowmelt period of 1991 was 0·8− 1·2 m per month and meltwater depth of runoff for this period was 150 mm.

The spring of 1992 was characterized by a short period of high air temperatures in the middle of May. A thick layer of ice was formed in the lower parts of the snowpack in gullies. This ice layer remained in the gullies up to the end of June. The main volume of meltwater flowed through the gullies above this ice layer and erosion rate was negligible.

11.3.3 Gully erosion during the period of rainfall

Summer and autumn rains have a duration of $74-171$ h per month on the west-central Yamal. Only two to four events per month are characterized by rainfall of more than 1 mm day^{-1} (observed maximum 40 mm day^{-1}). On $5-10$ August 1990 it was raining with low intensity over all the territory of west Yamal, but locally the rainfall intensity was relatively high. On 8 August on the KEH camp territory the depth of rainfall was $28 \cdot 6$ mm (20 year return period) and maximum 30 min rainfall intensity exceeded $0 \cdot 8$ mm min^{-1}. The runoff coefficient was $0 \cdot 42$ over the destroyed vegetation cover, with irregular microrelief and heavy loam soil, and the thaw layer was $0 \cdot 7-1 \cdot 2$ m thick. The soil was saturated and all surface microdepressions were filled by rain water from the $5-7$ August low intensity rains.

On gully 1 basin $2 \cdot 7$ m^3 were eroded from watershed slopes above the gully head during the period of maximum flow ($9-14$ h on 8 August 1990), and $14 \cdot 2$ m^3 of sediment were supplied from the gully mouth. Average erosion depth was $0 \cdot 16$ m, less than the thaw layer thickness.

On gully 2 basin the volume of erosion on the slopes was $9 \cdot 7$ m^3 and output volume was about 51 m^3. The average depth of erosion was $0 \cdot 58$ m, and in several places the depth of erosion was more than the thaw layer thickness.

The average rate of thermoerosion in the gullies during the rainfall period of 1990 was $0 \cdot 5-0 \cdot 6$ m day^{-1}, and depth of runoff was 12 mm. The rate of erosion was correlated with water supply (Figure 11.4).

11.3.4 Mass movement in gullies

A narrow rectangular trench in the gully bottom with depth up to $2 \cdot 5$ m and width $0 \cdot 4-0 \cdot 6$ m is formed by water erosion. This trench with vertical walls is stable only in frozen deposits. When the thaw layer reaches a depth of more than $0 \cdot 5-0 \cdot 8$ m, this cross-sectional shape becomes unstable. Shallow landslides transform the gully cross-sectional shape to triangular or trapezoidal, and this process lasts from several days up to weeks.

11.4 GULLY EROSION/THERMOEROSION MODELS

The field investigations shows that water flow behaviour and gully erosion/thermoerosion processes are very complicated. The lack of information about all the factors of these processes and insufficient knowledge about their mechanisms cause us to turn to rather simple models for water flow and erosion/thermoerosion prediction.

11.4.1 Water flow during the period of snowmelt

Komarov's (1969) model was used for water flow prediction during the thaw period. The thawed layer on the current day is given by:

$$H_m = K_m(T_+) \tag{1}$$

where K_m = coefficient of melting:

$$K_m = H_s / \Sigma T_+) \tag{2}$$

T_+ = sum of hourly positive air temperatures for current day, ΣT_+ = sum of hourly positive air temperatures from the beginning of thaw, H_s = storage of water in snowpack (mm).

At the beginning of the thaw period part of the meltwater is accumulated in snowpack pores. The daily layer of accumulation is:

$$H_a = H_m[0 \cdot 9^{(0 \cdot 1 H_m)}] \tag{3}$$

and daily depth of runoff is:

$$H_r = H_m - H_a \tag{4}$$

When the sum of H_m from the beginning of the thaw period ΣH_m becomes more than

$$H_{max} = 0 \cdot 2 \Sigma H_r - 4 \cdot 0 \tag{5}$$

the daily thawwater layer completely transforms into runoff with the addition of part of the previously accumulated water H_p:

$$H_r = H_m + H_p \tag{6}$$

H_p can be calculated from:

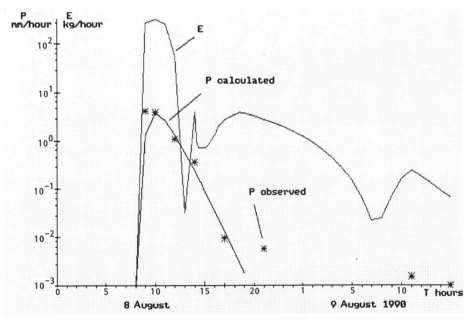

FIGURE 11.4   Erosion rate E and water supply intensity P in gully 2 during the period of summer rainfall

$$H_p = H_i - H_j \tag{7}$$

$$H_i = H_{max}/[\cosh(z_i)]^2 \tag{8}$$

$$z_i = \frac{\sum_i H_m}{0 \cdot 85 H_s - \left[\sum_i H_m\right]} \tag{9}$$

The index i means sum for i days from the beginning of thaw period; $j = i - 1$.

Calculation of meltwater supply must be processed day by day from the beginning of thaw (the first day with positive air temperatures) till the complete disappearance of snowpack.

11.4.2 Water flow during the period of rainfall

Field observation shows that the runoff hydrograph can be approximated by the Gudrich curve (Figure 11.4):

$$P = P_m 10^{-A[(1-x)^2]/x} \tag{10}$$

where P = runoff intensity (mm s^{-1}), P_m = maximum P value, $x = t_i/t_u$, t_i = current time (h), t_u = duration of water flow raise (h). The empirical coefficient A is $0 \cdot 9$ for periods of high surface storage (more than 1 mm) and $0 \cdot 15$ for periods of low surface storage (less than 1 mm).

11.4.3 Thermoerosion rate prediction

The most usual type of thermoerosion process consists of equal frozen deposit melting and surface lowering. This is called low-energy thermoerosion. Field and laboratory experiments (Malinovski, 1980; Dan'ko, 1982; Poznanin, 1989) show a simple relation for low-energy thermoerosion rate prediction:

$$dZ/dt = -K_t T \tag{11}$$

where T = water temperature (°C), Z = eroded surface altitude, t = time. The empirical coefficient K_t value is related to material texture (Figure 11.5). The scatter is related to the difference in texture of deposits and cryogenic structure (Table 11.1).

11.4.4 Erosion rate prediction

Erosion of thaw sediments takes place when the rate of permafrost melting is more than the eroded surface lowering. The rate of erosion is related to water flow velocity, depth and turbulence, and soil texture and mechanical pattern. The equations of mass conservation and deformation can be written in the form:

$$\frac{\partial Z}{\partial t} + (1/W)\frac{\partial Q_s}{\partial x} = 0 \tag{12}$$

$$(1/W)\frac{\partial Q_s}{\partial x} = uC_1 - wC_u \tag{13}$$

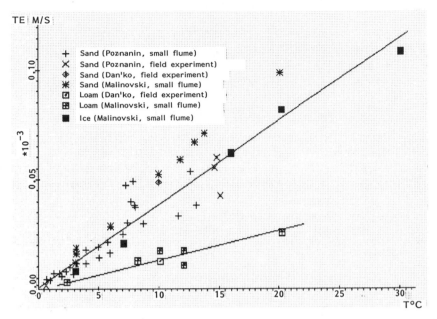

FIGURE 11.5   Thermoerosion rate *TE* versus water temperature *T*. Data from flume and field experiments of Malinovski (1980), Dan'ko (1982) and Poznanin (1989)

TABLE 11.1   Coefficients of thermoerosion for different
sediment textures and cryogenic structure
(from Malinovski, 1980; Dan'ko, 1982; Poznanin, 1989)

Sediment type		K_t (10^{-5} m s^{-1} °C^{-1})
Sand:	thin	5·16
	medium	4·30
	silty	2·50
	with vegetation remnants	1·44
	with peat	0·53
Loam:	laminated cryogenic structure	0·70
	massive cryogenic structure	0·55
	net cryogenic structure	1·25
	mainly horizontal lenses	1·40
	mainly vertical lenses	0·80

where W = water flow width, Q_s = sediment discharge, x = longitudinal coordinate, w = fall velocity, u = vertical bottom velocity, C_l = sediment concentration at lower boundary of the layer of sediment particle exchange, C_u = sediment concentration at the upper boundary of this layer. Experimental data of erosion rates in gullies of the Yamal peninsula show that upward sediment flux is proportional to specific discharge q and surface slope S (Figure 11.6):

$$uC_1 = K_e q S \tag{14}$$

The last term in equation 13 is negligible under conditions of gully formation and the equation of deformation can be written in the form:

$$\frac{\partial Z}{\partial t} - K_e q \frac{\partial Z}{\partial x} = 0 \tag{15}$$

The empirical erodibility coefficient (K_e) depends on soil texture and cohesion. For loams $K_e = 0 \cdot 0012$ and for sands $K_e = 1 \cdot 3$.

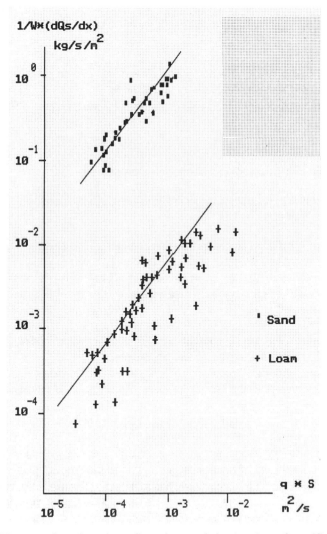

FIGURE 11.6 The rate of erosion versus flow characteristics (product of specific discharge q on slope S)

11.4.5 Gully cross-section shape prediction

Field investigation shows that shallow landslides transform the gully cross-section to a triangular or trapezoidal shape. The side walls of the gully become practically straight and a stable slope model can be used for wall inclination prediction. If depth of slides

$$D_s > \frac{2c}{gR}\cos(F)\Big/\sin^2\frac{1}{2}\left(F + \frac{\pi}{2}\right) \tag{16}$$

then the gully achieves stable side slope A_s, which can be calculated from:

$$\frac{c}{gRD_s} = \frac{\sin(2A_s)}{2} - \frac{R - mR_w}{R}\tan F\cos^2 A_s \tag{17}$$

where R and R_w = sediment and water specific weights, c = soil cohesion, F = angle of internal friction, m = water content in slide layer, g = 9·81. If soil mechanics characteristics are not available, the angle of stable gully walls can be estimated with field measurements.

11.4.6 Gully erosion/thermoerosion model composition

The main characteristics of the calculation algorithm are described in Figure 11.7. The topographic data include:

1. the longitudinal profile of initial basin slope along the main watercourse;
2. basin area distribution along the length of this profile;
3. longitudinal profiles of the lower boundaries of all layers of deposits with different thermoerosion and erodibility coefficient values;
4. values of these coefficients.

If the layer consists of vegetation remnants, or it is skin vegetation cover, the value of the velocity of erosion initiation must also be determined.

Hydrological data include: (1) number of flood events; (2) event type (thaw or rainfall) and duration; (3) for each event the row of water discharges and temperatures and each step duration.

The longitudinal profile transformation in space and time is calculated with the Lax predictor—corrector scheme. The stability criterion is determined for each calculation step and scheme stability is attained by time-step duration change. For the meltwater runoff period the rate of gully-bottom cutting is equal to the thermoerosion rate TE (if TE is more than erosion rate E) and equation 11 is used for calculation. If $TE < E$, then the rate of the gully-bottom cutting is equal to the rate of erosion and equation 15 is used.

After each flood event the rectangular bottom trench is transformed by the stable slope model to a trapezoid shape with the same total area of cross-section, and longitudinal distribution of the gully top width and depth is estimated.

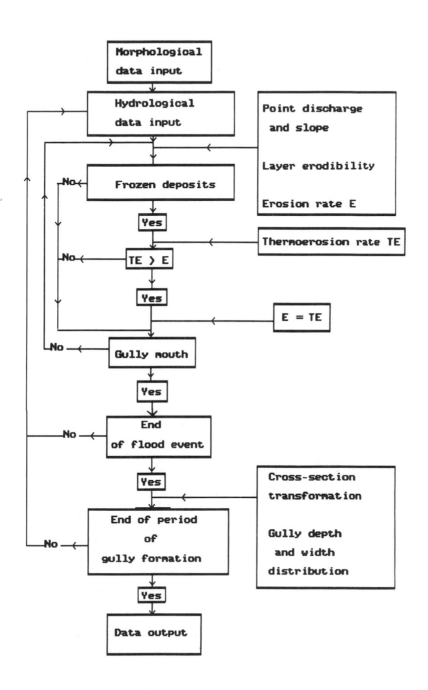

FIGURE 11.7 Algorithm of the gully erosion calculation

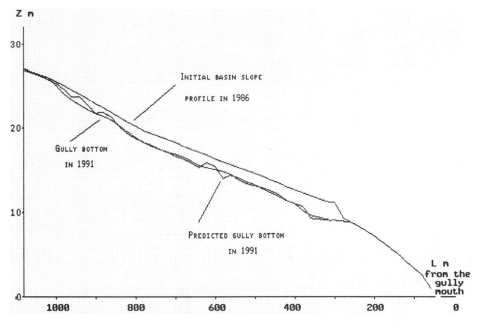

FIGURE 11.8   Actual and calculated longitudinal profile of gully 4

11.5 MODEL VERIFICATION

There are not enough data for complete model verification. The only gully for which initial and actual longitudinal profiles are available is situated in the territory of YaDE camp (4 km to the west of KEH). Before 1986 there was shallow linear depression with dense vegetation cover and ephemeral flow. From 1986 (YaDE camp construction) surface destruction and meltwater increase led to intensive gully erosion and thermoerosion. A gully about 1 km long was formed (Figure 11.8). In 1991 the longitudinal profile of the gully was measured. The initial profile was available from the map. The depths of runoff for thaw and rainfall periods for 1986–1991 were calculated on the basis of Marre Salye station meteorological data with corrections. The corrections were based on the meteorological and hydrological measurements of 1990–1991 on KEH camp territory. The calculated and observed altitudes of the gully bottom in 1991 are rather close. The calculated longitudinal profile is more irregular, but it can be related to the smaller number of points of altitude estimation in the actual gully than in the calculation (Figure 11.8).

11.5.1 Gully dimension prediction on the Bovanenkovskoye gas field territory

The longitudinal profile transformation was calculated for all drainage net thalwegs on the Bovanenkovskoe gas field territory (Figure 11.9). The period for calculation was equal to the operating period for the gas field (about 30 years). The topographic data were compiled from topographic and geological maps with field correction for some profiles. Hydrological characteristics were calculated on the basis of Marre Salye station meteorological measurements for 1957−1986. These flows were used as data for prognosis. The vegetation cover was assumed to be completely destroyed by human impact or skinflow.

Calculations show that all drainage net thalwegs would be transformed by erosion and thermoerosion processes. In more than 60% of thalwegs the depth of gullies would be more than 1·0 m (Figure 11.9). Some human-induced gullies would cross pipelines and roads, some would damage buildings and boreholes.

11.6 CONCLUSION

The gully erosion/thermoerosion model is based on the equation of deformation

$$\partial Z/\partial t + (1/W)\partial Q_s/\partial x = 0 \tag{18}$$

For erosion prediction a sediment budget equation combined with an empirical formula for incision rate estimation is used:

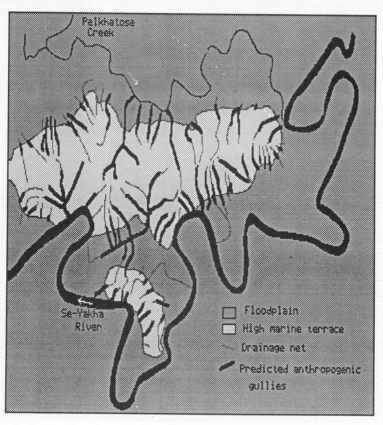

FIGURE 11.9 Predicted anthropogenic gully net on the Se-Yakha River−Pelkhatose Creek interfluve (west-central Yamal peninsula)

$$(1/W)\partial Q_s/\partial x + K_e q \partial Z/\partial x = 0 \qquad (19)$$

This equation is used when the rate of permafrost melting is more than the gully incision rate. Coefficients of erodibility values are $0\cdot0012$ for loams and $1\cdot3$ for sands.

For thermoerosion prediction, when the rate of permafrost melting is less than the gully incision rate, the sediment budget related to water temperature T is given by:

$$(1/W)\partial Q_s/\partial x - K_t T = 0 \qquad (20)$$

The coefficient of thermoerosion values are $0\cdot000052$ for sands and $0\cdot0000055$ for loams. The empirical coefficients are based on field measurements in Yamal peninsula conditions, and on flume experiment data. The model verification shows rather close values of predicted and measured altitudes of gully bottom.

REFERENCES

Dan'ko, V. K. 1982. *The Thermoerosion Process Behavior in North Western Siberia*. Author's abstract of dissertation for the degree of Candidate of Geological Science, State University of Moscow (in Russian).

Komarov, V. D. 1969. The hydrograph calculation for small plain rivers based on thaw intensity data. *Trudy Gidrometeotsentra SSSR*, **37**, 3–30 (in Russian).

Malinovski, D. V. 1980. *Permafrost Deposit Erodibility and Methods of its Study for Soil Mechanics Research*. Author's abstract of dissertation for the degree of Candidate (PhD) of Geological Science, State University of Moscow (in Russian).

Poznanin, V. L. 1989. The ground ice content and its influence on the thermoerosion process. *Materials of Glaciologic Research*, **59**, 11–31 (in Russian).

Voskresenskiy, K. S. and Zemchikhin, B. Ye. 1988. The main erosion–therkarstic relief patterns. In Solomatin, V. I. (ed.), *Northern Geosystems Stability Research*, Moscow University Publishing House, Moscow, 109–131 (in Russian).

12

Modelling and Monitoring of Soil Salinity and Waterlogging Hazards in the Desert – Delta Fringes of Egypt, Based on Geomorphology, Remote Sensing and GIS

MORGAN DE DAPPER, RUDI GOOSSENS

Department of Geography and International Training Centre for Post Graduate Soil Scientists, University of Ghent

AND

ABD-ALLA GAD, MOHAMED EL BADAWI

National Authority for Remote Sensing and Space Sciences, Cairo

ABSTRACT

This paper presents the results of a three year programme of the Belgian Ministry for Science Policy dealing with land degradation and remote sensing. In arid and semiarid climates the soil salinity hazard is an increasing problem. In this paper two types of simulation models are presented, allowing the prediction of risks for soil salinity and the interconnected problem of waterlogging. The method was elaborated in two test areas in Egypt. One model deals with delta soils, the other with desert soils in the New Reclaimed Areas.

12.1 INTRODUCTION

Salt-affected soils occur under a wide range of environmental conditions; however, they are more pronounced in the arid and semiarid regions. It has been estimated that about one-third of the cultivated land under irrigation in the world is already salt-affected (Framji, 1976). Moreover, salt-affected areas often occur in fertile alluvial plains. The inventory and mapping of soil salinity using remote sensing instead of the classical field methods has only occasionally been performed. In Pakistan (Rafiq, 1975) and India some case studies have been made to evaluate the possibilities of Landsat data for mapping salt-affected soils. Sehgal et al. (1988) are using Landsat MSS data for mapping salt-affected

Geomorphic Hazards. Edited by O. Slaymaker.

soils in the frame of a general soil map of India, while Sharma and Bhargava (1988) and Rao et al. (1991) are using, respectively, Landsat MSS and TM images for more detailed mapping in a limited area. Dwivedi (1992) used Landsat MSS and TM imagery for mapping and monitoring the salt-affected soils which are connected with bad drainage conditions in the Indo-Gangetic alluvial plain. A decrease in saline soils could be detected between 1975 and 1986. All these studies have in common that the salt-affected soils and the related waterlogged or poorly drained soils are mapped in a monoscopical and visual way. This paper, however, deals with supervised image classification. Until now the saline and waterlogged soils have mainly been studied using the classical field and laboratory approach (United States Salinity Laboratory Staff, 1954). This paper deals with the inventory and mapping of waterlogged and saline soils using digital image processing. El-Gabaly (1959) estimated the area of Egypt suffering from primary or secondary salinity at about 800 000 ha. This area represents approximately one-third of the entire area of arable land of the country. The extension of salt-affected soils is increasing as a result of the perennial irrigation without an adequate drainage system. Also, the need for irrigation water is increasing since the start of the reclamation of desert soils for agricultural purposes. This is obvious in the Baheira Governorate. The "good quality" irrigation water is partly derived from the New Reclaimed Areas, while the Old Land (the Delta Area) is receiving less "good quality" irrigation water. To avoid losing their crops the local farmers are sometimes obliged to irrigate with salty drainage water. In the future this could lead to an increase of the salt-affected soils in the delta region. Although the New Reclaimed Areas are receiving only fresh water, a lot of saline soils occur. Since Nasser's time, the reclamation of the desert fringes is operational. The wind-blown sands have been levelled and irrigation and drainage channels constructed. In some parts of the New Reclaimed Areas vast areas of saline and waterlogged soils occur at the present day.

The salinity and waterlogging was studied mainly by means of remotely sensed data linked to field observations (El Badawi et al., 1992; Goossens et al., 1993). Two test areas were selected, namely the Baheira Province and the Ismailia Province. In the Baheira Province two subtest areas are distinguished, one in the Old Land (Hosh Eisa) and one in the New Reclaimed Areas (Figure 12.1).

12.2 FIELD WORK FOR SOIL SALINITY AND WATERLOGGING

In the first phase the salinity was studied by field observations. During the field work 148 sample points were investigated. For each sample point the electrical conductivity of the soil paste (ECP) was measured. In suitable terrain conditions, the electrical conductivity of the irrigation (ECIR), drainage (ECD) and the soilwater (ECS) was also measured. In addition to the EC measurements, the depth of the oxido-reduction and reduction zone was measured, as well as the soil texture and the pH of the soil paste. The presence of calcium carbonate was checked by a HCl test.

The different parameters were stored in a data base (Reflex and Lotus). Correlations between the different parameters were calculated. Generally these correlations were weak or even absent. A correlation between ECIR and ECD could be proved; a more or less linear relation was found.

The most interesting relationship exists between ECP and the depth of the groundwater table. Two parameters were used, namely the depth of the oxido-reduction zone and the

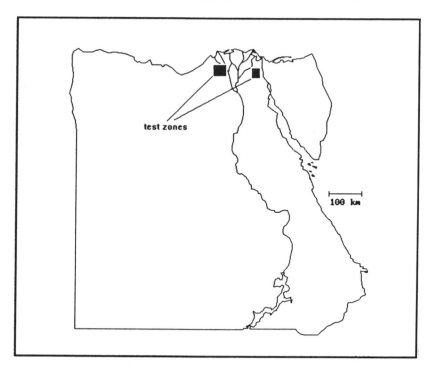

FIGURE 12.1 Locality of the study areas

depth of the reduction zone. A parabolic relationship was found between ECP and the depth of the oxido-reduction zone (Figures 12.2 and 12.3). Generally, the same relationship was found in the eastern as well as in the western test zone.

The nick point of these graphs indicates that the relation between ECP and the depth of the oxido-reduction horizon is situated around 40 to 50 cm for the clayey soils of the

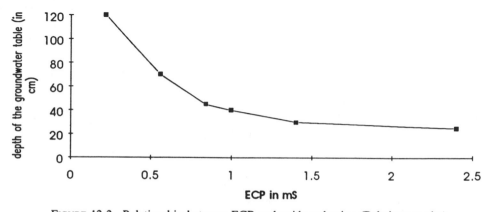

FIGURE 12.2 Relationship between ECP and oxido-reduction (Baheira test site)

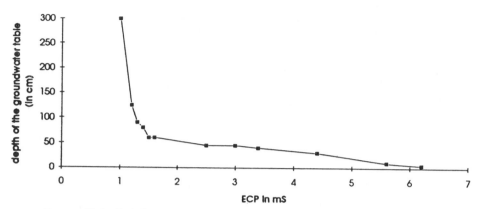

FIGURE 12.3   Relationship between ECP and oxido-reduction (Ismailia test site)

Hosh Eisa test area and around 75 cm for the sandy soils of the Ismailia test area. The major conclusion is that the salinity of the soil is in direct relation with the depth of the groundwater table. A high groundwater table results in a low leaching capacity leading to concentration of the salts in the upper parts of the soil profile. The critical depth seems to be 50 cm for the clayey soils and 75 cm for the sandy soils. The graphs also show that a groundwater level higher than 50 cm for clayey soils or 75 cm for sandy soils results in a strong increase of the soil salinity. This is important since the depth of 50 cm is also the mean root depth of most of the crops, so these salts can affect the growth of the plants causing losses in yield. In many places with a high groundwater table these soils are used for rice cultivation. Rice is a crop which needs wet soils and which is rather tolerant to salinity (Loveday, 1984). Therefore, rice is often the only crop which can be cultivated on these soils.

Comparable results were found by Kovda (1975), Rhoades (1975) and Halvorson and Rhoades (1974). They found the nick point of the relation between the EC of the soil and the depth of the groundwater table at a depth of 1 m. This difference could be due to the difference in soil texture, but it could also be due to the measuring methods, measuring the extract instead of the soil paste. The general trends of the two results are comparable: both show that the depth of the groundwater table is the decisive factor for soil salinity. Once the groundwater table rises above the nick point the soil salinity increases drastically.

It can thus be concluded that the problems of salinity are directly connected with the problems of soil drainage. Therefore, in the clayey delta soils, soil drainage conditions are the major salinity hazard factor. The waterlogging varies from poorly drained soils, with a groundwater table at a depth of approximately 50 cm, to completely submerged soils. The salinity of these soils can reach 18 mS.

It seems that the quality of the irrigation water is of minor importance. In fact all the irrigation water is derived from the Nile, except for some places in the Ismailia area where artesian groundwater is pumped.

12.3 THE HOSH EISA TEST AREA

12.3.1 Environmental settings

The study area is situated approximately 60 km southeast of Alexandria. The land is relatively low, situated between 1 and 5 m above sea level. The area is formed by an old braided river system; low ridges (former levees, so-called turtle backs, merging up to 5 m above the surrounding area) and microdepressions (former back swamps) alternate and give rise to a typical complex microtopography. As will be demonstrated further, this typical geomorphological setting will play an important role in the development and creation of waterlogged and saline soils. The soils are entisols and consist of heavy alluvial clay. The land is artificially drained by a dense network of elementary and master drainage channels. The irrigation water is derived from the Nile and is generally of good quality. The average EC is 1·4 mS. The farmers receive mainly fresh irrigation water twice a month during a five day period. The major crops are cotton, wheat and alfalfa.

12.3.2 Materials available

Three satellite images from three different sensors are available:

— a Landsat MSS scene of 29 January 1977
— a SPOT XS scene of 20 September 1989
— a Landsat TM scene of 19 February 1991.

Topographical maps of the area on a scale 1/25 000 with a contour interval of 0·5 m, dating from 1947, were also available.

12.3.3 Salinity by the lack of irrigation water

As mentioned above, the farmers receive mainly fresh irrigation water twice a month during a five day period. This is the irrigation scheme that is applied by the irrigation authorities in the area. The irrigation water is distributed by main irrigation channels from where primary channels tap the water. From here the farmers can tap the irrigation water and distribute it over the land. This is done by diesel pumps, the "sakia" or, seldom these days, by the "shadouf".

Since the reclamation of new land in the desert to the south of the study area, more and more irrigation water is needed. The traditional agricultural areas, mainly situated on the alluvial clay deposits, are therefore receiving less fresh irrigation water. Farmers who have their land close to a main irrigation channel are pumping the quantities of water they need, or even more. Farmers who have their land further away from an irrigation channel often lack the necessary amount of water. To avoid losing their crops they are obliged to irrigate with the salty drainage water. These procedures can lead to reductions of the yield, but this is still better than losing the crop. These practices inevitably lead to an increase of the soil salinity. The water will evapotranspire but the salts will remain in the soil, especially in the case of bad leaching. It can therefore be concluded that the greater the distance to a main irrigation channel, the greater the risk of increased soil salinity.

A map showing this risk was made by digitization of the main irrigation channels and calculation of the distances to these channels. This "distance map" can be considered as a risk map for soil salinity caused by the lack of fresh irrigation water. Since the higher parts of the landscape are seldom cultivated, and therefore not irrigated, these areas are masked in the map. This has been done using the digital elevation model (DEM) and a cut-off point at 0·5 m above sea level. The resulting areas with high digital values and at a level below 0·5 m can thus be considered as areas with a risk for soil salinity.

12.3.4 Salinity by drainage water

As stated above, a high groundwater table also results in high soil salinity due to a low leaching capacity. Waterlogging often occurs when a master drainage channel crosses a microdepression. The salty drainage water can seep into the soil of the surrounding areas resulting in a high groundwater table, waterlogging and eventually salinity.

A map showing the risk for soil salinity caused by waterlogging was generated. The master drainage channels were digitized from the topographical map and the distance map from the drains was calculated. A distance of 250 m away from the master drainage channels was chosen as a critical value. This criterion is compared with the DEM. Relatively high areas in the neighbourhood of a master drain can be considered as not sensitive for soil salinity. Using the DEM, a map is created showing the areas at a distance of 250 m away from the master drainage channels and situated below the 0·5 m level. This map (Figure 12.4A) can be considered as a risk map for soil salinity caused by the seepage of salty drainage water into the soil.

12.3.5 The combination of the two maps

Both maps were combined and superimposed on the DEM. A field check showed that the areas of waterlogging and salinity indeed occurred in the zones of risk predicted by the model.

12.3.6 Image classification

The three satellite images were classified using supervised techniques. The fact that the images are derived from three different sensors creates some classification problems due to differences in spatial and especially spectral resolution. The best classification results could be obtained using the Landsat TM imagery.

Since no field data from the period of 1977 were available, the image classification was performed using similarities in spectral characteristics as they were used with the image classification of the Landsat TM and SPOT images.

For the test area in the neighbourhood of Hosh Eisa village, seven different classes could be distinguished:

1. waterlogged 1: submerged soils with the groundwater table above the topographical surface;
2. waterlogged 2: wet soils within the capillary fringe;
3. waterlogged 3: wet soils above the capillary fringe where the top soil can be dried out and salt crystals are formed at the surface;
4. village: the centre of Hosh Eisa;

5. bare land: mainly situated in the neighbourhood of the saline and waterlogged soils;
6. irrigation: barren fields which were under flood irrigation at the moment of the image recording;
7. vegetation: fields with crops.

An attempt was made to distinguish all these classes on the three different satellite data. This was not always possible. For instance, in the classification of the SPOT image, only two classes of waterlogging could be obtained, namely wetland (shallow groundwater table) and salt crust. It should be mentioned that the SPOT image was recorded in the summer, so that a lot of surface water had already evaporated.

The best results, as controlled by the field data, were obtained using the Landsat TM imagery. The training data were checked by commission — omission matrices. The

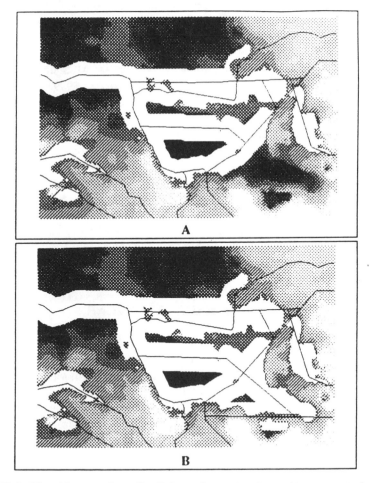

FIGURE 12.4 The risk zones for soil salinity and waterlogging (white areas), before (A) and after (B) the construction of new master drains. The background is the DEM

classification of the Landsat TM scene gave the best result: all seven bands, except for band 1, were used.

The Landsat MSS and SPOT XS images were classified as well. In general these classification results were comparable; only between the classes of waterlogging and irrigation did some confusion occur. The classified images were geometrically corrected and warped on the DEM.

12.3.7 Discussion

The classified images were checked in the field during a fieldwork campaign in February 1992. It could be stated that the classification of the waterlogging is correct. Moreover, all areas characterized by waterlogging are situated in the risk areas as predicted by the simulation model. This means that special attention has to be paid to the areas situated in the risk zones. In the case of poor maintenance of the master drainage channels waterlogging and salinity can occur in a very short time. So the model allows the creation of waterlogged soils and salinity to be predicted, but the opposite is also possible: the improvement of soil waterlogging and salinity can be simulated as well. This can be illustrated with the waterlogged area situated in the eastern part of the test area. This large area showed up on the image classification of the Landsat MSS image from 1977. Reactivation of the master drain which crosses the area started in 1989. The master drain was thoroughly deepened and at the same time, parallel to the master drain, a main irrigation channel was dug. The effect was that in a two year time span the groundwater table dropped by $1 \cdot 5$ m, allowing the salts to be washed out by the fresh water. This can be detected on the satellite images and the derived classifications. From 1991 it was possible to start with agriculture, and wheat and vegetables are now cultivated. By adding the new irrigation channel to the model it is noticed that the risk of soil salinity caused by the lack of fresh irrigation water has disappeared. However, the risk of waterlogging in the area still remains due to the fact that the master drain crosses a closed depression. In the case of poor maintenance the groundwater table will reappear in a very short time.

The model also allows checking of whether the risks for salinity and waterlogging are increasing or decreasing in the case of a new master drain (Figure 12.4B).

12.4 THE ISMAILIA TEST ZONE

12.4.1 Environmental settings

The waterlogged areas in the Ismailia area are localized between the Nile Delta and the Suez Canal. The surficial geology is characterized by aeolian sands on top of old alluvial Nile deposits. The latter are composed of alternating sand and clay layers (Figure 12.5).

The aeolian topography is composed of a complex of low dunes and blowouts. The blowouts reach the youngest alluvial clay layer. Because of the impermeability of the clay layer the lowest parts in the landscape form waterlogged areas, the so-called sebkhas or chotts.

The constantly increasing population pressure in Egypt results in an urgent demand for arable land. Here also the Egyptian government is trying to reclaim the desert as was the case in the western part of the delta—desert fringes. In cooperation with the Italian

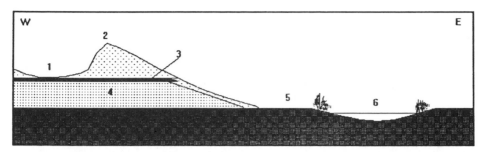

FIGURE 12.5   Transect through the topography of the Ismailia area. 1 = sebkha, 2 = aeolian sand, 3 = clay layer, 4 = alluvial sand, 5 = outcropping clay, 6 = open water and waterlogged soils bordered with reed vegetation

Development Aid Agency efforts are being made to reclaim the area between the eastern Nile Delta and the Suez Canal. In such schemes the dune topography is levelled and irrigation and drainage channels are constructed. Pivot systems are installed to provide the irrigation water.

In a first stage the waterlogging and salinity on the original topography were modelled. In a second stage an attempt was made to monitor and to predict the situation of waterlogging and salinity after the infrastructure works.

12.4.2   Materials available

One satellite scene was available: a SPOT XS scene dating from 16 July 1991.

Topographical maps were also available, dating from 1947, at a scale 1/25 000 with a contour interval of 0·5 m, and from 1985, on a scale of 1/50 000 with a contour interval of 2·5 m and indications of new roads and channels. The maps of 1947 were used to create the DEM and the maps of 1985 were used to digitize the road and channel network in order to use them for accurate ground control points.

12.4.3   Image classification

The SPOT scene was classified using supervised image classification techniques and the maximum likelihood algorithm. The following classes were retained:

1.   waterlogged 1: relatively deep water;
2.   waterlogged 2: wet soil at the surface;
3.   waterlogged 3: salt crusts at the surface;
4.   vegetation: green vegetation in the arable land area;
5.   desert sands.

After field control the classified image was further used as a land-cover map.

12.4.4   Creation of the DEM and ground control points

12.4.4.1   The DEM

The DEM was created by digitizing the contour lines of the topographical maps of 1947. Thanks to the small contour interval the microtopography, which is very important to simulate the waterlogging and salinity, could be modelled quite accurately. The 1947 maps are in Egyptian UTM (Universal Transverse Mercator projection) coordinates.

The raster format of the DEM consists of pixels of 40 × 40 m with DN (Digital Number) values every 10 cm. The DEM in UTM coordinates forms the master map in the Geographical Information System (GIS). Further created maps are inserted in the GIS and are georeferenced towards the coordinates of the DEM.

12.4.4.2   The ground control points

To obtain ground control points the road and channel network was digitized from the 1985 topographical maps. Since these maps are in geographical coordinates the coordinates of the ground control points (e.g. crossing of a road and a channel) had to be converted into UTM coordinates. The network was subsequently converted to the DEM. The ground control point file was used to warp the classified image on the DEM, so that comparison of the two documents became possible.

12.4.5   The modelling, simulation and prediction

As shown in Figure 12.5 two levels of alluvial clay are present. They show a height interval of approximately 3 m and give rise to two levels of waterlogging in the area, one at a level of 1 m a.s.l. and a second at a level of 4 m a.s.l. The lowest levels form the outcrop of a main alluvial clay body. The highest levels are considered as having a potential risk for waterlogging and salinity since the water can be stored in the sandy cover above the clay layer. This storage of water in the sand can be simulated using a density slicing on the DEM.

Comparison of the classified image with the potential risk areas for waterlogging and salinity, as simulated in the GIS, show that all present waterlogged areas are indeed localized in the indicated risk zones. It can be noticed that at present more areas are waterlogged as compared with the situation of 1947. However, the question of whether this represents a real increase in the surface area of waterlogging since 1947 or whether this is due to a lack of information on the topographical map of 1947 remains open.

Especially in the lower land along the Suez Canal, vast areas of waterlogging and salinity are present today which were not indicated on the topographical maps of 1947. In this area new drains and irrigation channels are being constructed. Further research is needed to prove the validity of the Hosh Eisa model for this test area.

On the higher level also, more waterlogged areas are present than indicated on the maps of 1947. This is confirmed by fieldwork, image classification and also from the 1/50 000 topographical maps of 1985. It is especially in this region that the Egyptian government started cooperation with the Italian Development Aid Agency to reclaim the area. The dunes in between the sebkhas are being levelled with bulldozers. The upper part of the dunes is used to fill the blowouts resulting in a relatively flat area. In this area one main irrigation channel and one master drain are being constructed. In the mean time a pivot system has been installed to provide irrigation water in the near future. This type of irrigation brings huge amounts of water into the soil. The sebkhas can be regarded as natural evaporation holes for the water stagnating upon the clay layer, but this is no longer the case after levelling the surface, because the groundwater table is entirely shielded from insolation. After the infrastructure work, the excess water stagnating on the clay layer can only be evacuated by the drain. Taking into account the increase of water input and the decrease of water evaporation, there is a risk of the groundwater table rising. A simulation model was developed to predict and simulate the risk of soil waterlogging and salinity after completion of the infrastructure works.

Additional documents were generated in the GIS. From field observation the depth of the clay layers was known. The field observation points where the clay layer depth could be observed (by drilling or by observation in pits and cuts) are digitized together with the depth value. Using interpolation techniques the clay surface could be generated in the GIS. This resulted in a map of the clay depth. By subtracting the depth of the clay layer from the DEM, a map is obtained indicating the thickness of the aeolian sands. This map is important since it gives an indication of the possible water storage capacity of the soil at different places. The thicker the sand sheet, the higher the water storage capacity.

From the area of the sebkhas on the plateau, a subimage was cut from the DEM corresponding with the planned New Reclaimed Area. From all the other files (image classification, etc.) an identical subimage was made. These files are further used to develop the model for prediction and simulation after the infrastructure works. The field work showed that the levelling of the terrain resulted in putting a 0·5 m thick sand layer on top of the clay outcrops in the sebkhas. This new surface was generated in the GIS by recalculating the "excess" volumes of sand in the upper part of the dunes and the "missing" volumes of sand in the sebkhas. First the amount of sand needed to fill up the sebkhas with 0·5 m was calculated The volumes required were extracted from the higher dune topography. In this way the new levelled surface was obtained. The differences between the two surfaces is illustrated in Figure 12.6.

In a next step the effects of waterlogging were calculated for the original surface as well as for the levelled one. In the first instance it is assumed that the project is a complete success and that no water table will develop above the clay layer. Subsequently the groundwater table in the GIS is increased by steps of 10 cm. This is done until a total rise of the water table of 2 m is obtained.

As indicated by Figure 12.7, the old surface is characterized by a linear function and the new surface by a discontinuous one. The intersection between the two graphs is situated at 80 cm. During the fieldwork it was observed that a groundwater table with a height of 40—50 cm is present above the clay layer, even after installation of the new master drain. As a consequence the future levelled surface cannot be considered as a well-drained soil. As was observed in the field, a capillary rise of 30—40 cm has to be taken into account. This capillary fringe has a high salinity risk since the water can evaporate as soon as it reaches the surface, giving rise to salt efflorescence in the upper layer of the soil. For all these reasons the results of this development project are rather doubtful. The efforts can even result in increased waterlogging and salinity.

It is clear that the relation between the rise of the groundwater table and the potential danger of soil salinity and waterlogging is linear. The levelled surface also experiences this linear relationship because the graph in Figure 12.7 has to be considered as three linear graphs; between 0 and 4 m, which is not levelled; between 4 and 6·6 m, the levelled surface; and higher than 6·6 m, again an unlevelled surface. The levelled part has a steeper slope on the graph compared with the original surfaces. The relation between the rise of the groundwater table and the potential danger of soil salinity and waterlogging can be considered as a linear function:

$$y = ax + b$$

where a = a "terrain rugosity" coefficient which can range from 0 to α, where α corresponds to a flat non-sloping surface and 0 corresponds to a (theoretical) vertical surface; b = the depth of the sand layer above the impermeable clay layer where the groundwater can be stored; x = the (artificial) rise of the groundwater table; y = the surface of the potential danger for soil salinity and waterlogging.

It can be concluded that the smaller a is, the smaller the risk of an increase in soil salinity and waterlogging. In other words, the higher the relief energy, the smaller the areas that will be affected in the case of a rise of the groundwater table. In the case of a strong undulating topography the risk of a strong increase in the area of soil salinity and waterlogging will be low. The bigger b is, the longer it will take before the groundwater table reaches the surface. The use of this model has some restrictions. The rise of the groundwater table cannot go on. Once the topographical surface is reached the

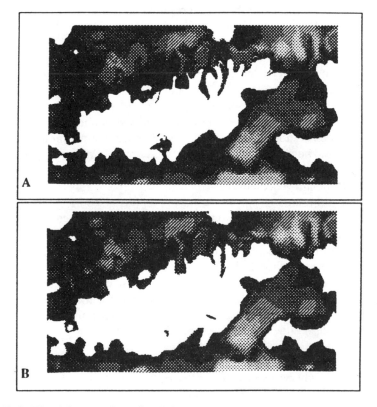

FIGURE 12.6 The risk zones for soil salinity and waterlogging (white areas), before (A) and after (B) levelling. The background is the DEM

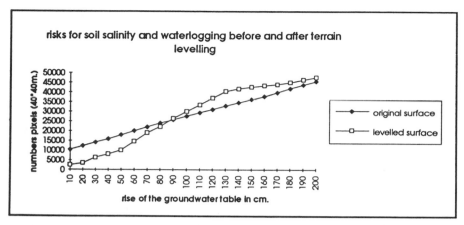

FIGURE 12.7   Relation between the surface extension of waterlogging and the possible rise of the groundwater table

evaporation starts. The surface of saline and waterlogged soil will become stable when the input of water (by irrigation) is equal to the evaporation.

This model allows the waterlogging and salinity to be monitored as well as allowing simulation and prediction in the case of infrastructure works.

12.5   CONCLUSIONS

It has been shown that the problem of soil salinity is in direct relation to the soil drainage conditions in the study area. The problem of soil salinity is also a problem of waterlogging. In areas of low relief, as in the Nile Delta and its fringes, both are closely linked to a geomorphological variable, namely microtopography. Two types of waterlogging could be distinguished, one in the clayey soils of the delta region and one in the sandy soils of the New Reclaimed Areas in the delta—desert fringes. In the delta region the waterlogging occurs where drains cross microdepressions leading to water seepage from the drain. In the desert area the waterlogging is caused by a rising groundwater table created above an impermeable (clay) layer. Both types of soil salinity can be simulated in a GIS. The basic layer of the GIS must be a detailed DEM. Other layers are the position of the irrigation and drainage channels, and possibly the depth of impermeable layers. The latter has to be derived from geomorphological fieldwork.

The effects on waterlogging and soil salinity by new public works such as the construction of new irrigation and drainage channels and the levelling of the terrain can be simulated.

12.6   ACKNOWLEDGEMENTS

This work could only be performed through the help, advice and organization of our research project by Prof. Dr Abdel Hady and Prof. Dr Hussein Younes, director and vice-director of the National Authority for Remote Sensing and Space Sciences, Cairo, Mr Laurent, director, and Ir. Decadt, coordinator, Ministry for Scientific Policy

(Belgium), and Prof. Dr L. Daels, director of the Laboratory for Regional Geography and Landscape Science, Department of Geography, University of Gent. They are gratefully acknowledged. Many thanks also to our colleagues Dr Beata De Vliegher and Dr Pascal Brackman for their help and advice.

REFERENCES

Abdel Salam, M. A., Abdalla, M. M., Zein El Abedine, A. and El Demerdashe, S. 1973. Comparative studies of soils in the Delta region and border fringes. *Desert Inst. Bull.*, ARE **23** nr. **1**, 59−89, El Mataria, Cairo.

Abdel Salam, M. A., El Kady, H. A. and Damaty, M. A. 1972. Soil classification of the Amriya−Maryut area, western Mediterranean coast of Egypt. *Desert Inst. Bull.*, ARE **22** nr. **2**, 281−293, El Mataria, Cairo.

Ayers, R. S. and Westcot, D. W. 1976. *Water Quality for Agriculture*. Irrigation and Drainage Paper 29, FAO, Rome.

Dwivedi, R. S. 1992. Monitoring and the study of the effects of image scale on delineation of salt-affected soils in the Indo-Gangetic plains. *International Journal of Remote Sensing*, **13**(8), 1527−1536.

El Badawi, M. M., Goossens, R., Ongena, Th. and Younes, H. 1992. The evolution of soil potentiality concerning salinity and waterlogging using multitemporal satellite image analysis in the NW part of the Nile Delta. In *International Space Year: Space Remote Sensing*, IGARSS '92, Houston, USA, 221−223.

El-Gabaly, M. M. 1959. Improvement of soils, irrigation and drainage in Egypt. In *Research on Crop Water Use, Salt-affected Soils and Drainage in the Arab Republic of Egypt*, FAO, Cairo.

Framji, K. K. (ed.) 1976. *Irrigation and Salinity: A World Wide Survey*. International Commission on Irrigation and Drainage, New Delhi.

Goossens, R., De Dapper, M., Ghabour, Th., Badawi, M. and Gad, A. 1993. The development of a GIS simulation model and the use of remote sensing for monitoring and prediction of soil salinity and waterlogging in the Nile Delta (Egypt). In *Proceedings of the Ground Sensing Conference*. SPIE, Bellingham, Washington, USA.

Halvorson, A. D. and Rhoades, J. D. 1974. Assessing soil salinity and identifying potential saline seep areas with field soil resistance measurements. *Soil Science Society of America Proceedings*, **38**, 567−581.

Kovda, V. 1975. Evaluation of soil salinity and waterlogging. In *Prognosis of Salinity and Alkalinity*. Soils Bulletin 31, FAO, Rome.

Loveday, J. 1984. Amendments for reclaiming sodic soils. In *Soil Salinity under Irrigation — Processes and Management*. Springer Verlag, Berlin, 220−237.

Rafiq, M. 1975. Use of satellite imagery for salinity appraisal in the Indus Plain. In *Prognosis of Salinity and Alkalinity*. Soils Bulletin 31, FAO, Rome, 141−146.

Rao, B. R. M., Dwivedi, R. S., Venkataratnam, L., Ravishankar, T. and Thammappa, S.S. 1991. Mapping the magnitude of sodicity in part the Indo-Gangetic plains Uttar Pradesh, northern India using Landsat-TM data. *International Journal of Remote Sensing*, **12**(3), 419−425.

Rhoades, J. D. 1975. Measuring, mapping and monitoring field salinity and water table depths with soil resistance measurements. In *Prognosis of Salinity and Alkalinity*. Soils Bulletin 31, FAO, Rome, 159−186.

Sehgal, J. L., Saxena, R. K. and Verma, K. S. 1988. Soil resource inventory of India using image interpretation technique. *Remote Sensing is a Tool for Soil Scientists*. Proceedings of the 5th symposium of the working group remote sensing, ISSS, Budapest, Hungary, 17−31.

Shainberg, I. and Shalhevet, J. (eds) 1984. *Soil Salinity under Irrigation — Processes and Management*. Ecological Studies 51, Springer Verlag, Berlin, 349.

Sharma, R. C. and Bhargava, G. P. 1988. Landsat imagery for mapping saline soils and wet lands in north-west India. *International Journal of Remote Sensing*, **9**(1), 39−44.

United States Salinity Laboratory Staff 1954. *Diagnosis and Improvement of Saline and Alkali Soils*. Agricultural Handbook no. 60, USDA, Washington, DC, USA, 160.

13

The Causes of Desertification in the Northern Algerian Sahara

MOHAMED TAHAR BENAZZOUZ

Institut des sciences de la terre, Université de Constantine, Algerie

ABSTRACT

Research on the causes of desertification in the northern Algerian Sahara indicates two sets of complementary approaches: (a) identification and localization of forms of degradation which can be observed in the field; and (b) a historical approach to the evolution of the human settlement in those predesertic margins until the present period. The confrontation of these two approaches allows a better identification of the causes of desertification which associate its natural aspects and its human effects.

The degradation of steppe through time constitutes a permanent indicator of evidence for human desertification. Many populations have successively colonized the Algerian steppe landscapes since Neolithic time: from the Berbers to the Romans (from the 2nd century BC to the 5th century AD), to Arabs (from the 7th century to the 8th century), to the eastern nomads (11th century) and lastly the French colonization in 1830. The consequences of these waves of colonizers led to an impoverishment of flora and fauna followed by a transformation and a degeneration of the steppe environments. Now, the traditional pastoral practices which are centred around the "Achaaba" system, based on customary law, have completely disintegrated due to rapid and dense pastoralism. This degradation and decline of the Algerian steppe results from these human effects superimposed on a set of natural processes and conditions which affect the territory of Northern Algeria:

- the permanence of climate perturbations of an Atlantic origin, from the north to north-west area;
- the consequences of the internal drainage of the High Plains, which explain the large extended aeolian accumulation on the sebkha margins. These sandy landscapes are considered as numerous stocks of mobile sand disposed directly in the axis of transatlas aeolian flux;
- the discontinuity of the Atlas mountains, which results in a corridor orientated north—south which is used as a sand transit area towards the Sahara.

So, desertification in the northern Algerian Sahara was initiated by natural causes and amplified by human activities. These human causes have contributed to the severe degradation of the sensitive predesertic environments in an irreversible way.

Geomorphic Hazards. Edited by O. Slaymaker.
© 1996 by John Wiley & Sons Ltd

13.1 INTRODUCTION

The Algerian Atlas Mountains form a natural barrier at the northern limit of the Sahara Desert. Surrounding these mountains there are two extremely sensitive environments, presently undergoing rapid degradation. Dune systems are developed equally well in the northern Sahara and in the corridor of the High Plains steppe (Figure 13.1). The steppes encircle the High Plains and the Sahara piedmont. This situation has encouraged the idea that desertification in North Africa results from movement of the desert from south to north. If this is the case, the Atlas Mountains do not function as a barrier to desertification from the south. It is therefore important to ask if the dunes of the High Plains and the surrounding slopes are of Saharan or of local origin. The answer to this question defines the role of the Atlas Mountains in relation to sand movement and consequently the direction of advancement of desertification in Algeria.

This study, on the one hand, defines the historical context of steppe utilization and the evidence of anthropogenic desertification; on the other hand, it presents the effects of natural causes of desertification and mechanisms of its growth.

13.2 COLONIZATION OF THE STEPPE: HISTORICAL EVOLUTION

13.2.1 Stages of colonization of the steppe environment

In the Neolithic times, the earliest people, the Berbers, grew wheat and barley but also raised domestic animals (Despois, 1953; Roubet, 1969).

During the Roman period (2nd century BC to 5th century AD) there was a large extension of agriculture protected from the nomads by a fortified wall or "Limès". Stock rearing in the Roman period was poorly understood but it is known that cultivation had driven back the nomads beyond the Limès (Leschi, 1943; Baradez, 1949).

The Roman period had otherwise been one of clearing of the forest which was an essential source of fuel for domestic hearths and city thermal baths (Camps, 1961).

The Arab conquests of the 7th and 8th century introduced changes with the resumption of the pastoral way of life and the extension of stock rearing at the same time as developing cultivation and irrigation (El-Edrissi, 1983; El-Bekri, 1965).

Invasions of eastern nomads from the middle of the 11th century had a negative impact on cultivated fields but favoured the growth of pastoralism and nomadism. These changes are evidenced by the disappearance of numerous villages and the neglect of numerous irrigation projects (Despois, 1953). The local population was greatly affected by this and forest clearing ceased, a fact which favoured rapid recolonization by the natural steppe vegetation on cultivated soils such as alfalfa (*stipa tenacissima*) and white artemisia (*herba alba*). Hence, the method of soil cultivation has led to stabilization during the centuries following the Middle Ages, and since the 16th century nomads and settlers have lived together.

Since 1830, French colonization has scarcely influenced the method of soil cultivation in the Saharan borderlands because the settlers monopolized the fertile lands of the northern plains. The contemporary period is characterized by rapid population growth which translates into impoverishment of the flora and fauna over 120 years (Le Houerou, 1968). Otherwise, the mechanization of ploughing introduced during the years 1920−1930 led to rapid regression of the steppe zones and continues today to transform the steppe landscapes (Chabin, 1982).

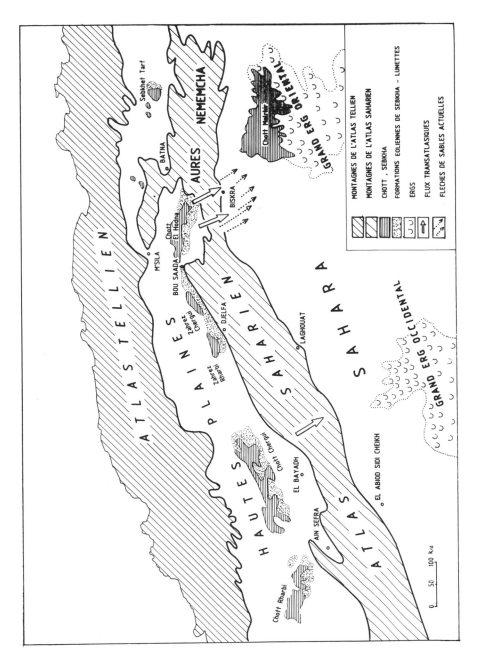

FIGURE 13.1 The internal drainage systems of the Algerian High Plains and the transatlas aeolian flux

Through this historical colonization of the steppe and the different ways in which the steppe has been utilized, it seems that the first desertification phenomena appeared as early as the Roman period following deforestation of large areas and intensive agricultural land use. During Arab times the vegetation cover was able to recover because of the pastoral and nomadic lifestyle. Since the opening of this century, these regions have been influenced by an acceleration of degradation of the natural vegetation and soils. Population growth, agricultural mechanization, intensification of tillage and increased pressure on settlement are universal factors (Chabin, 1982).

13.2.2 Human causes of desertification

Reduced vegetation cover is itself a direct cause of desertification. It is therefore interesting to analyse the factors which encourage reduction in tree cover and to infer the processes of desertification.

13.2.2.1 Overgrazing

The importance of overgrazing is indicated by the mean density of livestock on the steppe, equivalent to one sheep per 2−3 ha in Algeria. This represented an overloading by 45% in 1966 (Statistique Agricole, 1968). These densities are at least three times as high as the normal average in similar steppelands (in Australia, southern USA and South Africa) and generate a demand for fodder greater than the annual production of the steppe. Specifically, overgrazing affects land in the following ways:

- perennial vegetation cover is reduced;
- edible species become scarce by selective removal;
- resistant, inedible species develop, which replace forage crops selectively;
- trampling of the soil leads to reduction in permeability and soil moisture reserves. This deterioration of the soil is accelerated by development of concentrated runoff which produces incised gullies, especially well developed in areas of hydroaeolian activity.

13.2.2.2 Changes in surface runoff since the Roman period

Research by Birebent (1964) on the eastern High Plains and the Sahara piedmont shows that the Romans succeeded in their agricultural colonization of semiarid land by systematic development of hydraulic structures, as evidenced by remains of viaducts and canals visible on airphotos and on the ground. Since the Roman period, the neglect of these hydraulic structures has had disastrous consequences for soil conservation: water flows directly to the centre of depressions (the sebkha) and increases its erosive capacity. The Roman hydraulic structures are gullied and degraded, as evidenced by the lowering of wadis by 3−10 m since the Roman period (Birebent, 1964).

13.2.2.3 Effects of episodic cultivation

At the end of the autumn rains, the steppe dwellers extend their cereal cultivation further south where their chances of achieving a harvest are lower. Results are often catastrophic, followed by destruction of the silty sandy soils which are very vulnerable to aeolian erosion; as a result, large areas are denuded each year and are made even more barren than they would have become from mechanical cultivation alone.

13.2.2.4 Removal of woody plants

For their fuel needs, the inhabitants of the steppes uproot woody plants which leads to renewed aeolian activity over large barren surfaces each year. This type of denudation affects 30 000 – 100 000 ha of the margins of the Sahara each year (Statistique Agricole, 1968; Le Houerou, 1992).

13.2.3 The Algerian steppe — the current situation

13.2.3.1 Mean density of Algerian livestock

The mean density of livestock in the steppe zone has increased to about one sheep per hectare (Statistique Agricole, 1968) while the biological norm for Maghreb-like steppes is one sheep per 4 ha. The mean annual precipitation of this zone is 150 to 350 mm a^{-1}.

13.2.3.2 Total numbers of Algerian livestock

With the introduction of barley to the steppe over a period of 20 – 30 years, livestock numbers have increased markedly. In 1970, official government estimates were eight million head of livestock; today there are over 16 million (1990 estimate, Le Houerou, 1992). This growth is supported by a food base more and more dependent on cereal grains and concentrates, which represent more than 50% of the ration for cattle (Le Houerou, 1992; Statistique Agricole, 1968).

13.2.3.3 Present state of the Algerian steppe

For the whole of the Algerian steppe, the rate of recovery per year was 40 – 50% in the period 1940 – 1950, producing a biomass of 1000 – 1200 kg ha^{-1}. Today, the steppe is so degraded that the rate of annual recovery is only 2 – 5% based on a biomass of only 200 to 300 kg ha^{-1} (Le Houerou, 1968, 1992). The extension of cereal cultivation has led to a reduction in yield from 3·9 to 1·5 – 2·0 qha^{-1}, a reduction of 50% (Statistique Agricole, 1968). There is now a major retreat from the steppe. The catastrophic results that we are aware of today can be attributed to a single period, namely the contemporary period, but the evidence suggests that all these successive conquests have contributed to soil degradation in the Algerian steppe.

13.2.3.4 Evolution of pastoralism on the steppes

The practice of pastoralism on the steppe was subject to a "customary nomadic right" based on the duty to rotate land use. The nomadic breeders changed their land use each year with a view to restoration of the natural vegetation. Alongside their local pasture, the nomadic breeders practised transhumance or "achaaba" which set in motion two migrations per year of 2·6 million animals and 150 000 people (Statistique Agricole, 1968).

This regional complementarity is still kept alive by achaaba which links the northern High Plains and the southern Saharan piedmont (Figure 13.1). This traditional organization implies control of the pastoral activity on the steppes, mastery of the flock and rational use of the pasture systems. Now, since the loss of the customary right, there is a complete overturning of the steppe whereby everyone has the right to lead his flocks wherever and whenever he wishes. As a result the steppe is systematically broken up and today the traditional practice of achaaba is gradually disappearing.

13.2.3.5   *The imprint of society on the steppe today*

At the same time there is an increasingly common new type of pastoralism: "longitudinal pastoralism" (initiated by the Ouled Nail) which is characterized by rapid movement in the west−east direction. This form of modern pastoralism is linked to population densification and the increased means of transport which allows the richest owners to move their herds most quickly to the best pastures in the steppe. Consequences are catastrophic as there is no time for recovery of the natural steppe vegetation: grass does not even have time to develop before the herd is there. The imprint of society on the steppe is increased and natural resources are reduced. This sensitive and denuded natural environment becomes more vulnerable to agents of erosion.

13.3   EFFECTS OF THE ENVIRONMENT

In this sensitive environment, all kinds of interference and change can induce problems. This change is often accentuated by the strong influence of natural factors such that the combined effect of human and natural influences accentuates the desertification process.

13.3.1   Natural causes of desertification

13.3.1.1   *Seasonality of climate*

The climate of the High Plains includes an unsettled, cool and wet season in winter and a stable, warm and dry summer season. The Azores anticyclone determines the weather of this region. During the dry period, the Azores anticyclone affects the whole of the western half of the Mediterranean; the effects of continentality accentuate the warmth and dryness of the weather. The influence of the Tell Atlas mountain chain in intercepting rain from the north and northwest leads to even greater aridity in the High Plains and an increase in Saharan airmass influence. During the rainy period, the Azores anticyclone moves southwards and instabilities associated with the polar front affect the Mediterranean. North Atlantic unsettled conditions reach as far as eastern Algeria and northern Tunisia to produce sequences of rainy days (Sary, 1976). Mean annual precipitation in the Saharan piedmont and in the High Plains is presented in Tables 13.1 and 13.2, respectively.

13.3.1.2   *Wind*

Wind plays an important part in the formation of contemporary aeolian forms and in modifying older forms. In the basin of the Hodna, the dominant winds are westerly to

TABLE 13.1 Mean annual precipitation (*P*) on the
Saharan piedmont

Stations	*P* (mm a^{-1})	Period
Biskra	156	1913 — 1938
	140	1967 — 1984
Laghouat	167	1913 — 1938
	159	1960 — 1969
Brezina	84	1970 — 1977
El Abiod Sidi Cheikh	129	1913 — 1938
	84	1971 — 1976

TABLE 13.2 Mean annual precipitation (*P*)
in the High Plains

Aïn Sefra	192	1913 — 1938
	114	1978 — 1984
Djelfa	308	1913 — 1938
	335	1972 — 1984
Bou-Saada	270	1967 — 1974
M'Sila	226	1913 — 1938
	146	1981 — 1984
El-Bayadh	326	1913 — 1938

northwesterly. Analysis of diurnal variations indicates that the southerly, the westerly and northwesterly winds are most active from midday to the early evening and they are most effective in entraining fine soil particles from the dry soil surfaces. The northwesterly winds are most frequent. Their morphogenetic activity is important in the autumn when the winds blow over dry soil. Measurements in the Hodna indicate that, under light to moderate winds, surface wind speeds are one-half to two-thirds of those measured at 4 m above the ground (Sary, 1976). The predominant wind direction can be seen from the following four stations:

● at Ain Sefra, near the Moroccan border, the resultant direction is north to northwest;
● at the El Abiod Sidi Cheikh, on the Saharan piedmont south of the Atlas Mountains, the predominant direction is north to northwest (Callot, 1987);
● at Djelfa in the central part of the High Plains, the most frequent winds are west to northwest;
● at Barika, in the Hodna, the winds are west to northwest.

The turbulent erosional activity of the winds reaches a maximum towards the centre of the major depressions, where surface formations are completely desiccated.

FIGURE 13.2   Topographic discontinuity in the Atlas Mountains south of Hodna
(photo: Benazzouz)

13.3.2   Effects of the discontinuity of the Atlas Mountains

13.3.2.1   Topographic discontinuity

The topographic subdivision of the Atlas range gives the impression of a trellis pattern with large transverse gaps (Benazzouz, 1994). These passages develop at the site of topographic "saddles" or structural discontinuities (Figure 13.2) through which the Atlas wadis or those of the High Plains leading to the Sahara piedmont cut deep gorges (Guiraud, 1973). The "transatlas segments" of these wadis are characterized by canyons and gorges. The uniqueness of these Atlas "cluses" or transverse valleys lies in the presence of aeolian deposits in the form of hummocky slopes buried by the sand. Bou Saada, El Haouita and M'Doukal are good examples of such valleys.

13.3.2.2   Sand accumulation in the transverse valleys

These are essentially "aeolian plugs" which buried many transverse valleys during past periods of aridity when fluvial transport was inactive (Estorges, 1965). Indications of this aeolian activity are present in the whole of the Atlas chain and take different forms as a function of relief distribution (Mahrour, 1965; Trayssac, 1981). When the sands follow the route of the gorges of these wadis, they cause a blockage which influences fluvial activity to the point where rivers no longer flow. These areas of aeolian sand traps have functioned previously and at several times, as indicated by the characteristic sedimentation of alternating aeolian deposits and correlative fluvial deposits in the fill in the transverse valleys.

13.3.2.3 Water erosion

Often the accumulation of these sandy sheets across a valley orientated perpendicular to the Transatlas gap will block the bottom of the valley and stop water flow (Figure 13.3). Above this aeolian dam the valley soon fills up and becomes a zone of active fluvial reworking. The aeolian dam eventually gives way to the formation of a steep-sided gorge which then becomes the point of initiation of rapid and spectacular regressive erosion, developing into a heavily gullied and badlands-type landscape. This kind of hydroaeolian fill is particularly well developed in the southern part of the Hodna basin south of M'Doukal, and is the end product of the evolution of environments which are alternately arid and pluvial.

These kinds of valley fills are also common at the edge of the Saharan Atlas. Their location is dependent on the distribution of springs or of wadi sections with perennial flow. The fill is deposited in an arid environment, though the presence of a spring may reduce the climatic aridity locally. So, the vegetation favoured by the spring may encourage the accumulation of sand.

13.3.2.4 Holocene palaeoclimatic fluctuations across the Saharan Atlas

The edge of the Saharan Atlas is subject to climatic fluctuations, which are represented by a distinctive morphogenesis. At least four aeolian phases are recognized.

1. Sand fills of the "El Haouita, M'Doukal" type represent the oldest phase (12 000 – 8000 years BP) (Estorges et al., 1969).
2. Sandy aeolian veneers on the Atlas slopes are the second phase.
3. Formation of the first generation of ergs in the Zahreg and Hodna basin represents the third phase.
4. A second generation of ergs is developing today.

FIGURE 13.3   A sif dune barrier blocking a valley bottom (Djebel Saifoun, northwest of Biskra) (photo: Benazzouz)

This recurrence of arid phases consistently in the same location confirms the maintenance of aeolian fluxes under the same dominant wind direction as at present. Also, the relation of these climatic fluctuations with the aeolian morphogenesis appears to confirm the permanence of the transatlas aeolian flux from the northwest, at least during the Holocene (Ballais et al., 1989). The influence of this transatlas aeolian flux at considerable distances south of the Atlas has been well demonstrated by radar imagery (type SIR-A) in the region of the Chott Melrhir (Rebillard and Ballais, 1984).

13.3.3 Internal drainage of the High Plains and natural causes of desertification

The location of the High Plains — on the one hand, north of the Atlas barrier and, on the other hand, on the axis of aeolian fluxes from the northwest — represents an open area where wind can operate effectively (Figure 13.1).

In effect, and taking into account the state of denudation of the steppe, the intensity of aeolian phenomena is increased by the presence of many active sebkhas at the centre of the High Plains (Benazzouz, 1986). The seasonal functioning of the sebkhas involves two different mechanisms.

1. In the wet season, the sebkhas are flooded by surface and (or) subsurface water.
2. In the dry season, evaporation is important and results in the desiccation of the sebkhas which are the site of intense aeolian erosion. The drying out of the bottom of the sebkhas causes a cracking of the salty clays and development of patterned ground. The lifting of the dried clay particles by the wind leads to erosion of the sebkha hollow and deposition of material around the leeward edge in the form of clayey sandy or sandy accumulations. Lunettes, dunes, ergs or sandy sheets are thus developed.

The dynamics of sebkha evolution result in huge aeolian accumulations around the margins of the sebkhas or, in other words, the existence of a huge store of highly mobile material. The most important natural factor in the desertification process is seen to be the availability of the stored sand at the core of the High Plains and its location on the axis of aeolian flux from the northwest. These sands are in transit in the High Plains (Figure 13.4) and are dependent on the effectiveness of the winds (Benazzouz, 1994). This transit can be followed from north to south across the High Plains: (a) sandy ergs and lunettes surrounding the leeward margins of the sebkha can be recognized (Benazzouz, 1987); (b) aeolian veneers on the northern slopes of the Atlas; (c) sand sheets on the southern slopes of the Atlas (Figure 13.5); and (d) suites of dunes on the southern banks of the wadis of the Saharan piedmont which are orientated west−east.

This sand cycle, which is moving southwards (Figure 13.6), is an active environmental control. Increase of this aeolian activity is often due to an increased denudation of the steppe, which may in turn be anthropogenically induced.

13.4 CONCLUSION

In terms of this study, we wanted to show that the causes of desertification in the northern Algerian Sahara are partly anthropogenic, resulting from successive waves of colonization of the steppe, but are also strongly dependent on natural causes. The configuration and processes of the physical environment are especially important.

FIGURE 13.4   Sand movement in the High Plains; sand on its way from Zahreg Chergui to Chott el
Hodna (Bou-Saada) (photo: Benazzouz)

As for the process of desertification, indications and evidence exist in sequences of
aeolian deposits. Detailed study would reveal more precise details of evolution and
process of desertification.

It is important to emphasize the central importance of the process of removing from
storage sand that has accumulated during Holocene time in the High Plains.

FIGURE 13.5   Southern piedmont of the Atlas Mountains: sand moving from the High Plains across
the Atlas Mountains and forming sif dunes in the Biskra region (photo: Benazzouz)

FIGURE 13.6 Impact of the transatlas aeolian flux on the soil: an active aeolian corridor with movement of sand to the south from Chott el Hodna (photo: Benazzouz)

The desertification of the northern part of the Algerian Sahara is occurring due to the addition of sand to the Sahara from the north, carried by the major aeolian flux from the north and northwest. The sands of the dune systems of the High Plains do not come from the Sahara but have been developed in place following the erosion of steppe soils and by the dynamics of sebkha formation. The existence of free sand dunes across the High Plains represents a store of sand in transit and is also a serious hazard along the margins of the Sahara.

REFERENCES

Ballais, J. L., Dumont, J. L., Le Coustumer, M. N. and Levant, M. 1989. Sédimentation éolienne, pédogénèse et ruissellement au Pléistocène supérieur — Holocène, dans les Zibans (Algérie). *Revue de Géomorphologie Dynamique*, Paris, **2**, 39–58.

Baradez, J. 1949. *Fossatum Africae*, Arts et Métiers Graphiques, Paris, 377 pp.

Benazzouz, M. T. 1986. *Recherches Géomorphologiques dans les Hautes Plaines de l'Est Algérien*. Thèse Doctorat 3è cycle, Paris I, 268 pp.

Benazzouz, M. T. 1987. A comparative study of the lunettes in the Tarf and Hodna basins (Algeria). *International Geomorphology 1986, Part II*. John Wiley, Chichester, 1217–1229.

Benazzouz, M. T. 1994. L'endoreisme dans les hautes Plaines algériennes: Origine et impact dans les mécanismes de la désertification. In *Colloque en l'Honneur du Professeur R. Coque*, Publication du Centre de Biogéographie-Ecologie, Paris, 11 et 12 février 1993.

Birebent, J. 1964. *Aquae Romanae*. Thèse Université, Alger, 523 pp.

Callot, Y. 1987. *Géomorphologie et Paléoenvironnements de l'Atlas Saharien au Grand Erg Occidental: Dynamique Eolienne et Paléolacs Holocènes*. Thèse d'État, Paris, 412 pp.

Camps, G. 1961. *Aux Origines de la Berbérie. Monuments et Sites Funéraires Protohistoriques.* Arts et Métiers Graphiques, Paris, 628 pp.

Chabin, J. P. 1982. *L'Homme et le Milieu Naturel à l'Epoque Historique Contemporaine (1850—1980) sur les Confins Sahariens de l'Est Algérien: Région des Nememcha.* Thèse Doctorat 3è cycle, Dijon, 520 pp.

Despois, J. 1953. *Le Hodna (Algérie).* PUF, Paris, 409 pp.

El-Bekri, A. O. 1965. *Description de l'Afrique Septentrionale.* Trad. de Slane, Adrien-Maisonneuve, Paris, 405 pp.

El-Edrissi. 1983. *Le Maghrib au 6è siècle de l'Hégire.* Publisud, Paris, 187 pp.

Estorges, P. 1965. La bordure saharienne du djebel Amour: étude morphologique. *Travaux de l'Institut de Recherches Sahariennes, Université d'Alger,* **XXIV**, 1—16.

Estorges, P., Aumassip, G. and Dagorne, A. 1969. *El Haouita, un Exemple de Remblaiement Fini-Wurmien.* Libyca, Tome XVII, 53—92.

Guiraud, R. 1973. *Evolution Post-Triasique de l'Avant Pays de la Chaine Alpine en Algérie d'après l'Etude du Hodna et des Régions Voisines.* Thèse Doctorat et Sciences, Nice, 270 pp.

Le Houerou, H. N. 1968. La désertisation du Sahara septentrional et des steppes limitrophes. *Annales Algeriennes de Géographie, Alger,* **6**, 5—30.

Le Houerou, H. N. 1992. *Recherches Biogéographiques sur les Steppes du Nord de l'Afrique.* Thèse Doctorat d'Etat, Université Paul Valéry-Montpellier, 1992.

Leschi, L. 1943. Le "Centenarium" d'Aqua Viva près de M'doukal. *Revue Africaine,* **394—395,** 5—22.

Mahrour, M. 1965. Le versant méridional des monts des Ouled Nail. *Travaux de l'Institut de Recherches Sahariennes, Université d'Alger,* **XXIV**, 148—149.

Rebillard, P. and Ballais, J. L. 1984. Surficial deposits of two Algerian playas as seen on SIR-A, Seasat and Landsat coregistered data. *Zeitschrift für Geomorphologie, Berlin, NF,* **28**(4), 483—498.

Roubet, C. 1969. *Economie Pastorale Préagricole en Algérie Orientale: Le Néolithique de Tradition Capsienne. Exemple: l'Aurès.* CNRS, Paris, 595 pp.

Sary, M. 1976. *Géographie Physique d'une Haute Plaine Steppique Algérienne: le Hodna.* Thèse 3è cycle, Strasbourg, 284 pp.

Statistique Agricole. 1968. *La Steppe Algérienne: Enquête sur le Nomadisme.* No. 14, Avril 1974, Ministère de l'Agriculture et de la Réforme Agraire, 385 pp.

Trayssac, J. 1981. *Etude Géomorphologique du Bassin-versant de l'Oued Djelfa-Melah, Versant Nord des Monts des Ouled Nail (Algérie).* Thèse 3è cycle, Poitiers, 211 pp.

Index